T0389780

Seeing the World through Children's Eyes

Visual Pedagogies, Methodologies & Educational Research

Series Editor

E. Jayne White (*RMIT, Australia*)

VOLUME 1

The titles published in this series are listed at *brill.com/vper*

Seeing the World through Children's Eyes

Visual Methodologies and Approaches to Research in the Early Years

Edited by

E. Jayne White

BRILL

SENSE

LEIDEN | BOSTON

All chapters in this book have undergone peer review.

Library of Congress Cataloging-in-Publication Data

Names: White, E. Jayne, editor.
Title: Seeing the world through children's eyes : visual methodologies and
   approaches to research in the early years / edited by E. Jayne White.
Description: Leiden ; Boston : Brill Sense, [2020] | Series: Visual
   pedagogies, methodologies, and educational research, 2665-9034 ; volume
   1 | Includes bibliographical references and index.
Identifiers: LCCN 2020022007 (print) | LCCN 2020022008 (ebook) | ISBN
   9789004433304 (paperback) | ISBN 9789004433311 (hardback) | ISBN
   9789004433328 (ebook)
Subjects: LCSH: Early childhood education--Research. | Visual education. |
   Visual literacy.
Classification: LCC LB1139.225 .S44 2020 (print) | LCC LB1139.225 (ebook)
   | DDC 372.21--dc23
LC record available at https://lccn.loc.gov/2020022007
LC ebook record available at https://lccn.loc.gov/2020022008

Typeface for the Latin, Greek, and Cyrillic scripts: "Brill". See and download: brill.com/brill-typeface.

ISSN 2665-9034
ISBN 978-90-04-43330-4 (paperback)
ISBN 978-90-04-43331-1 (hardback)
ISBN 978-90-04-43332-8 (e-book)

To Elijah and Kayden
who help me see new worlds every day through their eyes

∴

Contents

Foreword

Over the past 20 years, the use and development of visual methods and media has increasingly become part of mainstream academia across social science and humanities research and dissemination. In 2001, I published my first book in this area, titled *Doing Visual Ethnography*. At the time, visual methods were still not necessarily treated seriously by many academics. Since then, I have both participated in and witnessed the growth of visual methods as a dynamic field of practice, distributed across various disciplines and interdisciplinary fields, informed by a range of different theories of knowledge and of sensory and visual experience, and accompanied by a keen interest in and commitment to ethical conduct and debate.

The new initiative, signalled by this first book in the new Brill Visual Methodologies series, is an important extension of the field as we move into the third decade of the twenty-first century. This is particularly so in a contemporary context, where it has become imperative that academic research and scholarship has an impact beyond its conventional scope in academia. Visual methods and media continue to play a significant role in academic research, and at the interface between academic, applied and public research agenda. They offer us modes of researching that create direct lines of continuity between the sites where research is undertaken and those where we seek to make critical interventions outside academia. That is, they offer us ways in which to broker connections between different stakeholders in our futures, thereby allowing for the potential to bring about new modes of understanding and practice.

Pedagogy and education studies have always been vibrant fields of practice in the development of visual methods internationally, and indeed they have provided some of the inspiration for my early work in this area. This area has, on the one hand, contributed insights into the question of how we know and learn, thus offering foundations for understanding not only how others learn, but also how researchers themselves learn, with visual materials. The field has also raised specific ethical questions relating both to the participation of children in research projects and their representation as well as to the rights of children to be able to make their own choices about participation and self-representation. These raise complex issues, which I do not pretend to be able to address myself, but leave to those who work in this area. I mention them, however, to highlight the way in which these, amongst other themes, suggest that researchers in the field of learning and pedagogy often need to be at the forefront of the key debates in which visual researchers are engaged.

This is also the case because learning studies constitute an applied field of research, which is designed to have an impact not only on academic debates but also on people's lives and futures. Therein lies a responsibility to uncover what matters and to enable the findings of research to play a role in shaping 'better' futures. I return to this question below in relation to the role of visual research methods and a 'seeing' approach in such an agenda.

Alongside the development of visual methods and media in academic research, the advent of mobile personal technologies – such as smartphones and tablets – the ways in which we experience our worlds through our sensory, affective and embodied relationships with technology have become part of our everyday lives and academic studies. As researchers, we use these technologies ourselves, as part of our fieldwork kit and in our personal lives; we study how others use them in their lives; and we engage them to produce and save the methods of knowing that our research participants co-create within projects. As such, the field of visual research methods is one that has grown and co-evolved with developments in visual technologies of recording and dissemination. In recent years, social researchers have expanded their use of visual and digital technologies, beyond still photography and video documentary, to experiment with the use of camera phones, GoPros, 360-degree cameras and drone photography within research. We grow up, live and learn in a world that is visually and technologically mediated in such ways that our research in and as part of this world and this visual-technological environment are likewise inextricable.

This means that still and moving images and the way in which children learn and know in the world, inside and outside of formal learning environments, are inextricable. This, together with more traditional drawing and other modes of visual engagement with materials, things and the environment, invites us to consider how the rich visuality of everyday life constitutes and expresses how we feel in the world. As the editor of this book notes, attention to such questions enables us to gain deeper understandings of others' worlds by seeking to see with them, or to at least acknowledge better how they see. Importantly, by learning to see as others do, and by developing new methodologies through which to do so, we can put these people's needs at the centre of our agendas for development and change. This is important because, as I explain further below, such agendas, when formulated from above, too often tend to rely on the idea that change could be driven by technological innovation.

The idea of *Seeing the World through Children's Eyes* therefore offers a way forward in theory, research and practice for the study of early learning. It invites us to ask what the world is like from the perspective of a child; to explore this as a matter of perception; and to put such questions relating to how the world is known, experienced and learned at the centre of the agenda. In doing so, researchers can establish a starting point that is resistant to contrary agendas that seek to impact on human lives and futures 'from above' because working from the ground up always demonstrates that what people see, experience and need in order to feel right, comfortable and confident in their everyday worlds should take precedence in the design of technologies, policies and services for learning.

Asking how people – and in the case of this book, children and teachers – create a window into what matters in everyday life, visual methods and media offer us ways of understanding people, their lives and their experiences. Seeing is never solely about the visual dimensions of experience but rather, similarly to other sensory categories, offers us a route into considering other elements of sensory experience or what it feels like to be in the world. Visual methods and media are particularly useful as modes of investigating, communicating and learning about those elements of human experience, knowing and feeling that are difficult or perhaps impossible to express verbally.

Early learning is an interdisciplinary field, and while associated perhaps most strongly with studies in education and pedagogy, it raises a series of interdisciplinary questions. It also brings to the fore insights that those from other disciplines, who seek to create environments and technologies for early learning, should consider. Indeed seeing the world through children's eyes offers a corrective, in various senses, to approaches that fail to put human experience and knowledge at the centre of their methodology. This is because it emphasises the importance of putting those people whose worlds we are seeking to design, improve or introduce new innovations into in some way, at the centre of our agendas.

In the present, it is perhaps even more important than ever that a sensitivity to the everyday, the sensory and the experiential, which is brought by qualitative visual methodologies, should be emphasised. We live in a context where data-driven design and policy are gaining favour with governments and industry, and where big data analytics appear to offer 'solutions' to the unpredictability of our futures. In this context, we need to be able to respond to the predictive stance of big data analytics and the certainties that risk-averse audit cultures seek to project, with all of the complexity and uncertainty that qualitative social sciences reveal. This is important because it is only an appreciation of this complexity that will enable the responsibility and ethics required to push forward in a context where the detail is obscured by big data. Moreover, in the contemporary context of emerging technologies of artificial intelligence and automated decision-making, this qualitative detail, which emerges from fine-grained visual studies in everyday life contexts, is also important. We need, for example, to know where, when and how human and artificial intelligence should meet, and where responsibilities should lie. We should also ask how human and machine learning might best work relationally, and what the ethics and responsibilities of such relationships might be. Today's early learners will grow up in an increasingly intelligent technological environment. Visual methods and media provide us with an entry point into such environments and a means of understanding the ways in which that they are experienced. Therefore, they offer us one method of producing ways of knowing that will support arguments that seek to ensure that the design of future technologies and policy are aligned with real human needs as we move on into as-yet-uncertain futures.

Sarah Pink
Monash University, Melbourne

Acknowledgements

I am ever indebted to the many children, teachers and families over the past 40 years who have granted me treasured glimpses into their lives through my seeing eye/I. I hope this book goes some way to 'paying forward' the many generosities you have extended to me.

To the contributors of each chapter in this book – each with a passion for seeing childhoods through their research efforts – I extend heartfelt thanks. The work these authors did in peer reviewing chapters, meeting in Melbourne in June 2019 to progress this work, and responding with good cheer to my many editorial requests, has made this book a joy to bring together. I have a feeling that the relationships that have developed out of this international collaboration are just beginning.

I am deeply thankful to colleagues from the Association for Visual Pedagogies, for the many lively discussions concerning the potential of visualities to shape educational thought and practice. I am also grateful to John Bennett and the Brill | Sense team for their positive and supportive work behind-the-scenes and in sharing our vision for visual pedagogies and its publishing potential. Thanks, too, to Courtney White for her careful edits of early chapter drafts; and to Adam and the team at Splash Editing – who helped me bring this book home under adverse circumstances.

Figures and Tables

Figures

Tables

Notes on Contributors

Dandan Cao

completed her Master in Education at Beijing Normal University (2009). She is nearing the completion of her PhD candidate at the University of Waikato (2017-2020). Her research focuses on exploring children's voices on their experience of touchscreen devices in a cross-cultural context from a dialogic perspective.

Julie Carmel

is a lecturer at RMIT University Melbourne, where she lectures in Early Childhood Education, Inclusive practice and 21st century issues impacting children. Julie is currently undertaking her Doctorate of Education by publication, researching how children with disabilities are framed in the media, with an emphasis on children's television, through a Derridean lens. Julie is a member of Australian Association for Research in Education (AARE), where she presented a paper based on her doctoral studies: Association Graduates in Early Childhood Studies (AGECS) and Early Childhood Intervention Australia (Melbourne/Vic branch) (ECIA).

Amanda Crow

is a Senior Lecturer and Early Years course leader at the University of Huddersfield, she is an experienced practitioner and manager having previously worked in a variety of settings. She has worked in higher education for 6 years, working with students on undergraduate and post-graduate programmes. Amanda is currently studying the Doctorate in Education with a research focus on partnership with parents and using digital documentation to facilitate collaborative discussions in early years practice.

Sheena Elwick

is a Senior Lecturer in Early Childhood Education (ECE) at Charles Sturt University, Australia. Her PhD study brought together philosophy and empirical data generated with six infants located in three family day care homes to interrogate the concept of infant participation in research. Her research interests include opening up the complexity of educational research with young children; identifying, measuring and improving ECE contributors to the development, learning and wellbeing of children aged under three; and, working with educators in prior-to-school settings to enrich practices and pedagogies.

Nicola Firth

is a Senior Lecturer in Early Years at the University of Huddersfield. She has worked in higher education for 14 years, working with students on undergraduate and post-graduate programmes. Prior to working in higher education Nicola qualified as a Nursery Nurse and worked in early years settings for 13 years as a Nursery Nurse, then Nursery Manager. Nicola is currently studying the Doctorate in Education with a research focus on boys' underachievement in their early years. Nicola has used a visual pedagogical approach to collect and analyse data with young children.

Amie Hodges

is a Senior Lecturer in the School of Healthcare Sciences, Cardiff University, she is a Sociologist with a previous clinical background healthcare. Amie's research interests focus around the sociology of health and illness; she uses participatory, visual and creative methods within her work with children, young people and families. She has used dramaturgy to explore the family centred experiences of siblings living in the context of cystic fibrosis.

Laura Jennings-Tallant

is a lecturer and researcher at Bath Spa University, Bath. Her PhD, from the University of East Anglia, was a Bakhtinian analysis of the place and nature of young children's carnivalesque humour within an early childhood setting. Laura's current research interests include interdisciplinary perspectives on children's humour and carnivality.

Liang Li

is a senior lecturer in the Faculty of Education, Monash University, Australia. Research interests are cultural-historical studies, infant-toddlers' education and care, family practices, play and pedagogy, children's speech development, science, technology and mathematics in early childhood and primary education settings.

Helen Lomax

is Professor of Childhood Studies at the University of Huddersfield. Her research is focused on understanding the everyday lives of children and the development of methods to enable their participation in research. Helen's publications bring together interests in creative visual methods, visual culture and ethics.

Dawn Mannay

is a Reader in Social Sciences (Psychology) at Cardiff University. Her research interests revolve around class, children and young people, education, identity and inequality; and she employs participatory, visual and creative methods in her work with communities. Dawn was the Principal Investigator on a Welsh Government commissioned project exploring the education of children and young people who are care experienced in Wales. She has worked on projects related to motherhood, health, poverty, migration, arts and heritage funded by the Wellcome Trust, the Welsh Crucible, Wales Millennium Centre and the Economic and Social Research Council. Dawn established a community of practice to improve the educational experiences of children and young people – ExChange: Care and Education. This online resource hosts free-to-access multimodal materials, case studies, and best practice guides to inform key stakeholders with an interest in the education of care experienced children and young people. Dawn edited the books *Our Changing Land: Revisiting Gender, Class and Identity in Contemporary Wales* (University Wales Press 2016); *Emotion and the Researcher: Sites, Subjectivities, and Relationships* (Emerald 2018, with Tracey Loughran); *Children and Young People 'Looked After'? Education, Intervention and the Everyday Culture of Care in Wales* (University Wales Press, 2019, with Alyson Rees and Louise Roberts); *The Sage Handbook of Visual Research Methods* (Sage, 2020, with Luc Pauwels); and wrote the sole authored text *Visual, Narrative and Creative Research Methods: Application, Reflection and Ethics* (Routledge, 2016). Dawn is committed to increasing the impact of research findings through the use of film, art work, music and a range of other participatory and co-produced multimodal materials.

Rene Novak

has had a strong interest in education for most of his life and has a strong passion for early childhood pedagogy and technology education. Through his Educational journey he gained teaching qualifications in all sectors, a degree in Pedagogy, a degree in Science, and he completed a Master of Education with the University of Waikato theorising the openness of the NZ ECE curriculum. For the last ten years he has been working for BestStart Educare and is currently supporting Tauranga centres as the Professional Services Manager. He is a published PhD candidate with his thesis focusing on developing new methodologies to study the importance of play involving modern digital technology, namely Virtual Reality, as a tool and a method.

Sarah Pink

(PhD, FASSA) is Director of the Emerging Technologies Research Lab at Monash University, Australia. She is also an Associate Director of Monash Energy Institute, International Guest Professor at Halmstad University, Sweden, Visiting Professor at Loughborough University, UK and Adjunct Professor at RMIT

University, Australia. Sarah is a design anthropologist and expert in innovative ethnographic methodologies. Her books in this field include the long established *Doing Visual Ethnography* as well as *Doing Sensory Ethnography, Advances in Visual Methodology, Visual Interventions* and *Refiguring Techniques in Digital Visual Research.*

Gloria Quinones

is a senior lecturer in the Faculty of Education, Monash University, Australia. Research interests are cultural-historical theory, visual methodologies, infant – toddler education, play and pedagogy and emotions.

Bridgette Redder

is Programme Leader of the Postgraduate Diploma of Infant and Toddler Learning and Development at Te Rito Maioha Early Childhood New Zealand. She is secretary of the *Association for Visual Pedagogies* and co-leads the New Zealand team of the International Study Social Emotional Early Transitions (ISSEET) research project. Bridgette's research interests focus on self study, early years, visual morality, answerability and teacher education.

Avis Ridgway

recent adjunct research fellow Faculty of Education, Monash University. Research foci: visual methodology; early childhood social, cultural and historical influences on learning; infant-toddler pedagogy; peer play and teacher education.

Elizabeth Rouse

is a Senior Lecturer in Early Childhood Education at Deakin University. Her research focusses on early childhood curriculum, pedagogy, professional practice, parent-school-community partnerships, and transition to school. Elizabeth is a member of the Australian Association for Research in Education (AARE), the European Early Childhood Education Research Association (EECERA), Early Childhood Australia (ECA) and the European Research Network About Partnerships in Education (ERNAPE). She has published extensively in both academic journals as well as professional texts.

E. Jayne White

is Associate Dean ECE at Royal Melbourne Institute of Technology (RMIT) in Melbourne, and Adjunct Professor at Western Norway Institute of Applied Science, Norway. She is founding member and current President of Association for Visual Pedagogies (AVP), Editor-in-Chief of the *Video Journal of Education and Pedagogy* (VJEP). Jayne is widely published in fields of ECE philosophy, visual philosophy, pedagogy and methodology, with a particular interest in dialogic theory and the very young. With Professor Carmen Dalli she co-edits the Springer book series *Policy and Pedagogy with Under Three Year-Olds: Cross-Disciplinary Insights and Innovations* and actively promotes scholarship across these intersecting domains.

CHAPTER 1

The Work of the Eye/I in 'Seeing' Children
Visual Methodologies for the Early Years

E. Jayne White

1 Introduction

Children all over the world are now seen long before they are heard. Before infants are born, their parents are often more interested in what (and who) their babies will look like than the sound of their voice. Photographs are readily taken to capture the earliest phases of life through ultra-sound technologies or images long before voice recordings (see, for example, the ground-breaking photography of Nilsson, 1965). Furthermore, the rise of social media (and platforms such as Facebook), coupled with the technologies of iPhone cameras and practices such as 'sharenting',[1] has meant that these visual glimpses are readily available for all who care to see them. This same emphasis is now evident in the early years, where larger numbers of younger children than ever before are located in early childhood education (ECE) institutions outside of the home (Gradovski et al., 2019), under the scrutiny of public gaze and various forms of surveillance (Rooney, 2017). Their teachers are widely utilising visual images (especially photographs and video) as a means of portraying learning and assessment as a ubiquitous source of pedagogical accountability to families and funders alike (White et al., 2020). Almost all children now have a portfolio of images that purport to narrate their earliest lives, and with the rise of social media, these are now readily published in public spaces for viewing. We should therefore not be surprised to discover that a similar emphasis now exists in early years research – as researchers utilise the same technologies as methods to grant them deeper insights into children, childhoods and associated pedagogies for ECE. These are widely viewed as a source of advocacy and empowerment – claiming to grant participatory rights for children as a consequence.

However, capturing images is no longer sufficient to meet the demands of representation (indeed, some might say it never was). Now, more than ever before, we are no longer required to take the word of authority figures who ask us to accept what they see without transparency or their account of the 'truths' they reveal. Visual essentialism borne out of traditional forms of observation in the absence of reflexive accounts of seeing have done great disservice to

© KONINKLIJKE BRILL NV, LEIDEN, 2020 | DOI: 10.1163/9789004433328_001

children (and teachers) in the early years. Pronouncing certain states of being or becoming based on these universal declarations of developmental limitation or immaturity – many of which are now being gradually eroded – can no longer be tolerated. The challenge we face in the early years today is neither a lack of visual access nor an absence of potential alternative sightings; rather, we appear to be caught between the scientific legacies that ask us for certainties concerning children's epistemological lives and the aesthetic potential of what we see (and the range of philosophies that we might summon, or promulgate, in order to see ontologically).

Furthermore, we cannot settle on seeing as an effortless event in the ocular age in which we live. Jay Martin (1993) reminds us that an inability to see beyond what is in front of us is one of the greatest dangers facing society today. As visualisers, we are called to account for what we see (and what we do not see) – making transparent the selections, technologies and interpretations we generate and/or receive. In consideration of the early years, we are also called to question the purposes of representation and our own motivations for production, and we expect to engage in difficult dialogues about what could or should be shown as a consequence. In short, we are compelled to engage in some serious work behind the scenes concerning what we bring into view, what we ask others to see as a consequence of our revelations and how we receive the seeings of others in critical ways.

Seeing beyond these taken-for-granted or universal portrayals is at the very heart of what I have come to call the 'work of the eye/I' as an important proposition for visual research for the early years (White, 2016a, 2017a). Mikhail Bakhtin (1986) first established this principle based on the writings of Goethe, who, upon viewing a mountain, suggested that there was more to his seeing than an image that appeared in front of his eye: Goethe asserts a seeing eye that distinguishes between the 'eye' and 'visibility' – placing *visibility* as the greatest authority because it is saturated with complex thought in time and space. Bakhtin explains that 'the seeing eye seeks and finds time – development, emergence and history. Behind the ready-made, it perceives what is emerging and being prepared' (p. 29). For this reason, he argued that no assertion could be made without implicating the work of the eye.

Throughout this chapter, I advance the work of the eye/I in two central ways that, together, orient the emphasis of this book. First, I implicate the work of the researcher's 'eye' that looks upon the early years, as Goethe viewed the mountain, through the visual lenses at his or her disposal. Second, I invoke the seeing 'I' as the thinking that brings forth particular seeings, frames others, and denies yet others still. I position this 'I' at the heart of the visual methodology, which I interpret as a series of lenses for seeing that are philosophically, ideologically grounded, and which inform the way research is visualised. The work of the 'I' is based on not only what is seen (how or who is seen) by the eye, but also the ideas, circumstances and ethics that frame such seeing, as well as its location in time and space (including outsider-insider perspectives). This is because, according to Goethe, one cannot exist fruitfully without the other.

In consideration of the early years, bringing the eye + I to bear on matters of importance concerning the child places the 'I' into consciousness with 'other' – since, as adults, we are implicated for our seeings regardless of whether we claim to see alone or in networked societies. It speaks to persistent issues concerning representation of the early years in a contemporary era of increased visualisation that holds much promise for the field. Summoning the work of the 'eye/I' into this space provides a means of undertaking visual research as an effort to see rather than a ventriloquised certainty. Without paying attention to the methodologies that orient our seeing, we will continue to rely on our existing assurances concerning the lives of children and the certainties we promote, or conversely abandon, about what is, and what can be, seen.

2   Eye Meets 'I': Visual Methods and Methodologies

Visual methods of the 'seeing eye' offer important and unique ways of seeing the world that are not available to text-based research. Visual methods now allow us to see and sense an image and its meaning(s) in ways that can be carefully scrutinised, retrieved and shared. For this reason, they are especially appealing to early years researchers who seek to understand the lived experiences of young children in increasingly public and therefore accountable spaces. However, the allure of the seeing eye – as a method – belies its potential for manipulative or strategic purposes. Reflexive accounts by the researcher are therefore increasing called for in early years visual research.

While a great deal has been written about the importance of reflexivity surrounding visual methods for seeing in early years research, less is proffered concerning the methodologies that orient what can (or cannot) be seen, or why this is the case.[2] Emphasis is typically placed on *what* to see, *who* to see (as well as who to see *with*), and the visual technologies of *how*, rather than on the methodological orientations that construct the very premise of visualities and their utilities in terms of representation, disruption, and advocacy. Methods, in and of themselves, are not necessarily the problem. They become problematic when employed to categorically determine what counts as knowledge that reinforces certain kinds types of dogma (e.g. in policy, curriculum, and pedagogies and so on). Little room exists to raise questions concerning the inadequacy of the treatment of an image. Moreover, the ability to pose alternative evaluations, ask different questions and even question the original assertions that oriented the issue in the first place is also lacking. Marion and Crowder (2013) suggest that visual research of this nature has had serious colonising effects in anthropological and ethnographic studies of 'other', and they argue strongly for the researcher's reflexive presence in images that are utilised and in their interpretations.

Paying attention to methodology shifts the emphasis from an exclusive focus on a method – in defense of a certain lens for seeing – towards complex thought (Conroy et al., 2008; Ruitenberg, 2009). Bringing methodological thought to bear in visual research provides a means of interrogating the meaning(s) granted to the image, rather than assuming its unquestioned assertions by the researcher, thereby bringing the work of the 'I' and the 'eye' into communion. The researcher is now called to elucidate (or conversely, dismantle) any claim to legitimacy based on careful scrutiny of what underpins and sustains it and to reflexively examine the alternatives that exist for its life in meaning. These may draw from interdisciplinary, philosophical and theoretical fields that will generate new ways of seeing and thinking about what is seen, rather than assuming an all-knowing, unquestionable interpretative truth concerning the image (Berger, 1972). For this reason, Gillian Rose (2012) suggests that visual research must pay more attention to 'the consequences of its implicit methodology, and to explore the interpretative possibilities offered by a range of other methodological strategies' (p. 553).

One of the challenges facing contemporary visual methodology is how to dissolve existing hierarchies of thought concerning text versus image while providing a means of making thought visible 'beyond semiotic representation and signification' (Sandywell & Heywood, 2012, p. 37). In his 2020 text, Pauwells emphasises the value in taking an integrated transdisciplinary approach to these topics and related methods as well as concepts in visual research – calling for 'more explicit and transparent methodologies' (p. 35) to do so.

A second challenge that warrants our attention in early years research is how to deal with the so-called subject of our gaze without merely duplicating ourselves or asserting what Rorty (1979) describes as 'the mirror'; based on narcissistic tendencies to mould others into our own image (a feat particularly prevalent in early years practice). New forms of ethical reflexivity are called for. These implicate us for our claims beyond the ocular culture within which we now exist. They signal the urgent need for what we have called a 'philosophy of the image' (Peters & White, 2018) and, with it, new means of 'thinking visually' with the technologies at our disposal.

3   Visual Research in the Early Years

Visual research in the early years is not immune to the allure of method-based investigations in the absence of methodological thought. There are many reasons for this – not least as a consequence of the desire to 'know' children as a form of accountability now highly evident in ECE assessment discourse. Many early years researchers justify their deployment of visual approaches as a means of granting 'voice' to the child (based on the idea that children have multiple non-verbal, highly visible ways of communicating). Other researchers in the field suggest that it is possible to gain access to children's perspectives through their own visual representations such as art and body movement or by giving them technologies that will allow them to offer their own images as 'buds', of meaning. In all cases, there is an unspoken assertion that images of or by children can accompany or even replace text as a means of representing childhood worlds – a point also raised by Chalfen (2020) in wider participatory visual research fields which grant "metaphorical voice" to the image (p. 248). The refrain 'seeing is believing – which is ... methodological thought – such treatment in the absence of methodological thought – risks serving the many commodification or production agendas that now orient the early years.

At this juncture, I should pause to re-state my earlier message that methods, in themselves, are not the problem. Indeed, you will read about a variety of creative, innovative methods used by the authors in each chapter of this book. I orient this chapter to their locatedness within certain, well argued, methodological claims concerning their significance. Paying attention to visual methodologies allows us to ask (and hope to read in the chapters that follow) some important, probing questions about not merely the methods employed but the meanings that are asserted concerning their significance for the early years. As Conroy et al. (2008) suggest, we can contemplate alternative causal explanations, outcomes and ethical engagements with the concept and its treatment within the discourse – beyond method alone. We might even begin to pose some of the questions raised by scholars concerning the extent to which visual methodologies can ever truly disassociate themselves from text (Agbenyega, 2014; Heywood & Sandywell, 2012) and, indeed, if the need exists for new ways of thinking about the visual that are yet to be thought of. These invite serious critiques of declarations concerning the capacity of the seeing eye to represent universal childhoods (see, for example, Burton, 1989; Higonnet, 1998; Holland, 2004) or to interpret young lives as knowable events of becoming (Gradovski et al., 2019).

Visual methodologies in the early years therefore allow us to ask probing questions of what we 'see' concerning the nature of reality, knowledge and the values that orient understanding or interpretation. We can contemplate what is produced as a consequence of the seeing eye – beyond any singular sayings about what is seen by the researcher alone. Methodological considerations allow us to think critically about what we are seeing and to make located research claims or critiques accordingly. Paying attention to visual methodologies thus implicates us fully for our seeing eye/I.

4   Methodological Lenses for Seeing

The orienting methodological fields for visual research stem from a long and complex legacy, drawing on interpretative philosophy, art history, media studies and film, to name but a few. Some of these parallel (and in other cases follow) philosophical epochs such as the linguistic versus pictorial turn (Peters & White, 2018), while others take an interdisciplinary approach to collapse traditional binaries of thought. Despite my claims concerning the dominance of visual methods, it is also true that the methodological 'I' is finding its way into early years research in various guises. In the section that follows, I propose four clusters of the seeing eye/I that orient visual research in and for the field – which I describe as 'lenses'.

I am in no way suggesting that these are the only ways of seeing in early years research, nor am I suggesting that there is some sort of methodological hierarchy at play in my inception; rather, there are diverse, methodologically located ways of seeing that co-exist in the field but which are all-too-seldom brought together for discussion. Too often, as researchers, we operate out of methodological silos, and this is no less true in visual research, which suffers from the same blinkered existence unless we are vigilant. The work of the I/eye is never singular by nature – it is contested and constructed, and it emanates from issues at hand rather than mere trends. Yet methodologies *are* discoverable in early years research – confessed or otherwise – and no declaration of plausible insight is ever without its 'I' in a research endeavour that professes to 'see' at its core.

5   Lens 1: Visualising 'Other'

Lens 1 has its origins in the twentieth century rise of the 'camera obscura', which grants the seeing eye (and the image captured accordingly) sovereignty. The camera, as a technical apparatus, operates as a site for truth telling – although, as Crary (1992) explains, it may also 'conceal, invert and mystify truth' p. 29 – based on the idea of visual 'data' as situated or 'lived'. Emphasis is placed on the authenticity of seeing through carefully constructed phenomenologist processes of 'visualising' (Haywood & Sandywell, 2012, p. 13), which are achieved by adopting 'an investigative orientation towards the conditions, mechanisms and structure of visual life' (ibid., p 15).

Regardless of the methods or technologies employed for visualising the child in this manner, the researcher frames what is seen and orients its meaning accordingly, while the child is the object of the gaze – as 'other'. Many contemporary texts concerning visual methods emphasise this turning point from camera obscura to an awareness of the person behind the image and the apparatus at his or her disposal (see, for example, Martens, 2012; Mannay, 2016; Rose, 2016) Central to this stance of seeing in early years research is that the child and/or his or her perspective can and *will be represented by the adult* through an analysis of existing images. Emphasis is therefore placed on an accurate, located portrayal of the child through the 'craft of seeing' technologies and techniques, which can capture discoveries for all to see (and validate). The researcher influences what is seen by the consumer (implicating such things as selection of image, angle, perspective and visual field) and calls for increased understandings of the systematic way in which their 'consciousness grasps an object or event of something, as it is meant' (Vagle, 2018, p. 7).

In early years research, the child is most often the object of this gaze – although significant claims have been made that such seeing grants 'voice' by proxy – generally by the researcher who keenly observes or seeks existing visual 'data'. This interest has resulted in considerable debate on the merits and methodological challenges of these approaches for early years research (Clark, 2020). It has also called for increased vigilance concerning representation and may go some way to explain the increased, and in some cases immobilising, sanctions now surrounding the ethical use of images (a point I return to later).

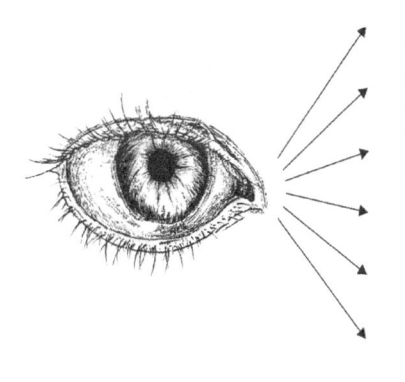

Observation

Technology + eye as craft

'Authentic' representation of 'other'
Child is object of gaze

Grants access to child's 'voice'

Heavy attention to ethics of representation

FIGURE 1.1   Phenomenological visualising

There are ample examples we might use to illuminate this form of representation in early years research. Traditional forms of observation have been more recently complemented and, in some cases, supplanted by video and photo-as-evidence in early years assessment and pedagogy, with teachers as researchers themselves – calling on the ubiquitous presence of visual media such as photographs and video. In taking up this methodological 'I', early years researchers construct alternative reflexive positionings to stake their claims in ways that attempt to bring children into partnership by accessing their visual modes of representation as 'voice'. As Sumsion et al. (2014) highlight – where this is necessary – researchers' awareness of the rhetorical forces at play in the deployment of visual methods that they bring to bear on such seeings is now an imperative for research of this nature. Throughout this book, you will see many examples of reflexive accounts on the part of early years researchers aiming to declare and justify their stance according to the participatory assertions they make in seeking to involve the child.

6   Lens 2: Visual Performance

Heywood and Sandywell (2012) describe this lens as 'the concrete enactments of visual forms and practices as ... signifying performances' (p. 21) – referring to the image as a means of representation through aesthetic insight, advocacy, provocation or production. Its origins lie in the spectacle (after DeBord, 1983) as a methodology for public resistance, advocacy, commentary or persuasion. In some cases, as Foucault might suggest, the 'eye of God' that is promulgated here can also represent a form of surveillance (utilised in ECE all over the world today).

More frequently utilised in popular culture than the academy, this lens summons artistic endeavour to its asserted 'I' – in forms such as visual narrative, documentary or art. We can recognise these approaches particularly through media – as a source of political activism and advocacy – which is becoming increasingly intertwined with educational research.

We are now witnessing a surge in translational research using visual media in the early years, thus responding to Biesta et al.'s (2019) call for inquiry that is characterised by 'ongoing public scrutiny' – a methodological tenet played out here that lends itself well to visual scrutiny. This is typically a mechanism for sharing visual 'data' (see, for example, White, 2019a) or, conversely, creatively re-interpreting visual research into consumer-accessible forms such as video or memes.[4] While not representing the research itself, these translations bring research into the public arena for all to see and consequently alter its meaning. Here, the visual representation needs no explanation or defense – it is, after all, the 'eye of God'.

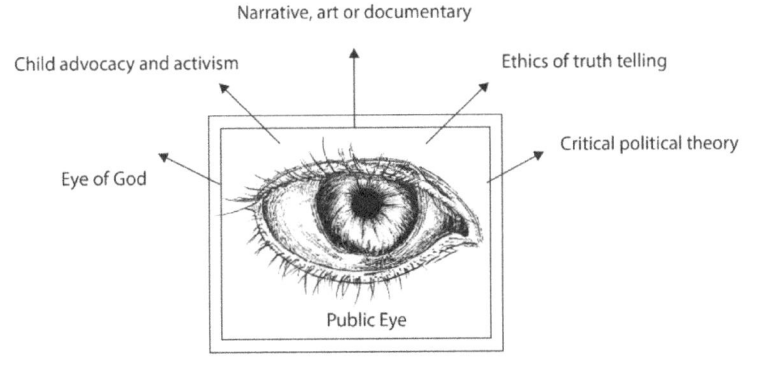

FIGURE 1.2   Visual performance

These modes of production lay the early years bare for adult scrutiny based on the representation and motivation of the artist or producer. Until now, there appear to have been few methodological limitations around this form of research, which – more than any other lens – sits on the periphery of the academy.[5] However, a number of methodologies can, and do, ask questions pertaining to what is posed from the outside that is important in highlighting the constructed nature of images and what they produce – wittingly or otherwise. Helen Lomax (2020) suggests a textual analysis of film, which is also explored by Julie Carmel and Elizabeth Rouse in this book concerning the popular children's television programme titled Playschool.[6]

7   Lens 3: Visibilising with the Subject

Visibilising refers to the effort of bringing visual worlds into contact with one another – in this case as a source of dialogue. Generating visibility with others turns towards the social process of seeing – seeking to place emphasis on the researcher seeing with the child or teacher, where the latter is now a 'subject with' his or her own representation rather than an 'object of or for' the interpretation of the gaze of others. We start to see the collapse of subject-object hierarchies and a fuller attention to the visual surplus offered by others (as opposed to the technology of the camera highlighted above). In accordance with this view, Rose (2012) highlights the interconnected sites of production

AND the site of the image AND the audiences, spectators or users – together constructing what can be seen based on its genesis, modality and reception. In this view, truth is not denied to the participants, but it is constructed out of the experience of seeing rather than as a received event of reality.

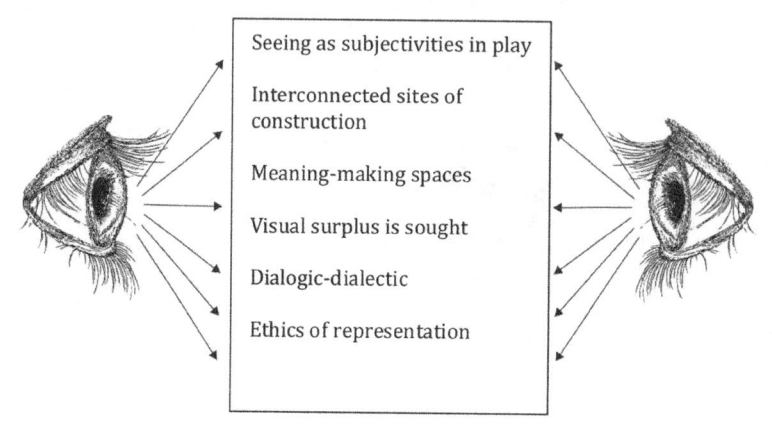

Seeing as subjectivities in play

Interconnected sites of construction

Meaning-making spaces

Visual surplus is sought

Dialogic-dialectic

Ethics of representation

FIGURE 1.3   Visibilising with the subject

Rather than relying on the technology to reveal meaning to the phenomenological researcher in the absence of others (who then report on it through rigorous techniques), the researcher enters into a dialogic or dialectic (depending on the methodological orientation) relationship with the 'seen' as a social construction of visibility. The technology and its image are insufficient in themselves for making claims within this view (although they may give rise to new forms of engagement, such as my use of headcams as a polyphonic method; see White, 2016b). Instead, the researcher seeks to understand the meanings granted to the images by those who are affected. In the case of a dialectic methodology, the aim is to generate shared meanings concerning child development, whereas through a dialogic route, the quest is open to multiple ways of seeing children as dialogic partners with whom to examine meaning-making spaces as a source of insight and possibility. As Carl Mika and I (2019) have argued elsewhere, an author seeking to understand earliest lives should be

> less concerned with making declarations of certainty but much more interested in continually acting within (and where possible beyond) the limits of his or her own perception while actively seeking to bring his or her ideas into play with all other things. (p. 69)

This approach, perhaps more than any other, poses considerable challenges concerning the authentic engagement of young children in research. In my own research with infants, I found myself caught in the delusion that by putting headcams on them, I was generating perspective, when, in reality, I soon realised I was merely generating a visual field. While this was important, it did not constitute a dialogic exchange with the infant – despite my best intentions. I thus began to explore dialogic alternatives, which opened my eyes to the complexities of this enterprise, with the only alternative I could see as 'voicelessness' (White, 2011, p. 80). Several researchers in this book take some interesting routes in this regard.

8   Lens 4: Co-Constituted Immanence

The final lens at our disposal (for now, since the field is evolving fast, and I cannot claim to see all) emphasises the co-constituted nature of seeing as an effort of many eyes (human and non-human in many cases) and in contemplation of multiple modalities and materialities at play. As a consequence these image networks implicate the researcher more fully as one 'who also takes shape in other, grayer practices and discourses, and whose immense legacy will be all the industries of the image and the spectacle' (Crary, 1992, p. 150). Given all our considerable efforts to 'know' the child or to grant him or her a 'voice', coupled with recent philosophical trends in early years research, it is perhaps unsurprising that this immanent eye/I is now upon us.

Co-constituted immanence is discoverable in multimodal, posthuman and protohuman methodologies that seek to address some of the limits of seeing by highlighting some of the not-so-obvious materialities and 'matters that

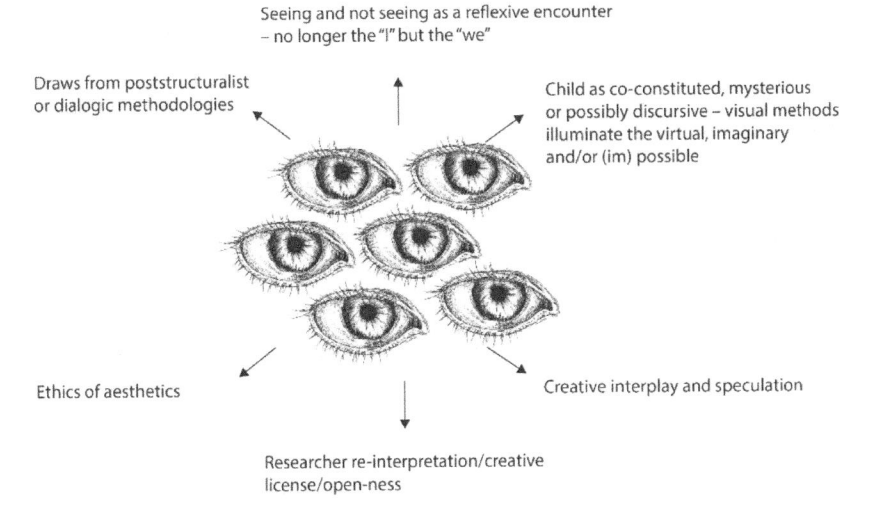

FIGURE 1.4   Co-constituted immanence

matter' that otherwise escape scrutiny, or by asserting the mystery of virtual becomings. In consideration of young children, it sets in motion a means of layering complex meanings and allowing interpretations to nestle against one another unproblematically. There is less emphasis here on truth telling, validating or representing, than on exploring possibilities or what St Pierre (2019) asserts as 'the not yet, the yet to come – the immanent' (p. 4), which she assigns to post-qualitative inquiry as an antidote to research methodologies that, in her view, have not fulfilled their promise.

Contemporary examples of this work can be found in posthuman and new materialism couplings that foreground visual assemblages of thinking and doing. The PhD materialist methodology (and its associates) offers an optimistic antidote to early years research that seeks to 'know' the child and childhood worlds – by engaging 'in world-making practices, to get into the thick of things' (Strom, Ringrose, Osgood, & Renold, 2019, p. 14). A recent issue of *Video Journal of Education and Pedagogy* Murris and Fin Menning (2019) locates such methodologies for the early years as a decolonising agenda 'whereby researchers (and children) are invited to meet the empirical material, not as a dead entity to be taken apart, but as a door to new possibilities of thinking, doing and becoming' (for an example see McRae's 2019 video). The ethical tenet to this lens is 'about mattering ... new configurations, new subjectivities, new possibilities – even the smallest cuts matter' (Barad, 2007, p. 384).

In various ways, each lens puts the eye/I to work in order to see children as active participants in research about, within and/or beyond their worlds through various methodological routes. The methodological treatment of each lens places emphasis on multiple seeing I's – empowering researchers to look beyond 'what merely is' to 'what more can be seen' in order to contemplate 'what could be' as a means of embracing more radical becomings.

It now behoves us to put these lenses into dialogue with one another as possible routes to the seeing eye/I– as is the case in the chapters that are now revealed.

9   Introducing the Chapters

Each seeing eye/I is discoverable throughout this handbook – sometimes within the same chapter as authors grapple with this complexity in their conceptualisations of visual research. Taken together, they draw from a range of methodological positionings and interesting combinations of theories, disciplines, approaches and, of course, technologies for seeing (including virtual reality film, camera and video) as methods. These chapters should be read as some of many possible (and yet-to-be-imagined) interpretations and applications for the work of the eye/I in early years research. They share a desire to understand aspects of early years practice and pedagogy and to better understand young children's perspectives on topics that researchers deem to be of great importance. These include 'free' play, nature, (dis)ability, space, touchscreen play and maths to name but a few orienting themes. Readers will be disappointed if they seek to find certain answers to any of these topics, as this was not the purpose of this book. However, the references provided by each author should contain sufficient links to the original research that is explored – by way of example – in each chapter.

The extent to which each chapter speaks cogently to the work of the eye/I is now a matter for the consideration of the reader. Each chapter seeks to do so in various ways – for some in the purported granting of 'voice' through visually stimulated dialogues with children, while for others through engagement with visual representations of children as a means of exploring the pedagogical practice of teachers. For others still, this is achieved through the eye of the researcher who draws on multiple visual and interpretative dialogues to draw conclusions that might otherwise be inaccessible to them. These methodologies in themselves are not necessarily new to the field, nor do they aim to grant a voice to children (or teachers in many cases); however, when addressing research questions that are best explored through visual means, coupled with a keen attention to the 'I', they open our eyes to new ways of seeing in early years research – an area where we have much to learn as teachers and researchers alike.

In preparing their chapters, each author was invited to present their visual research in response to the following questions:

- What methodological position is taken and why?
- What methods accompany this position and why?
- What can the method offer (or conversely, deny) concerning a critical analysis of the 'work of the eye'?
- What ethical considerations arise as a consequence?
- What are the future possibilities for visual research in the early years?

A series of summary statements end each chapter – as a referencing point for the reader. Readers are invited to determine for themselves what visual work is taking place in each chapter and what this contributes to the field. My hope is that these methodologies arise from probing questions facing the researchers and their early years communities rather than as cookie-cutter templates to be dutifully followed. What is particularly interesting here is that even though many of the visual methods are similar (photograph, video etc.), the way in which these are seen and therefore interpreted by the researcher differs radically. It is here that methodologies take centre stage.

Dawn Mannay and Amie Hodges take a child-centred approach to their eye/I – which they argue grants central authorship to children, while researchers play a facilitating role. Their emphasis is on hearing what children have to say, as 'voice' – a theme that will be repeated in many of the chapters and, indeed, in early years research more widely. They contend that this is retrievable through children's metaphorical engagement with physical (visual) worlds using object work and sandboxing to gain access to children's 'voice'. This sensory and reflexive turn calls for an awareness of the materiality of an image in real life. Their central claim is that this methodological approach provides a democratic view of children's perspectives regarding the present and the past, 'on their own terms', by upholding children's meanings over those of the researcher – a process called auteur theory, which centralises the subjective perspectives of the creator of visual constructions over those of the researcher. Mannay and Hodges seek to achieve this by paying careful attention to the contexts surrounding the child and ensuring that children's preferred communication styles are granted primacy, while suspending their own certainties about meanings that are generated.

Sheena Elwick puts philosophical-empirical inquiry into practise to posit a methodological approach that interrogates moments of seeing as 'epiphany' and 'depth' based on video footage of children in a home-based early childhood setting. She emphasises a critical approach to seeing in action research with early years teachers as an ontological imperative – summoning Merleau-Ponty to her inquiry. As Merleau-Ponty (1964, p. 159) famously asserts, 'I borrow myself from others'. Exploring the ways in which multiple visual perspectives can transform pedagogy through sequential viewings and the radical 'awakenings' that arise as teachers see their practice differently as a consequence, Elwick proposes a participatory approach to seeing. We can start to see here an alignment to other methodological points of connection regarding the relationship between the eye, the 'I' and the 'we' that orients this visual approach.

Helen Lomax also sets out to understand children's perspectives through an emphasis on voice as a sensory, embodied expression that can be accessed through what she calls a multimodal methodology. This methodology has been widely used in early years research as a lens through which to observe how young children communicate ideas across different modes. In this case, using creative methods of puppetry and photo-elicitation, Lomax investigates the ways in which children 'see' their environment. The engagement of families in these stimulated dialogues is important for Lomax, and she provides clear examples of the ways in which such co-engagements can generate more complex understandings of voice as a plural concept when everyone is involved, and implicated, in a research agenda that takes an activist stance in speaking to contemporary issues affecting children's lives.

Dandan Cao takes up the notion of 'researching with' children in her dialogic investigation of the competing voices that surround touchscreen use in ECE, including those of the child across home and ECE contexts. Her methodological orientation here is based on the concept of heteroglossia, or multiple dialogues. She expands on the notion of dialogue to prioritise body language. Furthermore, Cao utilises the idea of 'hidden dialogicity' to demonstrate how four year-old dialogues – discoverable through the body – can be altered in and across different spaces. In her ethnographic encounters with children and their peers as well as teachers (in a New Zealand ECE setting) and with children and their families (in the home), she explores how each talks about (and plays with) touchscreen devices. An additional complexity to Cao's study is that she focuses on Chinese children and their families who attend New Zealand ECE settings, thus conjuring up a range of potentially layered and plural competing voices across culture and space.

Adopting a different approach to examine how children are represented in public film on social media, *Julie Carmel and Elizabeth Rouse* introduce what they describe as a deconstructivist methodology to these practices to question the meanings granted to videos of children – as media – in the absence of the producer of the film, summoning a deconstructive framework to do so. They exploit Derrida's attention to textual layering in consideration of video that seeks to portray childhoods in certain 'logocentric' ways – seeking to privilege 'difference' through the image and its alternative readings. Their chapter shows their process of interrogating how disability is signified in media – offering a series of critical questions that ask, 'what is constructed?' accordingly. Video snapshots are considered against absences, hierarchies and exclusions that lead to dissonance rather than acceptance of what is presented as 'truth' concerning the construction of children and their (dis)abilities.

Taking into account the implications for adults in understanding children, *Bridgette Redder* turns explicitly to her own visualisations through a dialogic self-study methodology which, she argues, provides opportunities for greater meta-reflection of pedagogical practice. Studying her own 'self', as an infant ECE teacher in New Zealand, Redder proposes a method she describes as 'video-of-video' whereby video footage of teacher practice is critically analysed with colleagues – as critical friends – as a means of stepping back from everyday pedagogical events. She explains how this method allowed her to see her practice not only as answerable through the eyes of her peers, but also through a broader set of 'selves' in contemplation of the infants with whom she worked – leading her to 'see' herself in increasingly complex ways and accountable through a series of 'I's,– as well as highlighting their conflicted co-incidence in teacher pedagogy with infants.

Amanda Crow's phenomenographic study of young children's experiences in ECE settings through visual data – accessible through pedagogical documentation generated by teachers, and understood through what she describes as 'phenomenological interviews' – upholds the status of observation. She views it as an important means of engaging with children's 'voice' through visual provocations that act as 'plausible insights' rather than universal truths. Such declarations are now standard practice in early years research; however, the utilisation of pedagogical documentation as a phenomenographic route to seeing is an important methodological contribution to the field. Crow's chapter has important repercussions for teachers AS researchers in determining how children will be seen – calling for critical reflections concerning any claims that are made as a consequence.

Taking a less 'serious' approach, 'carnivality' is the orienting methodological concept that *Laura Jennings-Tallant* operationalises in her dialogic study of humour in ECE for three- and four-year-olds in a United Kingdom ECE setting. Using polyphonic video taken from the visual perspective of the children themselves, Jennings-Tallant sets out to identify what she describes as 'key moments' comprised of rich dialogues or utterances as 'sound bites' that are drawn from children's experiences as visual surplus. She locates these within the ECE chronotope, where alternative agendas are scoped out via dialogic encounters with children, based on the visual insights that are afforded. Through such means, a series of carnivalesque narratives are revealed. The meanings generated are both joyful and freeing – constituting new democratic forms of resistance for young children in ECE settings.

Nicola Firth's tentative approach to participatory research based on interpretative phenomenology sets the scene for visual encounters with young children's ECE 'lifeworlds' in England as lived experience. Firth's study seeks to extract boys' perspectives on their ECE lives through an interesting variety of visual prompts, such as walking tours, whereby children were offered cameras to convey their experiences of space and place, and photo production groups through which children were invited to share their collective perspectives.

Taking a *dialectic* methodological turn in an Australian ECE context, *Avis Ridgway, Gloria Quinones and Liang Li* adopt what they describe as a 'wholistic' approach to a child's activity of play by videoing from two different visual fields. They interrogate pedagogy as a meta-narrative means of understanding researchers perspectives through mutual dialogues concerning what is captured on film, as well as those of teachers. Their intention is to generate shared meanings or what they describe as 'intertwining flows' concerning relational pedagogy. As such, their visual emphasis is on understanding the motives for adult interpretations based on video that implies some degree of change as determined by the multiple researchers and/or teachers and which, by association, offers the opportunity for co-constructed meaning-making concerning toddler play through dialogue about what is see-able.

Rene Novak also employs phenomenology to study children's play in ECE – a common theme in early years research. In this case, his orientation is towards the combination of embodiment theory and immersive visuality as a new methodological contribution, which positions technology as an instrument to self-understanding and, again, pedagogy. Novak takes the virtual reality technology into ECE contexts in what he comes to discover is a dubious quest to capture the 'essence' of play. In a meta-analytical turn, he interrogates teachers ways of seeing through this lens – highlighting a series of interpretative layers that unfold when embodied ways of engaging pedagogically with play are accessed through a virtual reality lens. His claim that teachers see more, and differently, draws attention to the visibilisation offered through specialised forms of experience – providing a strong incentive for teachers to immerse themselves in play through this and other modes of inquiry. We can only imagine the alternative stutterings to seeing in certain ways, in the wake of these (and other) techno-humanist encounters within early years research.

10   An Ethical Yolking to the Seeing I

Accompanying almost every text[7] on visual methods is an attention to ethics and reflexivity, and this is even more so where young children are concerned. This is not surprising, since values lie at the heart of the 'I' that shapes meanings concerning what is seen. Yet the seeing 'I' is seldom granted its fullest presence in this space because the field is heavily tethered to a series of complex ideological and cultural assertions that seek to protect the innocent child from probing eyes. Sturm (2020) calls for a fundamental shift from this human-centric emphasis on responsibility to response-abilities (after Haraway) and their assemblages – these exceed text and may, in fact, serve children and other silent(ced) species better.

Against these contested revisions, researchers are guided by a surprisingly small set of statutes and guidelines concerning visual research (Derry, 2007), and authorities (such as academy ethics committees) often interpret those statutes and guidelines in the absence of rigorous methodological contemplation. In my view, this is a critical dialogue to be had across diverse cultural, historical, paradigmatic and moral domains – one that I continue to invite from my peers in early years visual research as a necessary step to represent the child in a methodologically attuned manner (White, 2017b). It seems I am not the only early years scholar calling for these and related critical dialogues concerning ethics (see, for example, Smith, 2020).

Having said this, it would be negligent (and foolhardy) on my part to deny the importance of ethical tenets that must be upheld in the interests of children; and which call for special consideration in visual research, especially when it is located in, about or around social media (Berman, Powell, & Garcia Herranz, 2018). It is not my intention to belabour the latter here (any visual research method book worth its salt will devote pages to this pursuit) except to say that they pose additional challenges for researchers in contemplation of the early years. The United Nations Convention on the Rights of the Child (UNCROC) calls upon all adults to protect children's interests and concerns as a matter of right. In some cases, we are called to question the extent to which visual representations, deconstructions, interpretations and assertions should be accessible to research consumers at all. Indeed, at the time of writing, it has become increasingly difficult to undertake international research involving video footage or images of children as a result of recent EU declarations and restrictions on data sharing, let alone dissemination (see Rutanen et al., 2018).

The researchers in this book take their ethical responsibilities seriously (perhaps too seriously at times): Laura Jennings-Tallant exposes the lengths to which she went to avoid toilet images when using head cameras, while issues concerning power are explored earnestly by Dawn Mannay and Amie Hodges, who claim that leading dialogues, rather than questions, prevents the researcher's agenda from dominating. Furthermore, you will read of Helen Lomax's tiered approach to consent in order to grant ongoing opportunities for withdrawal. Many authors also highlight the evolving nature of ethics in dealing with visual accounts concerning children. As Nicola Firth points out, what may at first glance seem to be empowering for children may, in fact, become disempowering when visual data is used out of context or when its purpose is not made explicit to young children in ways that make sense to them.

Elsewhere I have especially argued strongly for ethics committees to recognise the rights of children to be seen in representations of their lives and for researchers to be granted the opportunity to resolve ethical issues that arise in the communities of their lived experience, with consideration for the guidelines rather than in subservience to them (White, 2017b). I now wish to add to this plea a call for methodological transparency concerning what is to be claimed about what is seen – and summon the work of the eye/I to determinations regarding why, when and how visual data is used (or not). For while methodologies can be traced in terms of their orientation in order to understand how things got to be how they are, as well as why they are important in any specific time and place and what can be 'seen' as a consequence, so too can ethical approaches. Elsewhere I, with a writing collective (Peters et al., 2020), have explored some of these orientations for visual research; and argued for more nuanced understandings of the visual nature of childhoods that are lived out in increasingly public spaces today.

These are important considerations for visual research in the early years. In the absence of such thinking (and related dialogues with those who are affected the most), researchers are left to make ethical compromises to the integrity of their research. Summoning the work of the eye/I to ethics creates necessary spaces for methodological dialogues about what could, should and should not be seen, considering both the child AND the declared priorities of those who seek to see their worlds alongside internationally sanctioned guidelines. This is a creative space indeed.

11   Summoning *Your* I/eye

In this chapter, I have tried to locate the theme of this book within an overarching notion called 'The work of the eye/I' for early years visual research. In doing so, I presented a series of 'I' propositions that orient towards the methodological underpinnings concerning what the 'eye' sees, interprets, generates and disseminates as research into important topics concerning young children, families and teachers in particular. There is much optimism in these spaces as early years research seeks to realise its potential in seeing the child through different visual perspectives – often with a great degree of awe and appreciation that has betrayed many extant illusions generated through traditional forms of research concerning the limits of age. This researcher gaze is accompanied by significant ethical responsibilities that call for reflexive accounts concerning what is seen, how, why and who with, as well as declarations concerning the limits of seeing and its underpinning ideological constraints and opportunities. Where visibility is granted to the research audience, we can now invite new forms of validity and accountability, which call researchers to account for their seeings in ways that were not necessary before. We can see the impact of our own practices through a plural eye/I that may reveal new pedagogical insights or epiphanies, and we can engage in probing dialogues concerning our diverse interpretations.

For now though, it is time to put your eye/I to work. With these inspirations, this handbook sets out to establish a forward-looking agenda for visual research with and about the young and the ideologies that orient their legitimised presence in the field. A series of provocations are offered concerning ethical, social and moral agendas that underpin the potential of seeing to critically and authentically engage young children in their own representations and in dialogue with others or, conversely, to situate them beyond existing visualities. At the very least, this book will pose a challenge to any lingering representation that claims to see without accounting for what and how it is seen. It will also disorient the following claim that is all-too-often made in the case of early years research, pedagogy and policy: that we already 'know' all there is to know about our youngest seers who orient this book. Readers are invited to apply these critical lenses concerning the work of the eye/I – as a source of methodological insight in early years research – so that they might see for themselves what is revealed and, by association, concealed or congealed through the representations that are offered.

The stage is now set for a lively engagement with the methodologies, methods and ethical considerations that are raised throughout the book as a source of seeing. Reflecting on how children have been and are currently seen through the work of the 'eye/I', we can observe an important shift towards more complex methodologies and their yolkings for the field, which call the researcher to account. It will pose a challenge to any representation that claims to see and, by association, know all, or that fails to account for the impact of the researcher themselves – alongside others – in visual encounters. The glimpses we are offered through the pages of this book are, nonetheless, breath-taking.

Notes

1 Referring to the sharing of personal parenting practices and children online (Blum-Ross & Livingston, 2017).

2 An exception is noted in the 2014 text by Marilyn Fleer and Avis Ridgway. Here, the term 'post-developmental research methodologies' is asserted. In reality, it is based on cultural-historical theories that offer one (albeit important) route to seeing based on the work of Vygotsky, but other methodological routes to seeing are not proffered.

3 See publicly available television documentaries such as 'Babies', https://www.youtube.com/watch?v=vB36kohGxDM; 'Child of our Time' (US) https://g.co/kgs/eqikHJ; 'The Secret Life of Four and Five Year Olds' (UK)

https://g.co/kgs/6j4ZdB; and the recent Australian production 'Old peoples homes for four year-olds', https://www.youtube.com/watch?v=ih6q2ByW1-0

4 See e.g. https://me.me/i/research-indicates-that-babies-who-suck-on-pacifiers-are-more-3841109

5 Although readers may be interested to read the VJEP article Michael Gaffney and I wrote (2018) on the early video work of Anne Smith for an example of how video can contribute actively to research agendas concerning the rights of children to be seen as well as heard on matters of importance to them.

6 At the time of writing an interesting example of the work of the ethical 'I' in Playschool was posted on social media concerning children's access to social media https://www.youtube.com/watch?v=lrUSsWUQb68.

7 Some recent examples at the time of writing include Clark (2020); Lester (2018); Lomax (2019); Mannay (2019); Martens (2012); Sturken and Cartwright (2018); and Warr et al. (2016). This list is not exclusive.

References

Agnebyega, J. S. (2012). Beyond alienation: Unpacking the methodological issues in visual research with children. In M. Fleer & A. Ridgway (Eds.), *Visual methodologies and digital tools for researching with young children: Transforming visuality* (pp. 153–168). Springer.

Bakhtin, M. M. (1986). *Speech genres & other late essays* (V. W. McGee, Trans). University of Texas Press.

Berger, J. (1972). *Ways of seeing*. Penguin Books.

Berman, G., Powell, J., & Garcia Herranz, M. (2018). *Ethical considerations when using social media for evidence generation*. UNICEF Office of Research – Innocenti.

Biesta, G., Filippakou, O., Wainwright, E., & Aldridge, D. (2019). Editorial. Why educational research should not just solve problems, but should cause them as well. *British Educational Research Journal, 45*(1), 1–4.

Blum-Ross, A., & Livingstone, S. (2017). "Sharenting", parent blogging, and the boundaries of the digital self. *Popular Communication, 15*(2), 110–125.

Burton, A. (1989). Looking forward from Ariès? Pictorial and material evidence for the history of childhood and family life. *The Child in History. Continuity and Change (Special Issue), 4*(2), 203–229.

Chalfen, R. (2020). Methodological variation in participant visual media production. In L. Pauwels & D. Mannay (Eds.), *The Sage handbook of visual research methods* (2nd ed., pp. 241–253). Sage.

Clark, A. (2020). Visual ethics beyond the crossroads. In L. Pauwels & D. Mannay (Eds.), *The Sage handbook of visual research methods* (2nd ed., pp. 682–693). Sage.

Conroy, J. C., Davis, R. A., & Enslin, P. (2008). Philosophy as a basis for policy and practice: What confidence can we have in philosophical analysis and argument? *Journal of Philosophy of Education, 42*(1), 165–182.

Crary, J. (1992). *Techniques of the observer: On vision and modernity in the nineteenth century.* MIT Press.

deBord, G. (1983). *Society of the spectacle.* Black & Red Publishers.

Derry, S. J. (2007). *Guidelines for video research in education: Recommendations from an expert panel* (pp. 59–66). Retrieved from https://drdc.uchicago.edu/what/video-research-guidelines.pdf

Gaffney, M., & White, E. J. (2018). Video activism as political advocacy for social justice: The legacy of professor Anne Smith for ECE. *Video Journal of Education and Pedagogy.* Retrieved from https://videoeducationjournal.springeropen.com/articles/10.1186/s40990-018-0017-z

Gradovski, M., Eriksen Odegaard, E., Rutanen, N., Sumsion, J., Mika, C., & White, E. J. (2019). *The first 1000 days of early childhood: Becoming.* Springer.

Higonnet, A. (1998). *Pictures of innocence: The history and crisis of ideal childhood.* Thames & Hudson.

Holland, P. (2004). *Picturing childhood: The myth of the child in popular imagery.* I. B. Tauris.

Jay, M. (1993). *Downcast eyes: The denigration of vision in twentieth-century French thought.* University of California Press.

Lester, P. M. (2018). *Visual ethics: A guide for photographers, journalists, and filmmakers.* Routledge.

Lomax, H., & Fink, J. (2020). Understanding online images: Content, context and circulation as analytical foci. In L. Pauwels & D. Mannay (Eds.), *The Sage handbook of visual research methods* (2nd ed., pp. 591–603). Sage.

Mannay, D. (2016). *Visual, narrative and creative research methods: Application, reflection and creative research methods.* Routledge.

Mannay, D. (2019). Creative methods. In R. Iphofen (Ed.), *Handbook of research ethics and scientific integrity.* Springer.

Marion, J., & Crowder, J. (2019). *Visual research: A concise introduction to thinking visually.* Bloomsbury.

Martens, L. (2012). The politics and practices of looking. In S. Pink (Ed.), *Advances in visual methodology* (pp. 39–56). Sage.

McRae, C. (2019). Grace taking form: Re-animating Piaget's concept of the sensori-motor through and with slow motion video. *Video Journal of Education and Pedagogy, 4*(1). Retrieved from https://brill.com/view/journals/vjep/4/1/article-p151_151.xml

Merleau-Ponty, M. (1964). *The primacy of perception.* Northwestern University Press.

Murris, K., & Finn Menning, F. (2019). Introduction to the special issue: Videography and decolonising childhood. *Video Journal of Education and Pedagogy, 4*(1). Retrieved from https://brill.com/view/journals/vjep/4/1/article-p1_1.xml

Nilsson, L. (1965, April 30). Drama of life before birth. *Life Magazine.* Retrieved from https://time.com/3876085/drama-of-life-before-birth-landmark-work-five-decades-/

Pauwells, L. (2020). An integrated conceptual and methodological framework for the visual study of culture and society. In L. Pauwels & D. Mannay (Eds.), *The Sage handbook of visual research methods* (2nd ed., pp. 15–36). Sage.

Pauwells, L., & Mannay, D. (2020). *The Sage handbook of visual research methods* (2nd ed., pp. 3–23). Sage.

Peters, M., White, E. J., Besley, T., Locke, K., Redder, B., Novak, R., Gibbons, A., & O'Neill, J. (2020). Video ethics in educational research involving children: Literature review and critical discussion. *Educational Philosophy and Theory, 52.* Retrieved from https://tandfonline.com/doi/full/10.1080/00131857.2020.1717920

Peters, M., White, E. J., Grierson, E., Stewart, G., Devine, N., Craw, N., Gibbons, A., Jandric, P., Novak, R., Heraud, R., & Locke, K. (2018). Ten theses on the shift from the (static) text to the (moving) image. *Open Review of Education, 5,* 56–94. Retrieved from https://www.tandfonline.com/toc/rrer20/current

Rooney, T. (2017). Spy kids too: Encounters with surveillance through games and play. In E. Taylor & T. Rooney (Eds.), *Surveillance futures: Social and ethical implications for children and young people* (pp. 149–162). Routledge.

Rose, G. (2012). The question of method: Practice, reflexivity and critique in visual culture studies. In I. Heywood & B. Sandywell (Eds.), *The handbook of visual culture* (pp. 543–558). Berg.

Rose, G. (2016). *Visual methodologies: An introduction to researching with visual materials* (4th ed.). Sage.

Rorty, R. (1979). *Philosophy and the mirror of nature.* Princeton University Press.

Ruitenberg, C. (2009). Introduction: The question of method in philosophy of education. *Journal of Philosophy of Education, 43*(3), 315–323.

Rutanen, N., de Souza Amorim, K., Marwick, H., & White, E. J. (2018). Tensions and challenges concerning ethics on video research with young children – Experiences from an international collaboration among seven countries. *Video Journal of Education and Pedagogy.* Retrieved from https://videoeducationjournal.springeropen.com/articles/10.1186/s40990-018-0019-x

Smith, K. (2020). Rethinking informed consent with children under the age of three. In C. M. Schulte (Ed.), *Ethics and research with young children: New perspectives.* Bloomsbury Academic.

St Pierre, E. A. (2019). Post qualitative inquiry in an ontology of immanence. *Qualitative Inquiry, 25*(1), 3–16.

Sturken, M., & Cartwright, L. (2018). *Practices of looking* (3rd ed.). Oxford University Press.

Sturm, S. (2020). Response-ability in video research with children. In M. Peters, E. J. White, T. Besley, K. Locke, B. Redder, R. Novak, A. Gibbons, & J. O'Neill (Eds.),

Video ethics in educational research involving children: Literature review and critical discussion. Educational Philosophy and Theory, 52. Retrieved from https://tandfonline.com/doi/full/10.1080/00131857.2020.1717920

Strom, K., Ringrose, J., Osgood, J., & Renold, E. (2019). Editorial: PhEmaterialism: Response-able research and pedagogy, special issue: PhEmaterialism: Response-able research and pedagogy. *Reconceptualising Educational Research Methodology*, 2–3. Retrieved from https://journals.hioa.no/index.php/rerm/article/view/3649/3404

Sumsion, J., Bradley, B., Stratigos, T., & Elwick, S. (2014). 'Baby cam' and participatory research with infants: A case study of critical reflexivity. In M. Fleer & A. Ridgway (Eds.), *Visual methodologies and digital tools for researching with young children: Transforming visuality* (pp. 169–192). Springer.

Vagle, M. (2018). *Crafting phenomenological research* (2nd ed.). Routledge.

Warr, D., Guillemin, M., Cox, S., & Waycott, J. (Eds.). (2016). *Ethics and visual research methods: Theory, methodology and practice.* Palgrave Macmillan.

White, E. J. (2011). 'Seeing' the toddler: Voices or voiceless? In E. Johansson & E. J. White (Eds.), *Educational research with our youngest: Voices of infants and toddlers* (pp. 63–86). Springer.

White, E. J. (2016). More than meets the 'I': A polyphonic approach to dialogic meaning-making. *Video Journal of Education and Pedagogy.* Retrieved from http://videoeducationjournal.springeropen.com/articles/10.1186/s40990-016-0002-3

White, E. J. (2016a). A philosophy of seeing: The work of the eye/'I' in early years educational practice. *Journal of Philosophy of Education, 50*(3), 474–489. Retrieved from http://onlinelibrary.wiley.com/doi/10.1111/jope.2016.50.issue-3/issuetoc

White, E. J. (2017a). The 'work of the eye' in infant research: A visual encounter. In L. Li, G. Quinones, & A. Ridgway (Eds.), *Studying babies and toddlers: Relationships in cultural contexts* (pp. 123–136). Springer. Retrieved from http://link.springer.com/book/10.1007%2F978-981-10-3197-7

White, E. J. (2017b). Video ethics and young children: An editorial. *Video Journal of Education and Pedagogy.* Retrieved from https://brill.com/view/journals/vjep/2/1/article-p1_2.xml

White, E. J. (2019). *Dialogues about two year-old dialogues in 'preschool'.* University of Waikato, NZ. Retrieved from https://www.waikato.ac.nz/age-responsive/

White, E. J., & Odegaard, E. (2019). Ocular becomings in dangerous times: Special issue editorial. *Video Journal of Education and Pedagogy, 4*(2). Retrieved from https://brill.com/view/journals/vjep/vjep-overview.xml

White, E. J., Rooney, T., Gunn, A., & Nuttall, J. (2020). Understanding how early childhood educators 'see' learning through digitally cast eyes: Some preliminary concepts concerning the use of digital platforms for assessment. *Australian Journal of Early Childhood.*

CHAPTER 2

'Third Objects' and Sandboxes

Creatively Engaging Children to Share Their Understandings of Social Worlds

Dawn Mannay and Amie Hodges

1 Introduction

Childhood is often presented as a state of becoming constrained by discourses of ignorance, passivity and powerlessness, which negate the active role children can effectively play in research and policy; however, children should be supported to have a voice about their everyday lives, experiences and communities (Groundwater-Smith et al., 2015; Lomax, 2012a, 2015; Prout & James, 2015). The voice of the child needs to be heard to both comprehend historical periods of childhood and enable an understanding of the temporality of children's lived moments in contemporary society (Hodges, 2016). Consequently it is important to explore methodological approaches that centralise the subjective lived experiences of children.

Accordingly, this chapter explores the methodological techniques of object work and sandboxing as visual and creative approaches that can engage children and prioritise their views and meaning-making. The chapter draws from two studies undertaken in Wales, UK. One worked directly with young children who had siblings with cystic fibrosis and the other with children in foster care. The chapter argues that children have much to contribute to extending our understandings of childhood and its multiplicities. It outlines the practicalities, potentialities and limitations of working with visual and creative methods, and the data presented offers the reader an insight into innovative ways of seeing the world through children's eyes.

2 Theoretical Orientations

The research discussed in this chapter is embedded in a sociology of childhood, which moves away from 'seeing children as passive recipients of adult socialisation, to a recognition that children are social actors in their own right' (O'Kane, 2000, p. 136). In addition, it aligns with the Welsh Government's adoption of the United Nations Convention on the Rights of the Child (UNCRC),

© KONINKLIJKE BRILL NV, LEIDEN, 2020 | DOI: 10.1163/9789004433328_002

and other policymaking, which respects the perspectives of children and their capabilities to have a voice in matters that impact on their everyday lives (Welsh Assembly Government, 2004; Department of Health and Social Care, 2010. The Royal College of Paediatrics and Child Health, 2010). However, the techniques of data production adopted in these studies have been influenced by, and adapted from, therapeutic and psychoanalytical practice. Therefore, it is important to outline these foundational conceptual frameworks.

2.1   *Third Objects*

'Third things' (Winnicott, 1968, p. 70) or 'third objects' have traditionally been employed in psychoanalysis and other therapeutic work with young children (Isserow, 2008; Stanczak, 2007). In these therapeutic approaches, 'third objects' provide a visual and material point of reference for the patient or client to focus on. The 'third object' or 'third thing' is an activity or object in which a child is interested, for example a toy or game. Looking together is centralised, and the triangular relationship takes a priori the capacity of the patient to look at an object, together with the therapist, as an enactment of joint attention (Isserow, 2008). In therapeutic and clinical practice, the technique has been reported to reduce the stress and anxiety associated with talking about personal or sensitive issues (Winnicott, 1968).

Beyond these therapeutic spaces, objects have been used in social science research as tools of elicitation to build rapport and connection and to open up spaces of reflexivity. In these cases, it has been argued that reflecting on and discussing a topic is often easier if there is something to look at or hold, rather than being fixed within the gaze of the researcher (Dumangane, 2016; Pink, 2001; Shaw & Holland, 2014). The underlying principles of 'third object' approaches can also be seen in other research techniques that encourage metaphorical modes of engagement, such as sandboxing, where the visual is centralised.

2.2   *The World Technique and Sandboxing*

In the same way that the use of 'third objects' has been transferred from therapeutic practice into research spaces, 'sandboxing' was also developed and adapted from its original use in psychoanalysis to a technique of visual data production in the social sciences (Mannay et al., 2017, 2018, 2019; Mannay & Turney, 2020). While the term 'sandboxing' is used to distinguish the distinct development of this approach as a tool for visual qualitative research inquiry, many of its defining features were derived from the 'world technique' (Lowenfeld, 1939, 1950).

Margaret Lowenfeld was a pioneer of child psychology and play therapy; she designed the 'world technique' in which children create three dimensional scenes, pictures or abstract designs in a tray filled with sand and a range of miniature, realistic and fantasy figures and everyday objects. The 'world technique' (Lowenfeld, 1939) aligns well with approaches that centralise participants' meaning-making, as the discussion with the child about his or her sand scenes to some extent mirrors the elicitation interview approach, which is also a feature in work with third objects. Sandboxing retains this participant-focused understanding of visual data by including an elicitation interview in which participants explain the figures that they have set up in the sandbox and talk the researcher through their sand scenes.

In the following section, we discuss examples of our visual research, first with reference to toys as 'third objects' and second in relation to the specific approach of sandboxing. Importantly, in both cases, we are not aligning ourselves or our work with therapeutic or psychoanalytical practice. The objects were introduced to enable children to lead the conversations and introduce ideas that were important to them, rather than be confined by a set question-and-answer interview defined by the adult researcher (Kim, 2015; O'Kane, 2008), and to encourage visual, creative and metaphorical modes of engagement (Dumangane, 2016).

3 'Third Objects' and Sandboxes: Application of the Techniques

3.1 *Working with Siblings of Children with Cystic Fibrosis – 'Third Objects'*

Interested in the everyday experiences of the siblings of children with cystic fibrosis, I – Amie Hodges (2016, 2018) – worked with children's objects when interviewing them in their own homes.[1] I took a mosaic approach (Clarke & Moss, 2001), where children could draw pictures, create collages and use their own toys and objects to communicate their experiences of being the siblings of children with cystic fibrosis. The use of objects aligns with conceptualisations of the 'third object', and the material objects introduced by the children in the study formed the basis of elicitation interviews, where children shared their ideas about the actual or metaphorical meanings of their everyday playthings.

The introduction of toys proved to be useful for children to lead conversations about their possessions themselves and to link them with other facets of their everyday lives. For example, eight-year-old Elinor,[2] who had two siblings with cystic fibrosis, discussed her Barbie dolls at each of the four research visits and featured them in one of her collages. As a sibling of two children with cystic fibrosis, Elinor often had to 'get out of the way' when her siblings underwent treatments, an aspect of family life discussed by both Elinor and her parents. Therefore, her 'Barbie' bedroom took on a particular significance.

Elinor used her Barbie house and dolls to set up and discuss her daily routines with different dolls representing family members – the rooms in the doll's house aligning with rooms in the family home – and to re-enact family activity surrounding the provision of cystic fibrosis treatment. In watching Elinor play with the Barbie dolls, discussing their significance and moving them around the doll's house, I was able to gain an understanding of not only Elinor's relational experiences, but also elements of fantasy about the life that she could live, expressed within the Barbie world, as illustrated in Figure 2.1.

FIGURE 2.1   Barbie doll living space in Elinor's doll's house

Figure 2.1 illustrates the living space of the lounge area, where the Barbie doll was sat on the settee alone. The isolation that Elinor experienced when her siblings were undergoing their cystic fibrosis treatments would be when she was in her bedroom – a place she would often go to, but not always by choice. Based on my work with Elinor, including the talk around this activity, the drawings she made and conversations with her and her parents, the placement of the doll in the living room was a significant visualisation of her experience. Reflecting on the data generated and subsequent analysis, I read this scene as a way for Elinor to metaphorically be where she wants to be, where other family members are when she is not allowed to be with them because of the demands placed on the family by cystic fibrosis.

In addition, I noticed that the doll was not just placed alone in the sitting room, but alone within the whole of the house. Again, this placement could be read as representative of a feeling of isolation in relation to Elinor's positioning within the family. The use of the 'third objects', namely, the doll and accessories within the doll's house, enabled Elinor to provide a transformed view, thus giving her a voice as she was responsible for her own situated construction. This provided new insights into her family world and the socialisation and relationality within this familial space.

Edwards et al. (2005) identify the importance and use of differing rooms and spaces within the family home. Elinor arguably represented a metaphorical and fantasy world of a home with 'the Barbie house', which was located within the family home but at the same time was open to her direction and preferences. In this way, the doll's house moved from simply being a children's toy to becoming a useful tool in my researcher's methodological toolkit, enabling me to begin to see the world of the home and family through Elinor's eyes. Spending time getting to know Elinor both prior to and during the activities was important to gain trust and to give her the confidence to choose how and when to express and articulate her expression through object work. Timing and readiness to participate are important considerations for both child and researcher, particularly when exploring issues of a sensitive nature.

Another significant feature of object work was Elinor's interactive performance with her chosen objects and the ways in which she re-created scenes of her experience of family life, whilst living with siblings and journeying alongside the cystic fibrosis trajectory. Elinor was able to share her innermost feelings, worries and concerns as she created her own stage setting of the family home, focusing on the context of family life experience. It was through her interactive engagement with the object work that Elinor was able to create a narrative performance. This informatively represented her dialogic self (Hermans, 2001) that was relevant to the cultural and social interaction in the positioning of self and other, as she provided an insightful presentation of herself within her family world.

3.2   *Working with Care-Experienced Children – Sandboxing*

Resonating with the use of 'third objects' are the collection of objects, including people, houses, trees, fences, animals, transport, street signs and other miscellaneous items in the form of miniaturised figures, which feature in sandboxing. The figures themselves are not pliable or open to physical change, although metaphorically they can take on multiple and unrestricted meanings.

The sandbox, like the doll's house, acts as a frame for these figures, where they can be placed, raised or buried, and participants can decide how they are positioned and what this means in the visual communication of their experiences. This approach was offered as an option for care-experienced children and young people in a study by Dawn Mannay and colleagues (2015) exploring education, aspiration and everyday experiences.[3]

The research with primary school (aged 6–11) and secondary school (aged 11–16) children and young people was situated in all-day events, which included activities such as clay modelling; wall climbing; sport-based games; and jewellery, t-shirt and bag making, where participants could take home the items they created. Within these activity-based days, children and young people who wanted to be included in the research element told us they wished to join in, or they put their names on cards and pegged them on string to let us know they were happy to take part. This approach provided opportunities to get to know the children and young people and kept the activities open to everyone, regardless of whether they wanted to participate in the study. Children and young people who wished to be involved in the research could select one-to-one emotion sticker activities and/or sandboxing incorporating an elicitation interview, or they could simply have a conversation with the researcher.

Eight-year-old Spiderman[4] created a sand scene featuring what he listed as a 'bad knight and a good knight ... a ghost ... a horse, lion, house, fire and a pterodactyl' (see Figure 2.2).[5] Everyday objects matter to different people for different reasons and in quite different ways (Wagner, 2020), and in sandboxing, they are often used metaphorically (Mannay et al., 2017, 2019; Mannay & Turney, 2020). However, for Spiderman, they are what they depict in his initial descriptions, and the dinosaur is even given its particular name, which I – Dawn Mannay – did not know. When asked, 'what things do you think you might have when you're grown up?', the answer featured again 'a house, fire', and this time 'a pet', which may have been notionally represented by the horse, lion or pterodactyl. Horses and an experience of horse-riding feature in our later conversation, and Spiderman then commented that the horse in the sandbox represented future pets.

In reference to the building in the sandbox, Spiderman explained, 'my house would be ... bricks like this. But a bigger house', and he discussed the dog, called Ben or Bruno, that he would take for a walk. There was also an attempt to place one of the figurative pets inside the house: 'I think I'm going to put them by there ... so this is in the house. Pets'. The building usually opens but unfortunately the door was jammed in the session and could not be opened, neither by Spiderman nor by me, which meant that the imperative to place the pets inside the home remained unfulfilled. The centrality of 'home' was confirmed later when Spiderman explained, 'I'm happy where I am [foster home]', but then goes on to say, 'umm my ... social worker said she is having a look to see is there any foster carers up in [place name] so I can go with them so I can be closer to my Nan'.[6]

Spiderman's foster placement is not near his Nan's home, although he is able to stay with his Nan once a week. When he visits her, this also gives Spiderman opportunities to see his six siblings at different points and to call his best friend, who lives on the same street as his Nan. Through placement in the care system, Spiderman has been moved outside of his home town (see also Sebba et al., 2015; Welbourne & Leeson, 2012), and although he may be 'happy' there, it means he is distanced from supportive family relationships and friendship networks. This illustrates the complexity of 'home' for children in care, and it may go some way towards explaining Spiderman's choice of the house for his sand scene and his desire to open the house and place inside figures representing what he wants for his future.

FIGURE 2.2   Sand scene created by Spiderman[7]

The importance of home was notable in many of the care-experienced children and young people's accounts of their past and current experiences and in their future lives, and pets were also centralised. Pets are significant because, although they play an active role in fostering well-being (Briheim-Crookall, 2016), they are often left behind in the process of separation from the family home and later in placement-related moves to different foster cares. Within his current foster home at the time of the study, Spiderman did not have access to the type of pet he would like – 'No, nothing, we have fishes' – but as in the case with Elinor, the future-orientated nature of the scene allowed him to metaphorically be where he wants to be, in the security of a brick-built house with his ideal pets. In this way, the objects enabled Spiderman to visualise and communicate his ideas; however, there are both advantages and constraints associated with the use of these visual approaches that will be discussed in the following section.

4 Affordances and Limitations

Children form a heterogeneous group with a diversity of experiences, communication styles, preferences and 'voices' (Lomax, 2012b). Therefore, we cannot assume a one-size-fits-all approach where assumptions are made that creative methods are necessarily suited to all children. In both of the qualitative studies presented in this chapter, children were consequently offered a choice of visual activities, as well as the option to simply talk or not participate at all. For researchers considering applying visual and creative techniques, offering a range of options can be useful so that children are not constrained by a single approach (see Smith, 2019).

Object work did seem to confer particular benefits in working with the children. Participants in the studies had experienced moves away from their family or temporary dislocations as a result of their siblings' cystic fibrosis. Therefore, having an open activity, where children could create representations of their present and future on their own terms, allowed a safe space for exploring the complexities and uncertainties faced in the everyday lives of children. Hence, the consideration of space and environment is important when doing object work and creative activities, as it can enable a child to feel protected and safe, and it can allow for privacy from the outside world (Hodges, 2016; Lee, 2001). Providing a safe space for a child can be of particular value because of the emotional labour that can potentially be encountered when participating in a research study, as it can enable the child to visualise and externalise how he or she feels, and it can facilitate emotional growth and development within the research encounter.

Children valued having one-to-one attention during the activities, as it provided them with an opportunity to voice their worries, concerns and experiences relating to the context of their circumstances. Object work also provided a positive distraction from the uncertainties of daily life, and it enabled the children to feel supported, as an indirect platform for communication was provided. Moving away from a traditional question-and-answer style of interview also made it easier to reflect on and discuss topics, as there was something to look at or hold, rather than children being fixed within the gaze of the researcher (see also Ross et al., 2009). Using such techniques enabled children to have a choice in the objects that were selected, thereby permitting them to engage with the researcher and to present themselves through their own creative expression, on their own terms. For Buckingham (2000), children's choices are important in terms of their interactions and the influences that they encounter – and he maintains that choice is a child's right.

Furthermore, although activities such as drawing, collaging and Lego bricks have proved to be useful in previous research (Gauntlet & Holzwarth, 2006; Lyon, 2020; Mannay, 2010; Purcell, 2018), they rely on particular spatial and co-ordination skills, which could exclude some children. Object work does not demand any particular artistic skills or spatial capabilities, which suggests that it is potentially less threatening and challenging than other creative approaches. It is also important to note that no artistic or technological skills are required on the part of researchers, meaning that even when projects have limited research budgets and when teams have a lack of training in more technology-based techniques, opportunities still exist to employ creative methods of working with children. Furthermore, using creativity can allow for a synergistic way for children to consciously frame their existential self as well as expose the unconscious, unspoken, private, previously invisible, unacknowledged self (Leitch, 2008).

Enabling children to work with objects to creatively express themselves through visual manipulation also provides them with the opportunity to perform their lived experience. Therefore, it is important for the researcher to have greater awareness of the 'how' of the activity – how a child is performing his or her narrative in relation to the objects chosen, as opposed to just 'why' he or she has chosen those objects and their associated positioning (Hodges, 2016). Children's performance may manifest in the spoken or unspoken; it can be in a facial expression, a song, a dance or even silence. Observing their performance can offer more nuanced insights and understandings of children's worlds and their situated self (Hodges, 2016). This aligns with the premise introduced in the introduction to this chapter, namely, that children should be supported to have a voice about their everyday lives, experiences and communities (Groundwater-Smith et al., 2015; Lomax, 2012a, 2015).

In the interpretation of this data, however, the question of 'whose voice' needs to be further considered. In the work explored in this chapter, auteur theory was centralised – according to this theory, the most salient aspect in understanding a visual image is what the maker intended to depict (Mannay,

2010; Rose, 2001). Auteur theory was required on a practical level because the interpretation of researchers assessing visual representations is not necessarily the same as the narrative the image-maker aimed to communicate. The practice of asking children to explain the visual scenes they created enabled us to move beyond assumptions and invite them to offer their rationales and meaning-making. This is more difficult when children may not be able to verbally communicate with the researcher; here, consideration of other strategies is required to understand the motivations of those children through wider contextualisation, careful observation and an extended ethnographic time in the field getting to know individual children and their alternative communication styles (see, for example, Pickering, 2013).

5   Ethical Considerations

There are some specific benefits to working with objects rather than other visual approaches. For example, they do not have the ethical difficulties associated with the dissemination of film, photographs and other highly recognisable forms of data. Much mainstream engagement with the ethics of visual research focuses on the 'moral maze of image ethics' (Prosser, 2000) and the tension between revealing and concealing the contents of visual images, particularly when they feature young children. The generic nature of sandboxing figures, as well as the lack of attachment to individual participants beyond the situated and transient nature of the fieldwork, means that the associated photographs can be disseminated. However, the child-selected third objects in Hodges' (2016) research require more caution, and their recognisability must be assessed carefully on a case-by-case basis.

It is important to recognise that the third objects and sandboxing approaches have been drawn from therapeutic and psychoanalytical practice. Strong objections have been made to taking psychoanalysis outside of the clinical situation of the consulting room (Frosh, 2010), and drawing on methods used in therapeutic settings has been criticised for importing unequal power relations into social sciences research. However, the use of objects and sandboxing is an adaption that is clearly delineated from therapeutic practice. Furthermore, in considering power relations, object work and sandboxing arguably illustrate participatory potential because with the introduction of the objects, children have an opportunity to lead the discussions about their experiences with researchers, rather than being fixed and guided by set questions prescribed by the researcher.

Nevertheless, objects are containers of meaning, and the metaphorical and mnemonic qualities they engender mean that there is less control in the direction of the talk between researcher and participant. Therefore, it is advisable that researchers trial these techniques on themselves, as well as with colleagues and social networks, before they enter the field to work with children. This attention to carefulness and reflexivity is necessary prior to and within the process of creative data production with objects to ensure that children feel safe and supported in the research encounter.

6   Future Applications

The work with objects reported in this chapter was supported by photographs, fieldnotes and elicitation interviews. A further aspect that researchers adopting future applications could think about is other ways the data could be recorded. As illustrated by Spiderman's attempt to open the building represented as a home and Elinor's setting up of the doll's house scene, movement can be an aspect of analytical interest. Film could play an important role by documenting these processes: filming the making process would enable a higher level of reflexivity on participants' actions, facial expressions and movements (Knoblauch & Tuma, 2019), as it would capture their self-presentation through their performance and social interactions within the research experience (Goffman, 1990; Hodges, 2016). However, participants may not always welcome a video camera, as it could be viewed as a more intrusive presence than an audio recorder, which is a salient point for contemplation. In these particular studies, filming individual children was not possible in relation to institutional ethical requirements (Hodges) and the care status of the children involved (Mannay). Nevertheless, it is something that could be considered in future applications of object-based work with children.

7   Conclusion

Creative work with objects has much to offer in terms of the potential to engage children holistically and practically so as to engender reflection, as well as to enable more participant-led data production. Children can gain an identification and enjoyment of being involved in research when they are provided with an environment that offers freedom to express themselves through visual and creative activity and performance. Accordingly, using this approach enables movement beyond the confines of the set question-and-answer interview style to broaden and extend discussions of, and outside of, the topic under examination. This chapter explored the ways in which objects and sandboxes can creatively engage children in meaningful activities to share their understandings of their constructed and co-constructed social worlds, and it described how those elements can create opportunities to see the world through children's eyes. Hence, an understanding of the temporality of children's everyday lived experiences can be gained and, as such, can provide insights – not just concerning the child as an individual; but also into childhood in contemporary worlds.

8   Summary Statements

– Object work and sandboxing are research techniques that were adapted from therapeutic practice with third objects and the world technique.
– In social science research, these techniques can be useful in enabling children to lead interview discussions and engage with reflexivity and metaphor work.
– Object work moves beyond the confines of a set question-and-answer interview approach, and handling and viewing objects can provide a central focus so that the child does not feel held within the researcher's gaze.
– Object work enables the voice of the child to be heard, through creative expression, thereby allowing for an authentic presentation of self.
– Object work can facilitate the performance of an experience for children; this can be particularly beneficial if they are not fully able to express and articulate their spoken narrative.
– Object work can enable a greater understanding of the children's world, as it enables them to represent and enact their experiences, which can provide a holistic insight into their constructed and co-constructed presentations.
– The data generated has less ethical risks than those posed in film and photographs; however, researchers using these approaches should trial them and employ reflexive practice when working with children.

Acknowledgements

The authors would like to acknowledge all of the participants in the studies discussed, without whom there would be no research. In addition, we are grateful for the support of the Florence Nightingale Foundation, the Band

Charitable Trust, and the General Nursing Council and the Welsh Government. Thanks also to the book editor, Dr E. Jayne White, and to the reviewers, for their supportive and encouraging comments on earlier drafts of this chapter. Amie Hodges would also like to acknowledge her doctoral supervisors, Professor Daniel Kelly and Dr Katie Featherstone, and the Brocher Foundation.

Notes

1 The doctoral study was funded by the Florence Nightingale Foundation, the Band Charitable Trust and the General Nursing Council, and it was titled 'The Family-Centred Experiences of Siblings in the Context of Cystic Fibrosis: A Dramaturgical Exploration'. The research took place in England and Wales.
2 Elinor is a pseudonym selected by the researcher.
3 The study was commissioned by the Welsh government and was titled 'Understanding the educational experiences and opinions, attainment, achievement and aspirations of looked after children in Wales'. The research took place in Wales.
4 Spiderman is a pseudonym selected by the participant. The name is associated with a fictional superhero featured in magazines, books, film and television.
5 The fire is not a separate object but something visible in one of the painted window scenes on the building.
6 Nan is a term used in Wales as an alternative to grandmother.
7 The sandbox here is marked up with the pseudonym Spiderman because we took instant Polaroid photographs for participants to take home with them, and since only one camera was shared between researchers working in different areas, we wanted to ensure that all children went home with the correct photographic representations.

References

Briheim-Crookall, L. (2016). *How social workers can track and boost the happiness of looked-after children*. Community Care. Retrieved from http://www.communitycare.co.uk/2016/03/22/social-workers-can-track-boost-happiness-looked-children/

Buckingham, D. (2000). *After the death of childhood: Growing up in the age of electronic media*. Polity.

Clarke, A., & Moss, P. (2001). *Listening to young children: The mosaic approach*. National Children's Bureau Enterprises.

Department of Health and Social Care. (2010). *Getting it right for children and young people: Overcoming cultural barriers in the NHS so as to meet their needs*. A review by Professor Sir Ian Kennedy. Department of Health and Social Care, London.

Dumangane, C. (2016). *Exploring the narratives of the few: British African Caribbean male graduates of elite universities in England and Wales* (PhD thesis). Cardiff University. Retrieved from http://orca.cf.ac.uk/86927/1/Constantino%20 Dumangane%20-%20Final%20Thesis%20%28January%202016%29.pdf

Edwards, R., Hadfield, H., & Mauthner, M. L. (2005). *Children's understanding of their sibling relationships*. National Children's Bureau for the Joseph Rowntree Foundation.

Gauntlett, D., & Holzwarth, P. (2006). Creative and visual methods for exploring identities. *Visual Studies, 21*(1), 82–91.

Goffman, E. (1990). *The presentation of self in everyday life*. Penguin.

Groundwater-Smith, S., Dockett, S., & Bottrell, D. (2015). *Participatory research with children and young people*. Sage.

Hermans, H. J. M. (2001). The dialogic self: Towards a theory of personal and cultural positioning. *Culture Psychology, 7*(3), 243–281.

Hodges, A. S. (2016). *The family centred experiences of siblings in the context of cystic fibrosis: A dramaturgical exploration* (PhD thesis). Cardiff University.

Hodges, A. S. (2018). The positional self and researcher emotion: Destabilising sibling equilibrium in the context of cystic fibrosis. In T. Loughran & D. Mannay (Eds.), *Emotion and the researcher: sites, subjectivities, and relationships* (Studies in Qualitative Methodology, Vol. 16, pp. 49–63). Emerald.

James, A., & Prout, A. (2015). *Constructing and reconstructing childhood. Contemporary issues in the sociological study of childhood* (2nd ed.). Routledge.

Kim, C. Y. (2015). Why research 'by' children? Rethinking the assumptions underlying the facilitation of children as researchers. *Children & Society, 30*(3), 230–240.

Lee, N. (2001). *Childhood and society. Growing up in an age of uncertainty*. Open University Press.

Leitch, R. (2008). Creatively researching children's narratives through images and drawings. In P. Thomson (Ed.), *Doing visual research with children and young people* (pp. 37–58). Routledge.

Lomax, H. (2012a). Shifting the focus: Children's image-making practices and their implications for analysis. *International Journal of Research and Method in Education (Special Issue: Problematising Visual Methods), 35*(3), 227–34.

Lomax, H. (2012b). Contested voices? Methodological tensions in creative visual research with children. *International Journal of Social Research Methodology, 15*(2), 105–117.

Lomax, H. (2015). Seen and heard? Ethics and agency in participatory visual research with children, young people and families. *Families, Relationships and Societies, 4*(3), 493–502.

Lowenfeld, M. (1939). The world pictures of children. *British Journal of Medical Psychology, 18,* 65–101.

Lowenfeld, M. (1950). The nature and use of the Lowenfeld World Technique in work with children and adults. *The Journal of Psychology, 30*(2), 325–331.

Lyon, P. (2020). Using drawing in visual research: Materializing the invisible. In L. Pauwels & D. Mannay (Eds.), *The Sage handbook of visual research methods* (2nd ed., pp. 297–308). Sage.

Mannay, D. (2010). Making the familiar strange: Can visual research methods render the familiar setting more perceptible? *Qualitative Research, 10*(1), 91–111.

Mannay, D., Creaghan, J., Gallagher, D., Marzella, R., Mason, S., Morgan, M., & Grant, A. (2018). Negotiating closed doors and constraining deadlines: The potential of visual ethnography to effectually explore private and public spaces of motherhood and parenting. *Journal of Contemporary Ethnography, 47*(6), 758–781.

Mannay, D., & Staples, E. (2019). Sandboxes, stickers and superheroes: Employing creative techniques to explore the aspirations and experiences of children and young people who are looked after. In D. Mannay, A. Rees, & L. Roberts (Eds.), *Children and young people 'looked after'? Education, intervention and the everyday culture of care in Wales* (pp. 169–182). University of Wales Press.

Mannay, D., Staples, E., & Edwards, V. (2017). Visual methodologies, sand and psychoanalysis: Employing creative participatory techniques to explore the educational experiences of mature students and children in care. *Visual Studies, 32*(4), 345–358.

Mannay, D., Staples, E., Hallett, S., Roberts, L., Rees, A., Evans, R., & Andrews, D. (2015). *Understanding the educational experiences and opinions, attainment, achievement and aspirations of looked after children in Wales.* Project Report [Online]. Welsh Government. Retrieved from http://gov.wales/statistics-and-research/understanding-educational-experiences-opinions-attainment-achievement-aspirations-looked-after-children-wales/?lang=en

Mannay, D., & Turney, C. (2020). Sandboxing: A creative approach to qualitative research in education. In S. Delamont & M. Ward (Eds.), *Handbook of qualitative research in education* (2nd ed., pp. 233–245). Elgar.

O'Kane, C. (2008). The development of participatory techniques: Facilitating children's views about decisions which affect them. In P. Christensen & A. James (Eds.), *Research with children: Perspectives and practices* (pp. 125–155). RoutledgeFalmer.

Pickering, D. (2013). Creative mosaic methods: Hearing the 'voice' of children with disabilities. *International Journal of Therapy and Rehabilitation, 20*(7), 325.

Prosser, J. (2000). The moral maze of image ethics. In H. Simons & R. Usher (Eds.), *Situated ethics in educational research* (pp. 116–132). RoutledgeFalmer.

Purcell, M. E. (2018). Hubris, revelations and creative pedagogy: Transformation, dialogue and modelling 'professional love' with LEGO®. *Journal of Further and Higher Education.* https://doi.org/10.1080/0309877X.2018.1490948

Rose, G. (2001). *Visual methodologies*. Sage.

Ross, N. J., Renold, E., Holland, S., & Hillman, A. (2009). Moving stories: Using mobile methods to explore the everyday lives of young people in public care. *Qualitative Research, 9*(5), 605–623.

Royal College of Paediatrics and Child Health. (2010). *Not just a phase. A guide to the participation of children and young people in health services*. RCPCH.

Sebba, J., Berridge, D., Luke, N., Fletcher, J., Bell, K., & Strand, S. (2015). *The educational progress of looked after children in England: Linking care and educational data*. Rees Centre for Research in Fostering and Education and University of Bristol.

Shaw, I., & Holland, S. (2014). *Doing qualitative research in social work*. Sage.

Smith, P. (2019). A view from a Pupil Referral Unit: Using participatory methods with young people in an education setting'. In D. Mannay, A. Rees, & L. Roberts (Eds.), *Children and young people 'looked after'? Education, intervention and the everyday culture of care in Wales* (pp. 182–195). University of Wales Press.

Wagner, J. (2020). Seeing things: Visual research and material culture. In L. Pauwels & D. Mannay (Eds.), *The Sage handbook of visual research methods* (2nd ed., pp. 57–75). Sage.

Wartovsky, M. (1981). The child's construction and the world's construction of the child from historical epistemology to historical psychology. In F. Kessel & A. Seigal (Eds.), *The child and other cultural interventions* (pp. 188–215). Praeger.

Welbourne, P., & Leeson, C. (2012). The education of children in care: A research review. *Journal of Youth Services, 7*(2), 128–43.

Welsh Assembly Government. (2004). *Children and young people: Rights to action*. Welsh Assembly Government.

Wyness, M. (2012). *Childhood and society* (2nd ed.). Palgrave.

CHAPTER 3

Reaching beyond the 'Visual Givens' through Philosophical-Empirical Inquiry

Video, Depth and Epiphany

Sheena Elwick

1 Introduction

The objective of this chapter is to extend scholarly discussions of the research approach known as *philosophical-empirical inquiry* to include a visual element that affords visual researchers – and educational researchers more broadly – possibilities for 'reaching beyond the "visual givens"' (Merleau-Ponty, 1964, p. 166).

Using this as my starting point, I outline specific visual methods that are anchored in philosophical-empirical inquiry, and that in Merleau-Ponty's (1964, p. 166) words, 'give visible existence to what profane vision [the naked eye] believes to be invisible'. Of particular interest here is the use-value of Merleau-Ponty's (1962, p. 308) work, and more specifically his philosophical concept of *depth*: the existential 'dimension in which things or elements of things envelop each other', antagonise and encroach. Such a perspective offers a crucial alternative to the more typical perspective of video that suggests it 'serve[s] to depict only a limited and finite range of all possible content ...' (Banks & Zeitlyn, 2015, p. 52).

While it is not my intent to argue that video brings all 'possible content' into view, I draw on two completed early childhood education (ECE) philosophical-empirical inquiries to illustrate that video can, and should, serve to do much more in qualitative research than depict this or that. Rather, and somewhat contrastingly to Banks and Zeitlyn's argument, in this chapter, I put forward that when video is used to 'reach beyond the "visual givens"' (Merleau-Ponty, 1964, p. 166), it can facilitate what I refer to as an *epiphany*: a moment of sudden and great revelation or realisation that allows for self, other, and pedagogical evaluation and transformation.

I conclude the chapter by discussing the limitations and ethical issues that researchers might encounter when applying the outlined research approaches, as well as future possibilities.

2 On Philosophical-Empirical Inquiry

Philosophical-empirical inquiry is a term originally formulated by Stephen Kemmis (2011, p. 84) and used to describe an 'interpretive-critical mode' of working in action research and critical social science. The term has since been developed and enacted in several different contexts, including educational research with young children, where it has been conceived as a 'creative and expressive practice, and hence a practice of possibility' (Elwick & Green, 2019, p. 6).

Philosophical-empirical inquiry fundamentally, and as discussed elsewhere (Elwick & Green, 2019, p. 3), seeks to combine explicitly philosophical exploration with 'fieldwork' investigations, 'bringing together conceptual sophistication with empirical rigour' (Green & Hopwood, 2015, p. 5). It involves, amongst other things, a reciprocal and dynamic interaction between those involved in the research, the historical, social worlds they inhabit and the phenomena under investigation. In other words, when performing philosophical-empirical inquiry, a researcher begins with a 'concrete encounter with others in the field, not with a [pre-determined] research question' (St. Pierre, 2019, p. 12) or set of research methods that are applied top-down to the research context.

By doing so, the researcher aims to ensure that the investigations undertaken in a philosophical-empirical inquiry are always 'inter-activities, therefore, co-productive, and participatory' (Elwick & Green, 2019, p. 3). They also aim to ensure that rather than being something applied to empirical data after the fact, philosophy becomes 'an entering into' emerging (and often unexpected) empirical phenomena and questions, as well as emerging (and often unexpected) conceptual and methodological challenges, such that it 'take[s] part in their maturation and experience' (Merleau-Ponty, 1976, p. 58). The intersection of poststructuralist theory and philosophy, broadly understood, is of particular interest in this regard. Although it might be equally appropriate to point to St. Pierre's (2019) invention of 'post-qualitative inquiry' as a distinctive coming together of an 'ontology of immanence from poststructuralism as well as transcendental empiricism' (p. 3).

Importantly, in this chapter, the stimuli for what I write and think about originated from within actual moments in ECE research encounters that have stayed with me since – my 'ontological haunting[s]', as St. Pierre (2019, p. 12) puts it. By taking this approach, I ensure that the visual methods I discuss are anchored in philosophical-empirical inquiry, as well as illustrate some of the possibilities that philosophical-empirical inquiry might afford visual researchers interested in explicitly combining their own philosophical ponderings with fieldwork investigations in the future.

3　　Video, Depth and Epiphany

3.1　Video

The use of video in research situations concerning young children is not a new idea by any means. Likewise, it is not a new idea to use video filmed simultaneously from different camera viewpoints for various research purposes. White (2016), for example, synchronises four different visual fields of the same event to help operationalise what she refers to as a 'polyphonic approach to video data generation' (p. 6) based on visual fields and the dialogues that are generated out of this visual surplus. Part of White's reasoning for a 'polyphonic approach' is similar to what is put forward in this chapter: that when video is posited in this way, it 'allows one to perceive beyond one's own limits' (White, as cited in White, 2016, p. 1). In this chapter, I explore how such a 'deepened, transformed perception' (Hass, 2008, p. 71) might also eventuate when viewers watch different camera viewpoints of the same event *one after the other*.

I first realised the fruitful possibilities of consecutively viewing different camera viewpoints of the same event during a philosophical-empirical inquiry into infant participation in research (Elwick, 2016). It is fair to say the realisation came about accidentally and largely in response to difficulties encountered with the software used to synchronise the video, with the resultant decision being to use that software only on limited occasions.

In this particular inquiry, two cameras were used to simultaneously record the research environment: a tripod-mounted camera and a small digital camera system comprising a digital camera and sound-recording equipment worn by the infant on his or her head. The resultant video footage was later viewed by multiple audiences, including researchers and ECE professionals. On a few occasions, the images were synchronised so viewers were able to experience both camera perspectives simultaneously. However, on most occasions, the images generated by the tripod camera were displayed first, and viewers were then asked for their responses. The corresponding images from the camera worn by the infant were then presented and discussed.

A full discussion of the differences between both approaches of presenting the images to viewers is beyond the scope of this chapter. Suffice to say, it became evident that, in these particular research contexts at least, when viewers watched one camera perspective and discussed their thoughts prior to watching the second perspective, they often saw previously unnoticed and unsuspected phenomena. For many viewers, these revelations provoked what I refer to here as an epiphanic moment (discussed below).

At the time of the inquiry, I used Ihde's (1979) philosophy of technology and aspects of Merleau-Ponty's philosophy to interrogate this phenomenon (see Elwick, 2015). However, as an admirer and avid reader of Merleau-Ponty's philosophy, it later struck me that Merleau-Ponty's (1962) concept of depth might help to 'reorient thought' (St. Pierre, 2019, p. 14) and provide new insights. It also struck me that his commentary around the capacity of painting to 'give visible existence to what profane vision believes to be invisible' (1964, p. 166) would provide a productive line of inquiry.

A fascinating illustrative example (to me at least) of how technology 'give[s] visible existence to what profane vision believes to be invisible' (Merleau-Ponty, 1964, p. 166) is provided by artist Julian Beever.[1] For those who might not be familiar with Julian's work, he is known internationally for his pavement chalk drawings and, in particular, for his three-dimensional illusions drawn with a special distortion to create a three-dimensional image when viewed through either a camera, a mobile phone, an iPad or another screen – they do not look three-dimensional to the naked eye. *Swimming-pool in High Street* is one of Julian's drawings that particularly captured my attention.[2] When I viewed the image from what Julian calls the 'wrong' side (i.e. as the naked eye would see it), I could not quite work out what I was seeing. There was an especially long, pale appendage that seemed strangely out of place. The tripod camera that Julian had set up on the 'right' side for people to look through was also visible in the image. It was only after looking at the image from the viewpoint of that tripod camera that I was surprised to realise the 'long, pale appendage' that was 'out of place' was actually the leg of the swimmer in the pool. It is this capacity of technology to bring into visibility some of the hidden phenomena not always apparent to the naked eye that, for me, connects them to Merleau-Ponty's commentary on painting. Moreover, this capacity hints towards the possibility that watching different camera viewpoints of the same event one after the other might make multiple opportunities available for viewers to open upon the *depth* of being that Merleau-Ponty often refers to within that commentary (e.g. Merleau-Ponty, 1964).

3.2 *Depth*

Merleau-Ponty's articulation of depth is, in many ways, a response to its more traditional Cartesian treatment, where it is viewed as a third dimension derived from two other dimensions: height and width. Based on this account, depth is simply a juxtaposition of objects (or points or planes) detached from human experience (Merleau-Ponty, 1962, 1964). Translating this idea into video images suggests that the images are nothing more than a juxtaposition of objects on a screen that yield depth between them, but bear no particular relation to the viewer or the viewing situation. This standpoint has been widely refuted in visual methodology literature (e.g. Elwick, 2015; Martens, 2012) and film theory literature (e.g. Sobchack, 2004), albeit not from the outlook provided by Merleau-Ponty's concept of depth. While each of these cited scholars provides slightly different alternatives to the Cartesian standpoint, if we compared them, we would find agreement on the point that visual research is best conceived as 'an embodied and multi-sensory practice' (Martens, 2012, p. 42). We might likewise find a common groping toward an alternative to the concept of listening that enjoys widespread currency in educational research concerning young children. Within such approaches, vision is somewhat imbued with suspicion in relation to its proposed hegemonic role in positioning children as observable research objects, rather than as active participants. It is this Cartesian account of vision that 'turn[s] it into a view on the world, rather than in it' (Jay, 1993, p. 304) that depth helps to overcome.

Although Merleau-Ponty's treatment of depth is much too rich to be fully explored here, it too 'announces an indissoluble link' (1962, p. 298) between the embodied subject, object and world, such that they 'envelope' (1962, p. 308) or circuitously 'coil over' (1968, p. 140) one another through divergence (*écart*).[3] I have explored this 'indissoluble link' elsewhere in relation to visual research with young children, and educational research more broadly (e.g. Elwick, 2020), as well as its 'multi-sensory' features (Elwick, 2015). However, to put this difficult idea slightly differently, and in the context of the phenomenon being explored in this chapter, through the virtue of Merleau-Ponty's depth, images on a screen emerge in relation to the viewer and what he or she notices in a particular viewing situation. For example, part of my role in a recently completed philosophical-empirical inquiry included watching five different GoPro® camera viewpoints of the same event one after the other. A still-frame edited from the first camera viewpoint is presented in Figure 3.1.

FIGURE 3.1   Playing at the light table (still from video)

When I watched the video footage of this particular viewpoint, all of its elements – the educator sitting on the floor, the children standing around the light-table, the furniture in the room, the researcher sitting on the chair in the background, the light streaming through the window and so on – took on a significance and spatial configuration unique to my viewing situation. My gaze was drawn to the educator sitting on the floor and the child in the blue dress, perhaps because I could see and hear them both quite clearly through the technology I was using. However, the other children were much harder to see and hear, and they thus slipped into the background, so to speak. When I watched the second, third and fourth camera perspectives of the same recorded moments, the room and everything in it was transformed, as each camera perspective (along with my shifting viewer perspective) ensured the scene became reorganised in my visual environment. What was previously hidden was suddenly visible as objects or aspects of objects were pushed forward or held back – some attaining a position of prominence and others hidden or partially hidden in ways different than before. Other viewers who watched these same recorded moments noted similar experiences. For instance, one viewer stated, 'the multiple perspectives helped clarify what I was seeing and hearing – being able to hear the person that was further away in the first viewing' (Extract from Survey Report_14/8/18). Steinbock (1987, p. 340) eloquently describes this process in the following passage:

> ... it is through depth that things stagger out near and far, present and absent, rearranging themselves in diverse contexts in a struggle for recognition such that they can come to be for us ... [it] is a relation of antagonism: it holds things together while ensuring their integrity, their difference, without however resolving the openness and contingency of the antagonistic relationships.

It is also in this passage that Steinbock hints at the antagonistic qualities of depth that, for me, are important here. It is, we might say, suggestive of the idea that watching different camera viewpoints of the same event one after the other immerses viewers in multiple antagonistic relations. What they see in each viewing is similar, but at the same time, what they see is different: 'things stagger out near and far, present and absent ... in a relation of antagonism' (Steinbock, 1987, p. 340). In my experience, this relation of antagonism can bring about understandings that sometimes conflict with viewers' pre-conceived theories and expectations of the phenomena under inquiry – whether they are theories concerning young children's ways of being in the world, children's pedagogical experiences or otherwise. This conflict, in turn, often facilitates what I refer to here as an epiphany.

3.3   *Epiphany*

The concept of epiphany I am articulating here is similar to the concept of literary epiphany linked to authors such as James Joyce (Johnson, 2000), although I am not foregrounding the spiritual aspect of the epiphanic experience, as is often the case both in literary and philosophical contexts (e.g. Watts, 2019). My use of the term is also slightly different to the notion of the 'eureka effect' or 'Aha! Moment' that has captured the attention of psychologists and which is usually used to refer to the experience of understanding a previously incomprehensible problem or concept. A prime example of an 'Aha! moment' is the moment when I suddenly understood Merleau-Ponty's concept of depth, which had previously been incomprehensible in the context of writing this chapter. However, what I aim to signify through my use of the term epiphany in this chapter is not so much the solving of a previously unsolvable problem, but rather – and I borrow a phrase from Johnson (2000, p. xxxvi) here that captures the meaning well – to refer to 'a moment in which the radiant whatness and full significance of a thing suddenly becomes apparent'. To me, this phrase seems to point towards what can eventuate when visual methods are used to 'reach beyond the "visual givens"' (Merleau-Ponty, 1964, p. 166). While visual methods may, of course, enable viewers to suddenly make sense of a previously incomprehensible problem, this is not what I am emphasising here. Instead, I am interested in that moment when viewers are awakened by the 'radiant whatness and full significance' of something they had not previously noticed, as well as the transformative possibilities that emerge from that awakening.[4] The excerpt below, taken from my reflective notes written as I watched the five different GoPro® camera viewpoints discussed above, recounts one instance of such an awakening in me – a moment that, for me, was epiphanic:

> Having watched three camera perspectives of these recorded moments, I was completely taken by surprise when the fourth camera perspective made me realise that I had perhaps misinterpreted Emma's actions and expressions [child in red top shown in Figure 3.1]. I'm not even sure how to put this realisation into words, as it is simply a feeling that I may have got things quite wrong when I assumed she was just randomly placing objects onto the light box. Although I had heard her say, 'I made it, I made it' in each of the previous three viewings, it wasn't until the fourth viewing that these words jumped out at me as being important. Is it possible

that even though her creation appeared to me to be a random collection of objects, that it was in fact a carefully thought out design for her?

A full discussion of the importance of that realisation in that particular philosophical-empirical inquiry is beyond the scope of this chapter. Suffice to say that it was an inquiry focused on supporting educators to see the mathematics that features frequently throughout a young child's day. However, despite that focus, it was not until viewing the fourth camera perspective of the recorded moments that I came to realise I was quite possibly underestimating Emma's mathematical capabilities by limiting them to my expectations of what her 'design'[5] should look like. As a researcher supposedly supporting others to avoid such oversights, this was an extremely humbling and transformative moment – one that I have pondered since. Other viewers noted similar realisations in response to watching multiple perspectives of particular moments. For example, they commented that, 'it was really eye-opening to see things from the different angles. I realised I need to be more thoughtful about ensuring that I position myself at a level that doesn't overwhelm the children I work with'; 'it made me realise one mustn't assume the child's perspective – it was so different to what I expected'; and 'I didn't realise I wasn't looking at the child when they were playing with me ... I thought I was' (Extracts from Survey Report_14/8/18 and Field notes_4/3/18). All of these comments hint at the possibility that these viewers each experienced what could be described as 'a moment in which the radiant whatness and full significance of a thing suddenly bec[a]me apparent'.

Notably, in almost all instances, these viewers also reflected on and transformed their pedagogies and practices in some way. The last comment above – 'I didn't realise I wasn't looking at the child when they were playing with me ... I thought I was' – is particularly relevant in this regard. The educator who made this comment had been a participant in the inquiry and was therefore visible in some of video images she watched – each set of images lasting approximately four minutes. When watching the first two camera perspectives (high wide angle and low wide angle), the educator saw herself talking with a young child to her left, whilst another child (aged 2) was visibly placing a bandage on the educator's ankle. When watching the third perspective recorded from a camera located on her (the educator's) chest, she noticed that the child who placed the bandage on her leg also looked towards her on several occasions whilst simultaneously speaking.

When watching the fourth perspective recorded from a camera located on the 2-year-old child's head, the educator saw herself looking over her right shoulder towards something that is not visible in the recorded images (it was the young child who was visible in the first two perspectives). It was when watching this fourth camera perspective that the educator suddenly realised she had not looked towards the 2-year old for the full 4-minute duration of the recorded moments, despite thinking that she had at the time. Whilst this was a confronting realisation for this particular educator, it also reinforced for her the complexities of her work, including the necessity of being responsive to multiple children, often at the same time – something she told me she attended to carefully in her future interactions. Notably, this experience of seeing oneself behaving differently in video images to how one thinks he or she is behaving in practice was also evident in the philosophical-empirical inquiry into infant participation in research discussed earlier.[6] To me, this suggests that moments of epiphany, such as those outlined above, are significant events in the process of self, other, and pedagogical evaluation and transformation. As such, they form an important feature of video research and scholarship more generally, and they thus deserve further investigation.

4   Limitations

As with any research approach, there are limitations to using visual methods to 'reach beyond the "visual givens"' (Merleau-Ponty, 1964, p. 166). On the one hand, the use of such methods to consecutively view different camera viewpoints of the same event is emancipating insofar as it brings into visibility some of the not-so-obvious phenomena that otherwise escape scrutiny. Imaginary and habitual ways of knowing young children are challenged as the viewer, the images, the technologies and so on oscillate and antagonise one another during each viewing event. On the other hand, one could argue that it is an approach that relies heavily on what can be seen and recorded in the environment, albeit from different camera perspectives. This reliance on the visual is complicated further when working with young children. For example, children's behaviours and expressions that may not be visible in one camera perspective may be glaringly obvious in another camera perspective. While this gives rise to ethical issues such as consent to be recorded on multiple cameras, there is also a risk that what becomes seen adds weight to already existing 'evidence' relied upon to represent children, their experiences and their learning as either this or that.

It could perhaps be argued that decisions about what can be seen and recorded are somewhat moderated in a philosophical-empirical inquiry through its 'co-productive, and participatory' (Elwick & Green, 2019, p. 3) character. All of those involved in the research – including young children at times – work together to choose research foci and determine how visual methods are used in that specific context. Nevertheless, Banks and Zeitlyn (2015) remind us that the technologies used in producing images determine the form and content of those images, and they influence potential meanings and effects. In both of the philosophical-empirical inquiries discussed here, the technologies used to produce the images were challenging. Not only did we need to learn about the different technologies and their possibilities, but we also had to learn context-specific strategies such as how to keep track of the times when particular cameras were simultaneously recording. This issue of tracking recording times was complicated further in research contexts where participants' locations frequently changed, for example in settings where children frequently moved between rooms, as well as indoors and outdoors.

5   Ethical Issues

In addition to the ethical issues touched on above, some researchers might perceive the visual methods outlined in this chapter as an increased form of surveillance, potentially visually exploiting the children as they are filmed whilst they go about their explorations and play. White (2017, 4min50sec) outlines interesting questions to ask in this regard. For example, do these children 'know that they are being filmed in this manner? Could they have stopped the filming happening at any time in the process? Were they coerced ... or did the researcher sneak up behind?' There are no easy answers to these questions. On the one hand, in all of the examples reported in this chapter, the children were involved in filming decisions as much as possible. They were often actively involved in the unpacking, positioning, setting up and wearing of cameras. They were also able to indicate their assent or dissent through actions such as tugging at or removing the head camera. However, as I and others discuss elsewhere (Sumsion et al., 2014, p. 178), such actions might not indicate meaningful assent or dissent, as they may be 'based purely on the physical sensation of wearing the camera [rather than] any understanding of what the camera is, what it does, or why it is there'. Likewise, although the children were involved in unpacking, positioning and setting up cameras, those actions may have been based purely upon their willingness to help and be involved, rather than on any understanding of the implications of being simultaneously recorded from multiple perspectives.

This last point is also relevant to consider in relation to all participants, particularly given the focus of using visual methods to 'reach beyond the "visual givens"' (Merleau-Ponty, 1964, p. 166). As I have empirically illustrated, it is possible, and indeed quite likely, that what is brought into visibility through such methods is sometimes surprising for all involved, not just for children. This raises questions such as whether or not it is appropriate to share footage with large audiences, including via webinars and so forth. However, perhaps more importantly, it raises the question of what to do when something is brought into visibility that participants would rather not have seen, let alone shared.

6 Future Possibilities

Despite the above-mentioned ethical issues and limitations, we cannot overlook that video potentially enables viewers to 'reach beyond the "visual givens"' (Merleau-Ponty, 1964, p. 166), and in the process, it facilitates what I have referred to here as an epiphany. We also cannot overlook that such epiphanic moments are potentially significant events in the process of self, other, and pedagogical evaluation and transformation. As such, and as noted above, they form an important feature of video research and scholarship more generally, and they thus deserve investigation. In this chapter, I used Merleau-Ponty's (1962, p. 308) concept of depth and my early explorations of the concept of epiphany to start this investigation and to situate visual methods – especially the method of watching different camera viewpoints of the same event one after the other – as profoundly philosophical matters. By doing so, I have not only opened up the complexity of video research, but also created possibilities for others to draw on different philosophical concepts to explore the outlined approach to using video in research contexts, as well as other approaches.

Throughout the chapter, I also emphasised the 'co-productive, and participatory character' (Elwick & Green, 2019, p. 3) of philosophical-empirical inquiry, as well as the need for researchers to avoid applying visual methods top-down onto the research context. Furthermore, I highlighted that the illustrative examples used in this chapter were precisely that: illustrative examples. In those examples, I outlined two approaches to using multiple video cameras to simultaneously record research contexts: one approach used two cameras, and the other used five. What is important to note, however, is that the number of video cameras, their type and their locations were all decided in-situ and with the participation of everyone involved. Therefore, indefinite future possibilities exist for other researchers to explore different video camera configurations and their implications in practice – both philosophically and empirically.

7 Summary Statements

– This chapter extends scholarly discussions of the research approach known as *philosophical-empirical inquiry* to include a visual element that affords visual researchers – and educational researchers more broadly – possibilities for 'reaching beyond the "visual givens"' (Merleau-Ponty, 1964, p. 166).

- As part of this discussion, I drew on Merleau-Ponty's (1962, p. 308) concept of depth and my early explorations of the concept of epiphany to situate visual methods – especially the method of watching different camera viewpoints of the same event one after the other – as profoundly philosophical matters.

- Philosophical-empirical inquiry is the explicit bringing together of philosophical exploration with fieldwork investigations (Green & Hopwood, 2015). It is a 'co-productive and participatory' (Elwick & Green, 2019, p. 3) research approach that requires researchers to begin with a 'concrete encounter with others in the field' (St. Pierre, 2019, p. 12) and to avoid applying visual methods top-down to the research context.

- Merleau-Ponty's philosophical concept of depth 'announces an indissoluble link' (1962, p. 298) between the embodied subject, object and world, such that they 'envelope' (1962, p. 308) or circuitously 'coil over' (1968, p. 140) one another through divergence (*écart*). It is through the virtue of Merleau-Ponty's depth, images on a screen emerge in relation to the viewer and what they notice in a particular viewing situation.

- The term epiphany is used in this chapter to refer to 'a moment in which the radiant whatness and full significance of a thing suddenly becomes apparent' (Johnson, 2000, p. xxxvi).

- It is suggested that epiphanic moments are potentially significant events in the process of self, other, and pedagogical evaluation and transformation. As such, they form an important feature of video research and scholarship more generally, and they hence deserve further philosophical and empirical investigation.

- Two approaches to using multiple video cameras to simultaneously record research contexts were outlined in this chapter: one approach used two cameras, and the other used five. A vast number of future possibilities exist for other researchers to philosophically, and empirically, explore different video camera configurations and their implications in practice.

Notes

1 See http://www.julianbeever.net/
2 See http://www.julianbeever.net/index.php/phoca-gallery-3d
3 See Elwick, Bradley and Sumsion (2014) for a fuller discussion of *écart* in relation to educational research with infants.

4 In this context, epiphany can also be understood in terms of Hass's (2008, p. 71) "*virtue of sensibility*" [emphasis added] – I reserve for another occasion an elaboration of this matter.

5 Mathematically speaking, a design can be understood as the creation of an abstract or symbolic plan, structure or shape on a surface or space (Bishop, 1988).

6 See Elwick (2015) for a full discussion of this experience.

References

Banks, M., & Zeitlyn, D. (2015). *Visual methods in social research* (2nd ed.). Sage.

Beever, J. (2020, January 10). *Julian Beever's official website*. Retrieved from http://www.julianbeever.net/

Bishop, A. J. (1988). *Mathematical enculturation*. Kluwer.

Elwick, S. (2015). 'Baby-cam' and researching with infants: Viewer, image and (not) knowing. *Contemporary Issues in Early Childhood, 16*(4), 322–338. doi:10.1177/1463949115616321

Elwick, S. (2016). *A philosophical-empirical interrogation of infant participation in research* (Doctoral dissertation). Charles Sturt University, Australia. Retrieved from https://researchoutput.csu.edu.au/en/publications/a-philosophical-empirical-interrogation-of-infant-participation-i-3

Elwick, S. (2020). Merleau-Ponty's 'wild being': Tangling with the entanglements of research with the very young, *Educational Philosophy and Theory, 52*(2), 149–158. doi:10.1080/00131857.2019.1618275

Elwick, S., Bradley, B., & Sumsion, J. (2014). Creating spaces for infants to influence practice: The encounter, ecart, reversibility and ethical reflection. *Educational Philosophy and Theory, 46*(8), 873–885.

Elwick, S., & Green, B. (2019). Merleau-Ponty's body and beyond? Early childhood studies, philosophical-empirical inquiry, and educational research. *Qualitative Inquiry* (Advance online publication). https://doi.org/10.1177/1077800419836702

Green, B., & Hopwood, N. (Eds.). (2015). *The body in professional practice, learning and education: Body/practice*. Dordrecht: Springer.

Hass, L. (2008). *Merleau-Ponty's philosophy*. Indiana University Press.

Ihde, D. (1979). *Technics and praxis*. D. Reidel Publishing.

Jay, M. (1994). *Downcast eyes: The denigration of vision in twentieth-century French thought*. University of California Press.

Johnson, J. (2000). Introduction. In J. Joyce (Ed.), *A portrait of the artist as a young man* (pp. viii–xxxix). Oxford University Press.

Kemmis, S. (2011). Becoming critical at Deakin. In R. Tinning & K. Sirna (Eds.), *Education, social justice and the legacy of Deakin University: Reflections of the Deakin diaspora* (pp. 77–92). Sense Publishers.

Martens, L. (2012). The politics and practices of looking. In S. Pink (Ed.), *Advances in visual methodology* (pp. 39–56). Sage.

Merleau-Ponty, M. (1962). *Phenomenology of perception* (C. Smith, Trans.). Routledge.

Merleau-Ponty, M. (1964). Eye and mind (C. Dallery, Trans.). In J. M. Edie (Ed.), *The primacy of perception and other essays on phenomenological psychology, the philosophy of art, history and politics* (pp. 159–190). Northwestern University Press.

Merleau-Ponty, M. (1968). *The visible and the invisible* (A. Lingis, Trans.). Northwestern University Press.

Merleau-Ponty, M. (1976). Philosophy and non-philosophy since Hegel. *Telos, 29*, 43–105. doi:10.3817/0976029043

Sobchack, V. (2004). *Carnal thoughts: Embodiment and moving image culture.* University of California Press.

Steinbock, A. J. (1987). Merleau-Ponty's concept of depth. *Philosophy Today, 31*(4), 336–351.

St. Pierre, E. A. (2019). Post qualitative inquiry in an ontology of immanence. *Qualitative Inquiry, 25*(1), 3–16. doi:10.1177/1077800418772

Sumsion, J., Bradley, B. Stratigos, T., & Elwick, S. (2014). 'Baby Cam' and participatory research with infants: A case study of critical reflexivity. In M. Fleer & A. Ridgeway (Eds.), *Visual methodologies and digital tools for researching with young children* (pp. 169–191). Springer.

Watts, F. (2019). Mutual enhancement between science and religion: In the footsteps of the epiphany philosophers. *Zygon, 54*(4), 965–983.

White, E. J. (2016). More than meets the "I": A polyphonic approach to video as dialogic meaning-making. *Video Journal of Education and Pedagogy, 1*(6), 1–14.

White, E. J. (2017). Video ethics and young children. *Video Journal of Education and Pedagogy, 2*(2). Retrieved from https://videoeducationjournal.springeropen.com/articles/10.1186/s40990-017-0012-9

CHAPTER 4

Multimodal Visual Methods for Seeing with Children

Helen Lomax

1 Introduction

As a means of accessing voice, creative visual methods have become de rigour in research with children. However, their popularity can belie the multiple challenges inherent in their use. This includes how to meaningfully involve young children as knowledge producers and how to interpret children's meaning-making practices, particularly for young children who are only beginning to use spoken language. This chapter addresses these challenges to consider how visual methods, offered as part of a collaborative, multimodal methodology, can support children's participation and offer new perspectives on children's ways of knowing. The chapter sets out the principles underpinning this methodology, drawing on examples from research undertaken in the UK in which photo-elicitation and puppet-production were employed with children during farm visits and museum trips to explore children's experiences of agricultural landscapes. Data from the research (photographs, transcribed speech and body movement) are used to illustrate the ways in which visual methods within a collaborative, multimodal framework can support children's linguistic and non-linguistic, visual and kinaesthetic meaning-making practices. The chapter then considers how visual methods within such a framework might be developed in future research with children.

2 Theoretical Orientations: Seeing Children's Worlds

The last 20 years have seen burgeoning collaborative visual and arts-based methods designed to make research more appropriate and meaningful to children. However, this has been increasingly met with concerns about the ways in which children's voices in such research are articulated and understood (Canosa & Graham, 2020; Lomax et al., 2011). Within childhood studies, this includes questioning the degree to which such approaches are merely extensions of school-based pedagogy and whether, in such conditions, children can express their views and researchers can recognise and interpret them (Gallacher & Gallagher, 2008; Spyrou, 2018).

Alongside this critique, a body of research has emerged that seeks to elaborate the processes that produce children's voices and the broader ideological contexts that frame their construction (Canosa & Graham, 2020; Lomax, 2015; Mayes, 2016). An example is provided by McLaughlin and Coleman-Fountain's (2018) photo-elicitation study in which the authors suggest that to fully understand children's visual representations, it is necessary to see children's research practices as produced in response to wider visual iconography that values and devalues certain kinds of childhoods. Lomax et al. (2011) similarly explore how children's participation in visual research is mediated by the social dynamics of the research encounter, giving analytic attention to how children's voices are shaped by adult ways of seeing children.

For the purposes of this chapter and its concern with how children can be included in research and how their voices can be 'seen', these studies usefully highlight three key points: first, that the value of visual methods is located in their capacity to make visible how children (or indeed any participants) represent themselves visually, narratively or creatively; second, that such representations are mediated by the discursive and ideological processes that shape the research; and third, the importance of reflexive research practices for illuminating these processes (Christensen, 2004).

2.1   *Children's Embodied Meaning-Making Practices*

Concerns about how to enable and interpret voice are a key focus of a multimodal methodology. Within childhood studies, multimodal approaches are foregrounded in their acknowledgement of the multiple ways in which children communicate and the 'hundred ways of listening' (Clark, 2007). As Clark (2011, p. 311) elaborates, 'research(ing) the perspectives of children … requires a readiness to tune in to (children's) different modes of communication', a process that is enhanced by the use of creative visual methods that can support children to describe and give meaning to their experiences (Veale, 2005). Offering a range of creative visual media expands the interpretive emphasis on verbal communication to encompass a fuller range of communicative modes available to children (for example body movement, gesture, facial expression and touch), thus providing the multimodal researcher with important analytic resources through which to interpret children's meaning-making practices.

A theoretical focus on children's embodied meaning-making includes a recognition of the fact that these practices may not easily be disaggregated from their productive contexts but are rather produced in dialogue with their material and social environments (Christensen, 2004; Mayes, 2016; Mazzei & Jackson, 2017). Paying analytic attention to these tangible engagements – the things that children do and 'say' in the research encounter and the multiple ways in which they do and say them – offers rich insights to researchers seeking to understand children's worlds. More particularly, as Elizabeth Wood states, in attending closely to the production of children's diverse modal voices, the methodology acknowledges the possibilities and limits of children's voice in which children are:

> Social actors who engage with and experience their social, (im)material and cultural worlds on their own terms, and are (also) co-constituted by matter and discourse in complex networks that reflect the cultural politics of childhood. (Wood, 2015, p. 129)

The following section draws on influential work in contemporary childhood studies to consider how a multimodal methodology can constructively frame collaborative visual research and, in so doing, address some of the criticisms levelled at creative visual methods. This includes how the approach can not only provide opportunities for young children to be 'seen and heard' (Lomax, 2015), but also offer ways for the researcher to acknowledge and make evident the situated, multimodal character of children's voices and their entanglement in the research process (Canosa & Graham, 2020).

2.2 Creative Visual Methods in Collaborative Ethnographic Practice

> Qualitative researchers have long acknowledged that what participants say and do needs to be interpreted alongside the material and sensorial *settings* in which they say and do it. (Hurdley & Dicks, 2011, p. 277, original emphasis)

Multimodal approaches aim to make visible experiential knowledge, recognising that such knowledge is produced 'in situ through the full spectrum of sensory phenomena with which actors engage' (Hurdley & Dicks, 2011, p. 278). Attending to how research participants accomplish this in practice can provide an enriched understanding of children's interpretations and sense-making. In common with ethnographic methodology, this approach shares a commitment to more intimate, embodied, 'affective forms of knowing' (Hurdley &

Dicks, 2011, p. 277). Within childhood studies, this includes actively participating in children's worlds using methods that support children's embodied
sense-making. Examples include Hackett et al.'s (2017) arts-based research
using craft, rhyme and soft play and Blaisdell et al.'s (2019) creative research
encompassing fine arts, videography and puppetry. Each study considers how
offering children diverse visual and sensorial research experiences can support
deeper insights into their worlds.

The importance of enabling, and recognising, a fuller range of children's
linguistic and non-linguistic voices is exemplified in Blaisdell et al.'s (2019)
account of puppetry activities, in which children were supported to take control of the camera and the puppets in ways that appeared to suggest children's
agency, but which had the unintended effect of appearing to mute their voices.
In describing how the children sought to narrate their experiences individually
and collaboratively using these technologies, Blaisdell et al. (2019) offer important insights into the ways in which creative visual methods are not, in and of
themselves, voice-giving. They highlight the complexity involved in supporting
children's meaningful engagement and the importance of a reflexive interpretive approach in order to 'hear' the diversity of children's voices. In this way, the
researchers are able to build a vivid picture of children's interests, recognising
the relational character of research practice by reflecting on the participants'
indecipherable verbal utterances and interrogating data from their crafting
activities.

Blaisdell et al.'s (2019) articulation of how children's voices are produced
dialogically with the materiality (puppets, theatre props, cameras) and relationality (with the audience of adult researchers and children) of the research
echoes Hackett et al.'s (2017) reflections on how their understanding of children's literacy practices emerged through a collaborative co-shaping of activities with children participating in their research study. Hackett et al. (2017)
elaborated on how their own sensory immersion in children's learning spaces
(crawling, for example, through cardboard dens with glitter and blueberries
stuck to their knees) opened up the possibility of understanding children's
embodied ways of 'being in the world'.

Such work by Hackett et al. (2017) and Blaisdell et al. (2019) illustrate how
a collaborative, multimodal approach, in which the researcher is immersed
in and responsive to children's embodied experiences, can support children's
meaningful engagement in research and aid interpretation. In offering their
reflections, these researchers demonstrate the need for flexibility in terms of
what methods are offered and the importance of attending to children's verbal and non-verbal communication in order to generate new insights into

children's worlds. The application of this approach in practice is described in the following section, which draws upon research undertaken in the UK wherein photo-elicitation and puppet-production were employed with children.[1] It sets out the rationale for the creative visual methods used within a collaborative, multimodal framework, elaborating on how these were designed to support children to participate in ways that were meaningful to them and the insights this afforded about children's values and preferences for particular landscapes.

3 Multimodality in Practice: Application of the Techniques

A key aim of the research that forms the focus of this section was to explore how children experience agricultural landscapes. The dearth of research in this field (MacQuarrie et al., 2013) is such that policy-makers lack evidence to inform decisions about how agricultural landscapes should be managed in ways that can support ecological and human health in the long term and in contexts of climate change and fluctuating global food markets. The fieldwork, which was undertaken over a period of 18 months, included a series of collaborative visual activities carried out with a broad demography of adults and children. For the purpose of the chapter overall, the focus is confined to the research conducted with children aged 3 to 8 years that sought to explore their experiences using photo-elicitation and puppetry. The research took place at an open farm and a children's museum; these sites were chosen because they provided access to children outside formal education but, more particularly, because they are locations that children visit as part of their everyday lives and which offer environments conducive to creative visual activities.

3.1 Photo-Elicitation and Puppet-Production in Action

Photo-elicitation (Luttrell, 2010, 2020) and puppetry (Blaisdell et al., 2019; Mayes, 2016) were selected as methods which offer the potential for children to engage creatively with objects, materials and technologies in order to represent and communicate their ideas (Clark, 2011; Hackett et al., 2018; Mannay & Hodges, Chapter 2, this volume; Mannay et al., 2017; Van Aucken et al., 2010). Photo-elicitation, whereby children take photographs and, through the process of taking and talking about their images, add 'layers of story' (Templeton, 2020, p. 1), was used in the open space of the farm. Puppetry was offered as part of a repertoire of props that children could utilise to tell their stories in the museum (Mayes, 2016, p. 109). In such ways, the photographs and puppet props acted as an 'intersubjective medium … opening up conversations' between the adult researcher and the child (White, 2015, p. 185) while providing resources through which the children could develop and share their perspectives.

Methods were offered flexibly so that children could participate as much or as little as they liked, and activities were designed to support a full range of linguistic and non-linguistic communicative practices. The open farm provided an ideal location in which the use of photo-elicitation methods could be combined with children's 'sorties' (Fink, 2011) around what was a large agricultural space. Here, the method involved asking child visitors to take photographs of 'things they liked' about the farmed environment as they explored the farm independently and then, through the photo-elicitation interview, to reflect on the images they had taken. In this way, the research method meant that the participating children could exert a degree of control over the research process, deciding where to go and what photographs to take within the immediate boundaries of the farm. This flexible child-centred approach was supported by the use of tablets (iPads), which were issued to each child at the start of their visit and through which they could take as many or as few images as they chose, re-shooting and deleting images in order to frame their pictures as they saw fit.

It is also important to note how the photo-elicitation approach supported the children's embodied, playful participation. This support included the fact that the children were able to readily incorporate digital visual technologies (the iPad) into their activities as they engaged with the playful affordances of the farm. As Lomax (2012) notes in a study in which children used video and photography to capture their experiences of their local neighbourhoods, the children in this farmed environment research did not walk through the landscape; rather, they could be observed to run playfully between the farm buildings, paddocks and fields, pausing to stroke animals, contemplate the flora and fauna and scan the wider panorama as they composed their images. This flexible approach also enabled children to regulate the course and content of the photo-elicitation interview. In contrast to earlier, pre-digital approaches, wherein researchers tended to assemble, select and re-present images taken by children (Milne & Muir, 2020), here the children themselves led this process, talking the interviewer through the images on the screen and choosing which photographs to share and in what order by scrolling, pointing to and touching the images.

The museum, which had no direct access to farmed landscapes, required a different set of activities with which to engage children collaboratively. Here, the approach made use of the light, airy space of the museum to bring the landscape *into* the setting by using photographs, puppets and other props. This involved hanging five large (42.0 × 29.7 cm) photographs of agricultural landscapes of varying complexity (open pasture, fields with wild flowers or grass margins, and fields bordered by tree-filled and tree-less hedgerows). Images were placed at children's height, with soft grass-like matting placed beneath and baskets of plush finger puppets (of insects, animals and people) placed on the floor within children's easy reach. The materials were organised much like the museum exhibits to encourage children's spontaneous exploration.

The flexibility of the approach, in which children were encouraged to engage independently with the materials and complete the activity as they chose, is evidenced in the spontaneity and variety of children's embodied entanglements with the materials. For some young children, the cushioned mats provided a space to sit or sprawl on their tummies – an activity which included, in some cases, introducing toys from home into their play.

Other children chose to dart between the baskets of puppets and pictures, breaking off from the activity to run over to the museum window in response to the sounds of trains outside or to chat with the animated robot positioned nearby. Then, as Figure 4.1 illustrates, after approaching the research space and exploring the materials for themselves, children were invited to select puppets from the basket and to place these on the photograph/s they liked best in a location on the image of their choosing. Puppets were either magnetised or fitted with glue dots to facilitate this. Children were asked about their choices through questions such as, 'where would you like to put the caterpillar?' This approach generated complex verbal and non-verbal narratives about children's preferences for particular landscapes and their experiences of different landscapes in their everyday lives.

FIGURE 4.1
Olivia and Charlie engage in the museum puppet activity

3.2 *Interpreting Children's Visual Voices*

The use of photo elicitation and puppets within this multimodal framework enabled children to express their ideas symbolically, for example by placing their puppet selections on a particular photograph and in specific locations on that image. As 3-year-old Tom's puppet-image arrangement in Figure 4.2 illustrates, this involved putting insects in flowery (as opposed to grassy) field margins and 'family' groups (represented by a granddad, mummy, 'Tom' and 'Alfie' [dog] puppets, as illustrated) in pasture.[2] The use of the puppet objects thus enabled young children with limited verbal language to indicate their preferences, offering insights into their understanding of insect habitats and the importance of flower-rich natural environments for bees and butterflies. Other children verbally articulated their preferences as they placed the puppets on the images, remarking, for example, that 'insects live in hedges' (Asha, aged 7), that trees 'that make oxygen' are important (Seth, aged 8) and that fields were a 'good place to play with friends' and 'go for a walk with my dad' (Ralph, aged 8). In such ways, children's opportunities to 'voice' their complex emotional attachments to landscapes as places for social connection and their understanding of the importance of diverse flora for insect habitats were facilitated by the multimodal nature of the research.

FIGURE 4.2   Tom's representation of his family walk

At the farm, children took a large number of photographs, which included panoramic views of the landscape as well as close-up shots of smaller landscape features. These features included tree bark that was interestingly patterned and a glowing white mushroom (Figure 4.3), flowers, plants and insects.

FIGURE 4.3   'Mushrooms'

Viewed independently, the meaning of photographs in both the farm and museum locations is opaque, reflecting the polysemic nature of images (Rose, 2016; Templeton, 2020). As Mannay et al. (2017, p. 350) suggest, the meaning of images (and other creative outputs) are 'ambiguous' and offer the viewer little indication as to their significance for the child-creator. This means that 'to appreciate the interpretations of images ... it is also necessary to engage in dialogues with children about their significance' (White, 2015, p. 174). Children's multiple and varied appreciations of the qualities of landscapes is evident in Jordan's narrative, wherein he describes his pictures of mushrooms, which appear to him to 'glow' (Figure 4.3), and in his description of his images of trees and clouds in which he imagines the following:

> ... a dragon, that cloud. Look, if you look up there [pointing to the photograph], there's a little gap for the eye and then the sticking out nose bit,

there's a ... sticking out bit at the top, and there's a tiny bit at the bottom.
(Jordan, aged 8)

In eliciting these multi-layered, non-normative meanings (Spyrou, 2011, p. 1), the photo-elicitation process as practiced on the farm with sorties and iPads enabled children to articulate the 'strangeness' and 'wonder' they experience when looking at nature. As Luttrell (2010, p. 225) suggests, the different ways in which children express their ideas 'in bits and pieces and without the same sense of 'coherence' often associated with adult speakers' can make it difficult for adults to hear children's voices. However, the multimodal affordances of the technologies in which, in this case, the iPad becomes a communicative resource through which children can 'show' and 'tell' their ideas, can act as a form of 'cultural brokerage' (Clark, 2011, p. 326), thereby offering adults windows into children's worlds, which might otherwise be unseen.

The photo-elicitation process also prompted children's stories about where they liked to go, and with whom, in their everyday engagements with farmed landscapes. The children described farm tracks, fields and footpaths, as well as what they liked to do there with their families. Prompted by the pictures, children expressed how places make them feel (for example, 'happy' and 'calm') and their strong sense of connection to nature, which included the importance of maintaining habitats for animals and birds, expressed through sadness when wildlife is harmed:

It's heart-breaking when people like put a hole in the egg, and they put another hole in, and they blow so it takes the egg and the chick out. (Jordan, aged 8)

However, while the subject matter that children photographed and narrated can be seen to be powerfully motivated by deep feelings about nature, it is important to recognise how these narratives emerged in children's talk, including the ways in which they appeared to be shaped by familial scripts. The implications for children's voice are discussed in the following section.

4   Whose Voice? Methodological Affordances and Limitations

An important feature of both the photo-elicitation and puppet-production methods was that it enabled children to navigate their involvement in the research physically and metaphorically; they were able to make their own decisions about what to represent visually with puppets and pictures and what to reveal in the interview. However, it was also evident that at least some of what children photographed and narrated during the photo-elicitation interview was negotiated with family members, as illustrated in the following exchange between Jordan and his mum, Jenny, during an interview with the researcher.

4.1   *Extract from Photo-Elicitation Interview with Jordan*

Jordan (child):   So the next one [*scrolling through the images*] is about the landscape – we've got the ducks and then we've got the trees (and) [*looks over at mum, Jenny*] we've got a greenhouse, is it?

Jenny (Jordan's mum):   It is yes, *so* we took that one because we like growing things outside, I mean [pointing at the picture], that's quite a substantial greenhouse here ... I like that about the outdoors and you know making your own food, looking after yourself.

As can be seen from the transcript, Jordan's question *'we've got a greenhouse, is it?'*, appears to be a means of clarifying with his mum about what has been photographed, suggesting that the decision to take this particular photograph was a shared one. Jenny's response, 'we took that', confirms this, and she goes on to elaborate her own appreciation of the landscape and its affordances for growing food to the interviewer. The sense of emotional connection to the landscape and the importance of spending time outside resonates through this interview and can be seen in Jordan's father's later description of the way the landscape helps the family to relax, as well as in his sister Jane's comment about landscapes being 'peaceful':

> It's quite calming; it sort of takes your stresses away. We've both got fairly high-pressured jobs ... you're sat in an office all day, and it's just nice to get outside, and it takes a weight off. (John, aged 40)

> It's peaceful but it's also interesting so I like just looking at stuff. (Jane, Jordan's; sister, aged 14)

The ways in which these familial voices come together in the photo-elicitation interview – as each family member seeks to convey the meaning of agricultural landscapes through their recollections of time spent together on countryside walks and camping trips – is evident throughout this interview and in the wider data. Its visibility in these data demonstrates that children's voices are complex, situated and dialogical (Luttrell, 2011; White, 2015). Understanding parents' involvement in the research activities, and particularly the ways in which they can be observed, on occasion, to speak *with* children, has implications for how children's voices can be understood in these data and in creative visual research more generally. However, rather than see this as a problem for the research, the richness of the data and the analytic possibilities afforded by the multimodal framework offer the potential for a more robust understanding of how children's voices, both in research and in children's everyday lives, are routinely mediated and framed by adult's meaning-making. Examining these practices and how they shape children's participation can help researchers to better understand the limits of an 'authentic, autonomous speaking voice' (Mayes, 2016, p. 106) – recognising children's meaning-making as an inter-subjective experience rather than (an) individual act' (White, 2015, p. 185). In this way, rather than seeing these collaborative voices as problematic for the research, a multimodal analysis of children's (and their parents and others') meaning-making practices offers deeper insights into the relational nature of children's voices.

5   Ethical Considerations: Informed Consent and its Challenges

Visual research with children generates a number of ethical challenges, which have been well documented in the academic literature (Clark, 2020; Lomax, 2015; Wood, 2015). Concerns include the ways in which the visual can reveal information about children which may compromise their privacy (Nutbrown, 2011), and whether and how researchers should disseminate images of children, since these images have a permanent digital afterlife (Fink and Lomax, 2016; Mannay, 2015). As Lomax (2019) suggests, researchers need to think carefully about how images may circulate and be repurposed in ways that may distress participants. A significant challenge that remains for researchers of childhood is how these ethical challenges should be reconciled with children's wishes to be identified as the authors and creators of visual material. For the purposes of this research, this was managed using a tiered consent process (Clark, 2020) whereby consent was obtained for each of the following processes: taking photographs, disseminating images for publications and conducting secondary analysis. For further discussions about how to navigate these ethical challenges, including how to engage children in these conversations, see Edwards (2019), Ruiz-Casares and Thompson (2016).

6 Future Applications

This chapter has described how photo-elicitation and puppet-production methods within a collaborative, multimodal framework can offer richer understandings of children's lives. Drawing on a case study of food security funded research, the chapter highlighted that through collaborative, child-centred methods, children can have a say on a subject of global significance about which they are seldom consulted. Elaborating the possibility of this approach for involving children in research on topics that may be perceived to be beyond their capabilities, raises the question about the extent to which children can and should be involved in research addressing other global research priorities (for example on housing, climate change and digital identity). Therefore, a priority is for child-related researchers to work in partnership with research funders, academics and policymakers from across the social and natural sciences to consider how children can practically and ethically be involved in research in ways that support them to have a voice and in accordance with the tenets of the United Nations Convention on the Rights of the Child (UNCRC, 1989).

7 Conclusion

This chapter considered how creative visual methods within a collaborative, multimodal framework can support researchers to 'see' children's experiences, elaborating on some ways in which multimodal methods can offer richer understandings of children's lives. Through a focus on children's meaning-making practices and how these are constituted materially and relationally within the research encounter, the chapter draws attention to the immediate and wider discursive practices that shape children's contributions. Analytic attention to children's embodied meaning-making practices, as well as how these are shaped and supported by children's sensorial, tactile and discursive engagement in research practice, offers powerful ways to evoke children's rich, embodied, affective experiences and connections. Children's engagements with the puppet-production and photo-elicitation allowed access to individual and familial descriptions and recollections, which helped to bring to life children's relationships with landscapes and offered a unique window into these experiences.

8   Summary Statements

- Creative visual methods within a collaborative, multimodal framework, offer opportunities for children to participate in research in ways that are meaningful to them.
- Methods should be flexible and adaptable, providing opportunities for children to communicate their ideas linguistically and non-linguistically, for example using materials and technologies that can support a range of communicative practices.
- Researchers should make the following explicit and available: practical means by which children can engage, for example, by offering research tools directly to children and placing materials within easy reach of younger children.
- Multimodal approaches are enhanced when the researcher is immersed in and responsive to children's embodied experiences and when he or she is able to adapt methods responsively to children and reflect on their engagements in order to facilitate the interpretive process.
- Analytic attention to children's body movements, gestures, facial expressions and touch provide the multimodal researcher with important analytic resources through which to interpret children's meaning-making practices, thus offering richer insights into children's lived experiences.

Acknowledgements

Thank you both to the children and families who participated in this research and to the wider research team – in particular, Professor Simon Potts, Dr Tom Breeze, Dr Jeff Ollerton, Dr Jim Rouquette, Dr Emma Gardner, Kathrine Jensen, Victoria Benner, Paul Stroud and Dr Lisa Russell. Acknowledgements also to Research Councils UK and the Global Food Security programme for kindly funding this research and to Professor Jayne White, Professor Janet Fink and the other reviewers for their invaluable comments on earlier drafts of this chapter.

Notes

1 The research, 'Modelling Landscapes for Resilient Pollination Services', was funded by Research Councils UK as part of its Global Food Security programme and sought to model the impacts of climate and land use change on pollinating insects, food production and human wellbeing.

2 'Tom' is a pseudonym as are all participants names in this chapter.

References

Blaisdell, C., Arnott, L., Wall, K., & Robinson, C. (2019). Look who's talking: Using creative, playful arts-based methods in research with young children. *Journal of Early Childhood Research, 17*(1), 14–31.

British Educational Research Association (BERA). (2018). *Ethical guidelines for educational research* (4th ed.), BERA. Retrieved from https://www.bera.ac.uk/researchers-resources/publications/ethicalguidelines-for-educational-research-2018

Canosa, C., & Graham, A. (2020). Tracing the contribution of childhood studies: Maintaining momentum while navigating tensions. *Childhood, 27*(1) 25–47.

Christensen, P. (2004). Children's participation in ethnographic research: Issues of power and representation. *Children & Society, 18*, 165–176.

Clark, A. (2007). A hundred ways of listening: Gathering children's perspectives of their early childhood environment. *Young Children, 62*(3), 76–81.

Clark, A. (2011). Multimodal map making with young children: Exploring ethnographic and participatory methods. *Qualitative Research, 11*(3), 311–330.

Clark, A. (2020). Visual ethics beyond the crossroads. In L. Pauwels & D. Mannay (Eds.), *The Sage handbook of visual research methods* (2nd ed., pp. 462–493). Sage Publications.

Dicks, B., Flewitt, R., Lancaster, L., & Pahl, K. (2011). Multimodality and ethnography: Working at the intersection. *Qualitative Research, 11*(3), 227–237.

Edwards, V. (2019). *How might we work more ethically with children and young people: The 'case of ethics'*. Retrieved from http://www.exchangewales.org/

Fink, J. (2011). Walking the neighbourhood, seeing the small details of community life: Reflections from a photography walking tour. *Critical Social Policy, 32*(1), 31–50.

Fink, J., & Lomax, H. (2016). 'Sharing images, spoiling meanings? Class, gender & ethics in visual research with girls'. *Girlhood Studies, 9*(3), 20–36.

Gallacher, L. A., & Gallagher, M. (2008). Methodological immaturity in childhood research? Thinking through 'participatory methods'. *Childhood, 15*(4), 499–516.

Hackett, A., Pahl, K., & Pool, S. (2017). In amongst the glitter and the squashed blueberries: Crafting a collaborative lens for children's literacy pedagogy in a community setting. *Pedagogies: An International Journal, 12*(1), 58–73.

Hurdley, R., & Dicks, B. (2011). In-between practice: Working in the 'thirdspace' of sensory and multimodal methodology. *Qualitative Research, 1*(3), 277–292.

Lomax, H. (2012). Contested voices? Methodological tensions in creative visual research with children. *International Journal of Social Research Methodology, 15*(2), 105–117.

Lomax, H. (2015). Seen and heard? Ethics and agency in participatory visual research with children, young people and families. *Families, Relationships & Societies, 4*(3), 493–502.

Lomax, H. (2019). Consuming images: Ethics and integrity in visual social research. In R. Iphofen (Ed.), *Handbook of research ethics and scientific integrity.* Springer.

Lomax, H., Fink, J., Singh, N., & High, C. (2011). The politics of performance: Methodological challenges of researching children's experiences of childhood through the lens of participatory video. *International Journal of Social Research Methodology, 14*(3), 231–243.

Luttrell, W. (2010). 'A camera is a big responsibility': A lens for analysing children's visual voices. *Visual Studies, 25* (3), 224–237.

Luttrell, W. (2020). *Children framing childhoods.* Policy Press.

MacQuarrie, S., Nugent, C., & Warden, C. (2015). Learning with nature and learning from others: Nature as setting and resource for early childhood education. *Journal of Adventure Education and Outdoor Learning, 15*(1), 1–23.

Mannay, D. (2015). Making the visual invisible: Exploring creative forms of dissemination that respect anonymity but retain impact. *Visual Methodologies, 3*(2), 67–76.

Mannay, D., Staples, E., & Edwards, V. (2017). Visual methodologies, sand and psychoanalysis: Employing creative participatory techniques to explore the educational experiences of mature students and children in care. *Visual Studies, 32*(4), 345–358.

Mayes, E. (2016). Shifting research methods with a becoming-child ontology: Co-theorising puppet production with high school students. *Childhood, 23*(1), 105–122.

Mazzei, L., & Jackson, A. (2017). Voice in the agentic assemblage. *Educational Philosophy & Theory, 49*(11), 1090–1098.

McLaughlin, J., & Coleman-Fountain, E. (2018). Visual methods and voice in disabled childhoods research: Troubling narrative authenticity. *Qualitative Research, 19*(4), 363–381.

Milne, E. J., & Muir, R. (2020). Photovoice: A critical introduction. In L. Pauwels & D. Mannay (Eds.), *Sage handbook of visual methods* (2nd ed., pp. 282–296). Sage.

Nutbrown C. (2011). Naked by the pool? Blurring the image? Ethical issues in the portrayal of young children in arts-based educational research. *Qualitative Inquiry, 17*(1), 3–14.

Rose, G. (2016). *Visual methodologies: An introduction to researching with visual materials* (4th ed.). Sage.

Ruiz-Casares, M., & Thompson, J. (2016). Obtaining meaningful informed consent: Preliminary results of a study to develop visual informed consent forms with children. *Children's Geographies, 14*(1), 35–45.

Spyrou, S. (2011). The limits of children's voices: From authenticity to critical, reflexive representation. *Childhood, 18*(2), 151–165.

Spyrou, S. (2018). *Disclosing childhoods.* Palgrave Macmillan.

Templeton, T. (2020). "That street is taking us to home": Young children's photographs of public spaces. *Children's Geographies, 18*(1), 1–15.

United Nations. (1989). Convention on the Rights of the Child (UNCRC). Office of the High Commissioner for Human Rights. Retrieved from https://www.unicef.org.uk/what-we-do/un-convention-child-rights/

Van Auken, P., Frisvoll, S., & Stewart, S. (2010). Visualising community: Using participant-driven photo-elicitation for research and application. *Local Environment, 15*(4), 373–388.

Veale, A. (2005). Creative methodologies in participatory research with children. In S. Greene & D. Hogan (Eds.), *Researching children's experiences: Approaches and methods* (pp. 253–272). Sage.

White, E. J. (2015). Seeing is believing? Insights from young children in nature. *International Journal of Early Childhood, 47*, 71–188.

Wood, E. (2015). Ethics, voices and visual methods. In E. Stirling & D. Yamada-Rice (Eds.), *Visual methods with children and young people.* Palgrave.

CHAPTER 5

Competing Voices

Hidden Dialogicity through Visual Encounters with Children's Play with Touchscreen Devices

Dandan Cao

1   Introduction

Researchers in early childhood education (ECE) are increasingly advocating for a shift from *research on* children to *research with* children, which means children's voices are actively sought and highly valued in research (Mayall, 2008). Despite this widespread recognition of the importance of children's active participation in research, the question of *how to* achieve this remains to be explored, especially for children in early childhood who are largely excluded from *research with* them because of their lack of language literacy within the traditional definition (Irwin, Moore, Tornatore, & Fowler, 2012). As a result, exploring methodological considerations and innovative methods, which go beyond this limitation, is essential for *research with* young children. Examining young children's language not only in its verbal form but also in its non-verbal form introduces new and important insights into the field. Given the multi-form feature of language, visual research methods (video recording and reflective talking) serve as ideal ways in which to examine children's voices, accompanied by their rich expression of body language, regarding their own experiences. This principle orients the methodological approach presented in this chapter.

In this chapter, I introduce a visual approach that examines how children's voices express their own experience, using an example from my studies of children's engagement with touchscreen devices in ECE. I set out to interrogate touchscreen use in a deeply social and aesthetic way, drawing on Mikhail Bakhtin's theory of *Dialogism* (Bakhtin & Emerson, 1993; White, 2009a) because of its effective method of exploring the plural competing voices and visualities that form four-year-old children's touchscreen use in a diverse cultural context. Bakhtin's notion of *hidden dialogicity* (hidden dialogue) is adopted as an orienting concept within this methodology, as it provides a way of interpreting children's rich non-verbal voices as a plural concept with both others and self. Importantly, hidden dialogicity facilitates the recognition of invisible speakers, and it provides a means of examining the values underpinning language use.

When different internal and external voices – visible and invisible – gather and conflict with one another, another important Bakhtinian term then becomes indispensable: *heteroglossia* (multiple voices). Bakhtin's concept of heteroglossia introduces an analysis framework that can be readily applied to multi-voice discussions in the diverse social-cultural context, as it provides an opportunity for examining the extent to which voices are shut down or invited to join the chorus.

This dialogic framework combines traditional methods of ethnographic observation and interviewing with the introduction of participatory tools, including the use of cameras, touchscreen devices, and touchscreen game-playing. Each of these participatory tools can serve as a means of evoking and reframing conversations, thus providing a rich basis for the examination of children's voices concerning touchscreen use. Regarding children's voices in their different forms, competing voices can be discerned, where multiple voices, as Bakhtin claims, compete with one another under the constantly conflicting influence of centripetal and centrifugal forces in the construction and destruction of the meaning-making process.

1.1   *Bakhtinian Dialogic Methodology as a Route to 'Seeing' Voice(s)*

A strong emphasis has recently been placed on the visual experience as a source of understanding children's learning in ECE. According to White (2016), such 'seeing' has the potential to offer an authorial gift of 'other-ness' when brought to bear on evaluative relationships with children. From Bakhtin and Emerson's (1993) view, voice is plural; that is, voice is a response to its own past while at the same time awaiting a response from its future. Even in an utterance or a word, audiences can hear two or more competing voices. The plural feature of the 'voice' is of particular importance for researchers who conduct research with children, as this concept of the voice allows researchers to 'see' children's voices in the non-verbal forms of their embodied expression. This plurality furthermore leads researchers to 'see' the 'hidden dialogue' between the child and an invisible speaker.

To answer the question of how a dialogic methodology provides the means of seeing this non-verbal voice, we need to isolate the 'form' of gesture from its 'content'. According to Bakhtin (1981), this is best achieved by understanding how the chronotype (cited in White, 2009b) – the ideological space in which the gesture is expressed – comes to constitute the development of a dialogic genre in the actor. For instance, in an early childhood setting, children will act according to the manner in which ECE is conducted, to the culture of the centre and to the idiosyncrasies of centre life; this knowledge leads the children to orient their actions in multiple ways and according to the micro context in which each child finds him- or herself. This multiplicity of genres and the production of gestures that these genres produce demand that teachers learn to see the hidden voices in the 'form' of these gestures. Without learning to see the 'multiple forms' that children employ, teachers will not understand the intentions behind children's actions or their particular dialogic interactions. For instance, the interactions during children's encounters in their touchscreen play – both verbal and non-verbal – often highlight the differences, diversity and conflict that characterise the presence of multiple voices. To begin to recognise the genres that characterise children's actions, it becomes important to recognise the nature of such differences, diversities and conflicts. One way in which to see the 'form' in the gestures that populate such differences, diversities and conflicts implies the need, according to Bakhtin (1981), to describe such conflicts as involving centripetal and centrifugal forces – phenomena Bakhtin describes as involving heteroglossia, which is the presence of multiple voices. In taking this analysis a step further, the researcher can employ Bakhtin's notions of heteroglossia and hidden dialogicity to provide a means of understanding the competing voices that characterise visual encounters with others – children; the micro contexts in the centre; and the technologies in use, for instance touchscreens.

1.2 Hidden Dialogicity: An (In)visible Speaker

Hidden dialogicity was described in Bakhtin's book, *Problems of Dostoevsky's Poetics* (1984), as follows:

> Imagine a dialogue of two persons in which the statements of the second speaker are omitted, but in such a way that the general sense is not violated. The second speaker is present and invisibly, his words are not there, but deep traces left by these words have a determining influence on all present and visible words of the first speaker. (Bakhtin, 1984, p. 197)

Bakhtin (1984) claims that 'hidden dialogue' is a form of double-voiced discourse where 'the other's words actively influence the author's speech, forcing it to alter itself accordingly' (p. 197). Bakhtin's notion of hidden dialogicality – terminology that supposes the protagonism is half our own and half someone else's – involves a type of discourse entailing a struggle between two equally valid voices that harbour an element of internal dialogisation. Hidden dialogicality characterised by an invisible speaker allows children to take a metacognitive perspective that leads them to internalise the other speaker's words. To Wertsch (1991), for example, hidden dialogicality supposes that 'the meaning of a child's utterances reflects the outside interference of another's voices (p. 91). Bakhtin's notion of hidden dialogicality has also been used in ECE research.

For example, Cohen (2015) analysed pre-schoolers' use of double-voicing in the context of block play and found evidence of different types of passive double-voicing: 'unidirectional and vari-directional', as well as active categories of 'hidden dialogicality, parody, and skaz'. Cohen claims that hidden dialogicality accounts for children's voices directed to self in children's play. Similarly, a recent study by White (2020) highlights the ways in which young children in ECE settings navigate the rules whilst upholding their own priorities for play. Where children's voices come from and how their voices are formed are not well understood; however, these visual explorations are beginning to shed some light on the complexities of children at play in ECE contexts (see also Jennings-Tallant, Chapter 9, this volume).

In this study, I attempt to make children's voices better understood by identifying the invisible speaker who has exerted an influence on the expression of their voices; that is, how others' voices actively influence children's voices. Hidden dialogicity has been located within the dialogic methodology for the purpose of exploring the plural expressions of children's voices – verbal and non-verbal –toward both self and the invisible speaker. The hidden dialogue accounts for the influence of adults' voices on children's voices with respect to the ways in which children play when using touchscreen devices. This means that not only are children's voices their own, but they can also sometimes be the expression of someone else's (an adult's) voice – a voice conveyed by an invisible speaker in the form of a child's internal dialogisation. During such an internal dialogue, contradictions, conflicts and psychological struggles are experienced as internally persuasive and authoritative discourses that become the subject of the centripetal and centrifugal forces and battles that seek to attain priority, can be seen in Redder's self-study reported in this handbook. During this interplay, competing voices can be discerned in this multi-voiced (heteroglossic) arena.

1.3   *Heteroglossia: A Route to Understanding*

Bakhtin (1981) has described the concept of heteroglossia (*orraznorečie*) as 'another's speech in another's language, serving to express authorial intentions but in a refracted way' (p. 324). Bakhtin claims that language is 'always populated – overpopulated – with the intentions of others' (p. 293) and that this multi-voiced interplay is determined by the particular social context in which it occurs. Heteroglossia represents the 'concrete, living totality' of language in everyday social events (Bakhtin 1984, p. 181), and it represents the social and linguistic diversity – the multiple voices that people use in social and cultural life – and their corresponding values and views of the world. From a Bakhtinian point of view, linguistic and social communities are the sites of a struggle between centripetal and centrifugal forces. Centripetal forces seek to unify and establish one common language for everyone to utter, while centrifugal forces regard common understanding as a problem and attempt to voice multiple languages that represent social and linguistic diversity. Heteroglossia brings to light the fact that cultures and societies are diverse rather than unified.

A number of researchers have operationalised these ideas for the early years. White (2009b) examines heteroglossia and its relationship to metaphoricity and invites a re-conceptualisation of language use in education. In her 2009 study of block play, Cohen analysed Bakhtin's discourse typologies, using video data, to evaluate children's utterances. Rosen (2015) focused on the presence of heteroglossia in responses to play that has violent themes and points to the importance of the heteroglossic space of play. ECE researchers are now beginning to recognise the complexity of language use for children who draw from increasingly pluralistic contexts, which influence their education. Children's voices in touchscreen play have not been examined in a way that locates the children themselves within the wider heteroglossic arena alongside the multiple voices of their parents, teachers and peers inside and outside the centre.

In this study, heteroglossia was used to understand children's voices on a more subtle level, through observational work performed in relation to the invisible speaker and the multiple voices – the influence of adults' voices on children's voices – through the different genres children use when they play using touchscreen devices.

1.4   *Visual Method: An Approach to 'Seeing' the Voices*

While Bakhtinian notions of dialogic and heteroglossic voices have proved to be richly suggestive of everyday events within language and cultural studies of young children (Marbin, 2006; Sperling & Appleman, 2011), they do not, in themselves, offer a method of examining children's voices in the social and cultural context. While their voices have gradually gained the attention of ECE researchers (Spyrou 2011, Canning, Payler, Horsley, & Gomez, 2017; Fane, Jovanovic, Redmond, & Gibb, 2018), the following question is still to be explored: how should one explore and understand children's voices? Some scholars (James, 2007) provide an arena within which children are seen as social actors who provide a unique perspective on the social world about matters concerning children, while others actively look for ways to elicit children's voices in relation to their everyday experiences (Fane et al., 2018). Vochdt (2015) uses video to explore children's replication of teacher 'voice' in the absence of the teacher – highlighting the plural dialogues that take place for children in ECE.

Focussing on competing voices across settings grants us a way to 'see' children's voices – not only for what they said but also for what they expressed through their gestural expressions. The plural feature of the voice offers possibilities not only to 'listen' but also to 'see' children's voices by examining them in their different forms – verbal and non-verbal, and visible and invisible. I argue that there is merit in using a visual method to explore children's voices, as this method opens up possibilities for interpreting a visual moving image as a dialogic interaction. Video is used in this study not only as a means of recording both verbal and non-verbal dialogues in different spaces, but also as a means of stimulating children's voices through the reflective dialogue between the researcher and the child. By doing this, new meaning-making can be generated, and children's voices and perspectives can be further explored.

2   Context of This Study

2.1   *Children's Use of Touchscreen Devices*
The study took place in a New Zealand early childhood centre where touchscreens were regularly used as part of the curriculum. Touchscreen devices such as tablets, iPads and smartphones have garnered increasing interest and presence in young children's everyday experiences in the digital age key references needed here – suggest the Suzi Edwards stuff rather than Khoo. Given both the early introduction and the current use of touchscreen devices in the everyday experiences of young children, authoritative voices on this topic emphasise guidelines for safety rather than user perspectives.

Fieldwork involved 30 days of visits to both the centre and each child's home, during which time I videoed examples of engagement with touchscreens and initiated many dialogues surrounding children's use of touchscreen devices. The participants were (i) four-year-old children from different cultural and language backgrounds, with a specific focus on (ii) three four-year-old children of Chinese descent, in addition to (iii) teachers and (iv) parents. Multiple methods were employed to examine the different voices and stimulate further dialogue, including video recordings of children playing using touchscreen devices, reflective dialogue with them based on the previous video and interviews with teachers and parents, along with my informal observations and journaling. Together, these methods afforded me the opportunity to engage deeply with hidden dialogicity surrounding touchscreen play in the ECE context (there is insufficient scope in this chapter to report on the home – suffice to say that additional interanimating dialogues were taking place therein).In the example below, I demonstrate, in three parts, how the same touchscreen play is dialogised across time and between ECE players.

2.2   *Part 1: The Voice of an (In)visible Speaker*

In the scene that unfolds, the ECE teacher has put in place a rule that all children are to take turns playing with touchscreen devices in the centre. The teacher spoke about this rule before play began; therefore, it can be said that the children were already familiar with it.

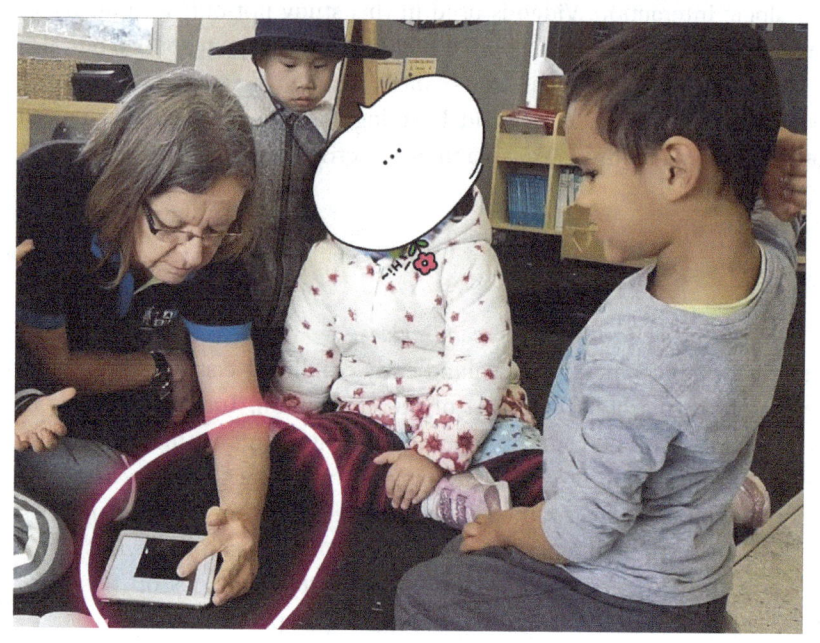

FIGURE 5.1   Jayden's internalisation of the teacher's voices (verbal and non-verbal)

The teacher maintained the rule of playing in turns by stopping other children from playing when it was not their turn. That said, the focus of my discussion is not on the story itself (which I will discuss later in the next section), but on the four year-old boy (Jayden) standing behind the teacher and the verbal and non-verbal voices he had 'seen' and then 'internalised as his inner voice' in this dialogic space. The following questions arise:

1.   In what way did Jayden respond to this scene he experienced in this public space that he shared with his teacher and peers?
2.   How did he respond to the teacher's voice (words and gestures)?
3.   Did the teacher's voice exert an influence on Jayden's ways of playing with the touchscreen device in future?
4.   How does the teacher's voice influence the child?

2.2.1   Example 1: An Invisible Speaker (Video No. JC-04)

It was Jayden's turn to play with the touchscreen device. He was surrounded by his peers but without the company of a teacher.

FIGURE 5.2   Jayden moved other children's hands and covered the iPad screen

L1 Jayden: (*Jayden clicked on the screen*)
L2 Child A: (*Child A also made a quick, random click on the screen*)

Jayden clicked on the screen, and Child A also attempted to play by making a quick, random click on the screen.

L3 Jayden: (*Jayden moved Child A's hand away and covered the screen with both hands*)

Here Jayden imitates the teacher's previous body language (see Figure 5.1) by (i) moving other child's hands away and (ii) covering the iPad screen. From Jayden's imitation, we can see the influences of the teacher's voice on his ways of playing with the touchscreen device. The teacher's voice was present here even if she was invisible (not physically present); that is, the teacher's voice had an influence on the child's thoughts and behaviours, despite her no longer being present.

Even though Jayden did not use words here, it appears to express his voice through the use of body language – hand gestures. The child's imitation of the teacher's hand gestures can be viewed as his active response to the teacher's voice (through body language) and his internalisation of the rule set by the teacher.

L4 Child A: (*She kept clicking on the screen randomly*)
L5 Jayden: (*Jayden moved Child A's hand away again*) No!

With an utterance of 'No!', Jayden moved Child A's hand away each time she randomly clicked. Both his spoken and unspoken voices can be viewed here as representing a hidden dialogue with his teacher – the invisible speaker who presents (the influence of) her voice – in a peers-shared public space. Even though there was no audible voice of the teacher, we can still sense her invisible presence through the influence of her voice on the child's thoughts and behaviour. His behaviour can be recognised through the employment of the invisible speaker genre, and we might also assume that this voice has been internalised both in the child's own thoughts and behaviours and in his autonomous and conscious choice-making. Table 5.1 summarises these points.

TABLE 5.1   Hidden dialogicity: An invisible speaker

Space	A public space shared by the child and his peers (without the teacher)	
Genre	The genre of an invisible speaker	
	Content	Jayden: 'No!'
	Form	i) Jayden moved Child A's hand away and covered the screen with both of his hands. ii) Jayden moved Child A's hand away again.
Competing voices	Between Jayden (behind whom is the voice of the teacher) and his peer (Child A) regarding the rule the teacher set for children's play with the touchscreen device.	
Dominant voice	The invisible speaker's (the teacher's) voice was dominant, as it presented and influenced the child's behaviour even though the speaker was not visible.	
Hidden dialogicity	Hidden dialogue between the child and the speaking teacher, who is invisible in a peer-shared public space without the teacher's physical presence, regarding the maintenance of the rule the teacher had set before.	

However, from a dialogic perspective, we cannot assume that this voice is the only one that holds sway during this event. Taking up Bakhtin's notion of heteroglossia (multiple voices), we can also explore the potential conflict between centripetal and centrifugal forces at play in this dialogue.

2.3   *Part 2: The Voice of Resistance*

As soon as the teacher turned the iPad on, a group of children were attracted to it and all sat next to the teacher. While the teacher set the rule that children must play in turns, one of the children, Korben, wanted to play when it was another child, Anna's, turn. Korben poses a resistance to the rule set by the teacher as presented in Figure 5.3.

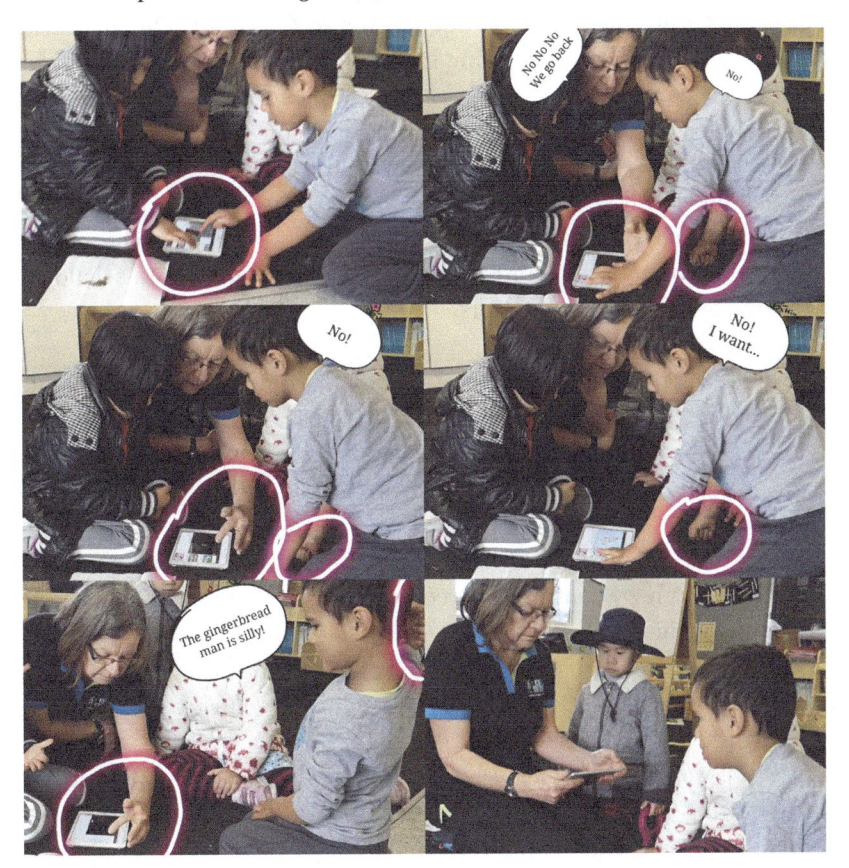

FIGURE 5.3   The teacher moved the child's hand and covered the iPad screen

L1 Korben: (*Korben reached out towards the iPad and clicked on the screen*)

From Korben's gesture of reaching out and clicking on the screen, we see that he wanted to play or join in on this play, even though it was not his turn.

L2 Sharon (Teacher):   No, no, no, we go back. (*Teacher Sharon moved Korben's hand away and covered the screen to protect it from Korben's touch*)

Teacher Sharon wanted to maintain the rule she previously set, so she moved Korben's hand away when he tried to touch the screen, and she even covered the screen to prohibit him from touching it again.

L3 Korben: No! (*Korben clenched his right fist and beat on the ground*)

Korben demonstrated his resistance not only through his words ('No!') but also through his body language (clenching his fist and beating on the ground) in response to teacher Sharon's actions of moving his hand away and covering the screen. However, observing this dynamic on a deeper level, what Korben was resisting was not only the teacher's specific action, but also the rule that the teacher had previously set and, in fact, the power the teacher had to set rules. Here, the child voiced his resistance to fight for his right to play when there was a conflict between his interest and the rule the teacher set in this dialogic space shared by his teacher and peers.

L4 Sharon (Teacher):   She [Anna; it was Anna's turn] wants the gingerbread man, then maybe you too have one [chance to choose what you like]. (*Teacher Sharon continued her action of covering the screen with her hand*)

Teacher Sharon explained the rule again to Korben while simultaneously maintaining the rule by continuing to cover the screen with her hand to stop Korben from touching it.

L5 Korben: No! I want ... (*Korben raised his right hand*)

Korben expressed his resistance again through both his words (L5) and the gesture of raising his right hand.

Korben's body language, in my interpretation, is illustrated (i) by clenching his fist and beating the ground (L3) and (ii) by raising his right hand (L5), which demonstrates that he is fighting for his own interest by using the genre of resistance. His frustration is palpable.

In this excerpt of a video on touchscreen play, evidence of competing voices between the teacher (the rule the teacher set, the need to speak with a unified voice) and the child (resistance to the rule, the need to speak with a different voice) was observed. Their hidden dialogue was evident: the teacher maintained the rule she set, while the child attempted to resist both the rule and the power the teacher had to set it. Through his voice of resistance, the child fought for his interest and his right to engage in touchscreen play.

TABLE 5.2   Heteroglossia: Competing voices and the use of a genre of resistance

Space	A public space shared by the child, the teacher and peers	
Genre	A genre of resistance	
	Content	Korben: 'No!' 'No! I want ...'
	Form	i) Korben clenched his fist and beat the ground. ii) Korben raised his right hand.
Competing voices	Between the child and the teacher regarding the rule that the teacher set for children's play using the touchscreen device.	
Hidden dialogicity	i) The child's resistance to the rule the teacher set and the power she had to set it, and ii) The child's fight for his interest and his right to play.	

2.4   *Part 3: The Whispered Voice*

Bakhtin draws the researchers attention to 'the whisper of the precursor' (cite in Jones, 1990, p. 149) as a clue to hidden meanings. The whisper embodies the whisperer's psychological state, contradictions and struggles. It is used in the excerpt that follows and refers to the strategic purpose of creating a relatively private space (versus a public space) between the whisperer and the recipient (the listener to whom the child whispers) in order to express a voice that is different from a public expression. The whisper is presented here as a tactical manoeuvre to move from the public space (with the common understanding shared by all the children) to the intentionally created private space (where different voices are expressed by only two of the children).

Example 1: The whispered voice and its dialogic response (Video No. JC-04)

A group of children played with the iPad together in the centre. It was Jayden's turn, but Madison also wanted to play.

L1 Madison: (*Madison made a quick click on the screen*)

Madison reached to quickly click the screen, expressing her voice of wanting to join in the play. Her action of 'a quick click' instead of 'playing in a leisurely, unhurried and relaxed way' revealed that she acknowledged the voice of the common rule that the teacher had set regarding the use of touchscreen devices.

FIGURE 5.4   Jayden moved Madison's hand away in a public space

L2 Jayden: (*Jayden moved Madison's hand away*)

Jayden moved his peer's hand away (again) to stop her from clicking on the screen.

An inner heteroglossic moment for Madison

After she was denied the possibility of playing on her first click request, Madison looked as though she was lost in thought, considering the strategy of her next move.

L3 Madison: (*Madison whispered something in Jayden's ear while covering her mouth with her hand*)

Madison strategically changed her communicative style by approaching Jayden and speaking into his ear in a whispered tone while covering her mouth with her hand. Her action of whispering transformed their dialogic space from a public one into a relatively private one, shared between only the two of them, so that she could express a voice that was different from her public expression (see Cresswell & Sullivan, 2020).

Later, during our reflective conversation after viewing the video, when Madison was asked, by me (the researcher), what she had whispered to Jayden,

FIGURE 5.6   Madison whispered to Jayden

she said she had asked him to play the iPad game with her. Here, Madison's whispered voice expressed her intention to break the unified rule and form a new rule, which reflected the conflict between centripetal force and centrifugal force. Therefore, Madison's whispered voice can be reasonably interpreted as her quick-witted shift between different communicational genres across different spaces with the intention of building a new rule for playing together with Jayden.

L4 Jayden: (*Jayden concentrated on the iPad and made no response to Madison's whisper*)

Despite Madison's efforts, Jayden did not display any response to Madison's first whisper and continued to concentrate on the touchscreen game. This suggested to me that Jayden was not ready to move to the private dialogic space that Madison had created and that he was still located in the public space that he shared with his peers. As such, he continued to use the communication style that he normally used in this space. Here, the voice of the invisible speaker was stronger than the voice of the whisperer.

L5 Madison: (*Madison whispered to Jayden again*)

Madison did not give up on her new strategy and enhanced the power of her voice by making a second attempt to whisper to Jayden, urging him to respond in the private dialogic space she had created.

L6 Jayden: (*Jayden responded with a slight smile, while still concentrating on the iPad game*)

Jayden received her whispered voice (with her friendly signal) this time, and he gave her the positive response of a slight smile (an affirmation of the effectiveness of her whispered voice and her creation of this private dialogic space that was shared by the two of them). However, he still concentrated on the touchscreen game (his actions still focused on his peer-shared public space). This demonstrated that Jayden positioned himself on the boundary between the public space and the private space, his style of dialogue corresponding to the nature of these spaces.

L7 Madison: (*Madison whispered to Jayden for the third time*)

Madison continued to whisper to make her voice stronger than the voice of the invisible speaker.

L8 Jayden: (*Jayden responded with another slight smile but continued to concentrate on the touchscreen game*)

Jayden was still hesitant about crossing the boundary line from the public space (indicated by his concentration on the touchscreen and his respect for the common rule set by the teacher) to the private space (by the gesture he shared in giving the voice of the whisperer a positive response). In my interpretation, this was the moment of inner heteroglossia for Jayden. The voice of the teacher (execution of the rule), the voice of the whisperer (seeking an exception to the rule), the voice of resistance (resisting or breaking the rule) and the voice of the 'good child' (following the rule) all gathered together in his mind, competing fiercely with one another in their fight for greater importance and priority. This was a moment for Jayden to listen to a multitude of competing voices and make a judgment as to what his priorities were.

L9 Madison: (*Madison made an attempt to click the screen*)

Madison further enhanced her voice by her action of clicking the screen.

L10 Jayden: (*Jayden stopped all his playing movements on the screen and patiently waited for Madison's click, without interruption*)

FIGURE 5.7   Madison played with a big smile, and Jayden waited patiently

This was the magic moment. Even though he did not make an utterance, Jayden provided a positive answer to the voice of the whisperer. Through his body language, he discontinued all his playing movements on the screen and waited patiently for Madison's click. It would appear that in this moment, the voice of the whisperer won out.

Instead of stopping Madison's click as he had done previously, Jayden stopped his action of play to give way to her play and patiently waited for her click. This illustrated that Jayden had stepped into a different dialogic space (the private space shared by the two of them), where a different strategy or policy was employed. They shared a new game rule of playing together in this private space, which was contrary to the teacher's rule that the children should play one at a time – a rule that was understood and shared by all the other children in the public space.

Even though no actual words were spoken, I could discern the actively hidden dialogue between these two children.

TABLE 5.3   Heteroglossia and the whispered voice

Space	The shift between the public space shared by peers and the private space shared by two children.	
Genre	The genre of a whisper	
	Content	... (no uttered words)
	Form	i) Madison whispered something into Jayden's ear while covering her mouth with her hand. ii) Jayden responded with a slight smile.
Competing voices	Between two children regarding the execution of the rule and the exception to the rule.	
Dominant voice	The whisperer's voice finally dominated as she achieved her goal of playing together on the touchscreen device.	
Hidden dialogicity	Hidden dialogue between the two children regarding the negotiation of playing with touchscreen devices, even though no words were uttered.	

L11 Madison: *(Madison continued clicking on the iPad screen a few times, with a big smile on her face)*

From Madison's big smile and numerous clicking actions, it is evident that she had happily immersed herself in this play and that she was trying to make the most of the opportunities afforded by the new rule that had she created through creating a private space. She was the master of her own play in this moment of joint play.

L12 Jayden: *(After waiting patiently for some time, Jayden clicked on the screen and played together with Madison on the touchscreen device).*

Jayden used new strategies here (waiting patiently without interruption and clicking on the screen together), which indicated that the new rule of playing together had been applied in this newly private space.

Taken together, these examples highlight the struggle that results from the presence of powerful social forces when engaging in touchscreen play – as an arena of difference and conflict. While conforming to rules set by adults, children's own voices emerge, often with an interest in changing the rule and seeking an exception or in creating a rule of their own making.

4   Affordances and Limitations

This dialogic method, with respect to the visual understanding of children, allows us to better understand children's voices – not only verbal voices that require speech, but also non-verbal voices that, while unspoken, are expressed through children's body language – and the values and views hidden behind those voices. In this way, a visual methodology makes the hidden dialogue of an invisible speaker visible to us. It helps us to discern the competing voices surrounding children with regard to their use of touchscreen devices and with respect to the value that is carried in each non-verbal form of a hidden voice. This methodology also helps us to grasp the moment of inner heteroglossia, which children experience as a consequence of the conflicts that result from competing centripetal and centrifugal forces. Lastly, this methodology assists us in recognising children's strategic employment of multiple voices across different spaces, through both what is said (content) and how it is said (form).

Despite the affordances of this methodology, some limitations exist for researchers to contemplate with respect to the dialogic approaches to such 'seeings' involved in research of this nature. To interpret children's verbal and non-verbal voices properly, this visual method requires the researcher to have a sound understanding of the child-participants and the context of their dialogue. However, given the complexity of the language itself, the danger of misinterpretation exists. Therefore, it is vital that the researcher does not fall into the trap of speaking on behalf of children or ascribing meaning with any certainty at all. As a consequence, dialogic researchers can do little more than add to the voices with their insights as a primary source of seeing anew.

5   Ethical Issues

This brings us to the need to discuss the ethical issues of using a dialogical methodology in the practice of engagement with children's play involving touchscreen devices. Ethics, as a problematic in the early childhood setting, relates to researchers' responsibility for their own actions. Therefore, ethics is about (i) their responsibility for the way they condition the actions of the individual children with whom they interact and (ii) their responsibility for the actions that make relations palpable or not between children. This notion of responsibility in Bakhtin's (1981) thinking is perhaps best discussed in the context of his concept of answerability. Answerability refers to

> ... the social encounters that occur as a result of being in the world and the fact that these encounters suppose 'the importance of a moral and ethical obligation to carry responsibility towards relationships'. (Bakhtin, as cited in Redder & White, 2017, p. 424)

This responsibility for the relationship with self, for the actions of children in one's charge and for the relationships between children essentially pertains to 'answering *to* and *for* the other "without alibis"' (Ponzio, 2008, cited in Redder & White, 2017, p. 424, emphasis added). 'Without alibis' means that 'every action is answerable' (Bakhtin, 1981, cited in Redder & White, 2017, p. 424) – the ethical problematic being that because no two actions are the same, researchers must make themselves answerable to the uniqueness of every action that can be categorised as pertaining to the relationships described above. These relationships are, however, interconnected, which means that a single action changes everything for all beings in the same social context. As such, researchers are implicated in all decisions that produce actions, whether their encounters with children are direct or indirect (Redder & White, 2017).

As previously intimated, researching children's use of touchscreen devices involves not only an ethical problematic when using a dialogical methodology, but also a moral problematic. The moral problematic in the context of this research supposes a concern for how we think about education, what its purpose is and how it should be conducted. For example, what does freedom mean in terms of how we regard a child's independence of thought and action in the early childhood setting? I have taken this dialogic standpoint in my research on account of my sense of moral responsibility to value children's voices and their freedom to think, speak and act for themselves while at the same time needing to protect them from potential harm that might occur when exercising such freedoms. A conflict sometimes arises when, for example, I confront children's requests to 'play one more game' in the context of parents and teachers thinking children's play using touchscreen games needs to be restricted and guided by a learning purpose. The extent to which we should listen to children's voices, value their rights by addressing their voices and respond to their request with full trust and confidence in their abilities to self-manage is a challenge for a dialogic researcher.

In addition to the above-mentioned concerns, I also experience tensions as a researcher with respect to my own situatedness and my experience of my participants' 'voices'. Although I try to give equal and careful consideration to each voice, including children's voices, parents' voices, teachers' voices and my own voice as a researcher, I am concerned that my voice might involve misinterpretation, especially on account of my being a Chinese researcher and an outsider in the New Zealand ECE setting. As a mother of two young children, there might also be the 'hidden voice' of a parent in my voice.

6   Future Possibilities

Hidden dialogicity, as a dialogic methodology, provides possibilities for hearing and understanding children's voices in different forms, especially those that are not spoken out loud. Possibilities also exist to assist teachers and parents in paying greater attention to children's inner voices and their real needs, which in turn can lead to the development of corresponding pedagogies and teaching methods that might benefit children's learning to a greater extent. As a result, hidden dialogicity offers possibilities of exploring the formulation of more complex and nuanced teacher-student and parent-child relationships.

Heteroglossia, as a dialogic framework for analysis that provides possibilities for understanding the rationality of a diverse range of voices by bringing them together such that they debate in conflict and collaboration with one another with the purpose of asserting the value of their rationalities. This is especially important in such a multicultural society as the one in which we live. Heteroglossia offers us a way of understanding and respecting the variety of viewpoints and the richness of our multicultural experience.

'Seeing' voices, from a dialogic perspective, offers possibilities of understanding the voice in its multiple forms – verbal and non-verbal, hidden and spoken out loud – and in relation to the nature of a broader chronotope. Moreover, 'seeing' voices offers us a way in which to understand the origin, interaction and internalisation of voices and furthermore learning about the values underpinning the voices with which we interact.

7   Summary Statements

- The plural feature of the voice makes it possible to 'see' children's voices in their non-verbal forms of embodied expression.
- By listening to children's 'hidden dialogue' when observing an invisible speaker, their inner heteroglossia and the conflicts that occur in the dynamic between centripetal and centrifugal forces that children experience can be understood.
- Through children's prioritising of multiple voices, the origin of voices and the underpinning values can be explored.
- To be answerable to our relationships with children, we should take care to avoid ascribing our own meanings to their unspoken dialogues.

Acknowledgements

I wish to thank the teachers, children and parents who participated in my doctoral study, I will always appreciate your active response and support. I would also like to thank the University of Waikato for awarding me a doctoral scholarship to complete this research. I want to express my heartfelt thanks to Professor Jayne White, as the editor of this book and my supervisor, for being not only an excellent academic guide, but also a caring and understanding life mentor. And last, I want to thank my two children Yuan and Lan for giving me unconditional love, courage and inspiration, and to my parents and other family members for offering me support from all aspects.

References

Bakhtin, M. M. (1981). *The dialogic imagination: Four essays*. University of Texas Press.

Bakhtin, M. M. (1984). *Problems of Dostoevsky's poetics*. University of Minnesota Press.

Bakhtin, M. M., & Emerson, C. (1993). *Problems of Dostoevsky's poetics*. University of Minnesota Press.

Canning, N., Payler, J., Horsley, K., & Gomez, C. (2017). An innovative methodology for capturing young children's curiosity, imagination and voices using a free app: Our story. *International Journal of Early Years Education, 25*(3), 292–307.

Clark, A. (2011). Breaking methodological boundaries? Exploring visual, participatory methods with adults and young children. *European Early Childhood Education Research Journal, 19*(3), 321–330.

Cohen, L. E. (2009). The heteroglossic world of preschoolers' pretend play. *Contemporary Issues in Early Childhood, 10*(4), 331–342.

Cohen, L. E. (2015). Layers of discourse in preschool block play: An examination of children's social interactions. *International Journal of Early Childhood, 47*(2), 267–281.

Cresswell, J., & Sullivan, P. (2020). Bakhtin's chronotope, connotations, and discursive psychology: Towards a richer interpretation of experience. *Qualitative Research in Psychology, 17*(1), 121–142.

Duncan, R. M., & Tarulli, D. (2003). Play as the leading activity of the preschool period: Insights from Vygotsky, Leont'ev, and Bakhtin. *Early Education and Development, 14*(3), 271–292.

Fane, J., Jovanovic, J., Redmond, G., & Gibb, L. (2018). Exploring the use of emoji as a visual research method for eliciting young children's voices in childhood research. *Early Child Development and Care, 188*(3), 359–374.

Irwin, J., Moore, D., Tornatore, L., & Fowler, A. (2012). Promoting emerging language and literacy during storytime. *Children & libraries, 10*(2), 20.

James, A. (2007). Giving voice to children's voices: Practices and problems, pitfalls and potentials. *American Anthropologist, 109*(2), 261–272.

Jones, M. V. (1990). *Dostoyevsky after Bakhtin: Readings in Dostoyevsky's fantastic realism*. Cambridge University Press.

Khoo, E., Merry, R., Nguyen, M., Bennett, T., & MacMillan, N. (2015). *iPads and opportunities for teaching and learning for young children*. Wilf Malcolm Institute of Educational Research, Hamilton, New Zealand. Retrieved from https://www.waikato.ac.nz/__data/assets/pdf_file/0003/257025/Ipads-and-Opps_For-website_2015-03-18-1.pdf

Marbin, J. (2006). *Children's voices: Talk, knowledge and identity*. Palgrave MacMillan.

Mayall, B. (2008). Conversations with children: Working with generational issues. In P. Christensen & A. James (Eds.), *Research with children: Perspectives and practices* (pp. 109–124). Routledge.

Palaiologou, L. (2016). Children under five and digital technologies: Implications for early years pedagogy. *European Early Childhood Education Research Journal, 24*(1), 5–24.

Radesky, J., Kistin, C., Eisenberg, S., Gross, J., Block, G., Zuckerman, B., & Silverstein, M. (2016). Parent perspectives on their mobile technology use: The excitement and exhaustion of parenting while connected. *Journal of Developmental & Behavioral Pediatrics, 37*(9), 694–701.

Redder, B., & White, E. J. (2017). Implicating teachers in infant-peer relationships: Teacher answerability through alteric acts. *Contemporary Issues in Early Childhood, 18*(4), 422–433. doi:10.1177/1463949117742782

Rosen, R. (2015). Children's violently themed play and adult imaginaries of childhood: A Bakhtinian analysis. *International Journal of Early Childhood, 47*(2), 235–250.

Sperling, M., & Appleman, D. (2011). Voice in the context of literacy studies. *Reading Research Quarterly, 46*(1), 70–84.

Spyrou, S. (2011). The limits of children's voices: From authenticity to critical, reflexive representation. *Childhood, 18*(2), 151–165.

Vochdt, L. D. (2015). Reconceptualising teacher-child dialogue in early years education as a moral answerability. *International Journal of Early Childhood, 47*(2), 317–330.

Wertsch, J. (1991). *Voices of the mind.* Harvester Wheatsheaf.

White, E. J. (2009a). *Bakhtinian dialogism: A philosophical and methodological route to dialogue and difference?* Retrieved from http://citeseerx.ist.psu.edu/viewdoc/summary?doi=10.1.1.359.7435

White, E. J. (2009b). *Assessment in New Zealand early childhood education: A Bakhtinian analysis of toddler metaphoricity* (Unpublished PhD thesis). University of Monash, Melbourne, Australia.

White, E. J. (2016). More than meets the "I": A polyphonic approach to video as dialogic meaning-making. *Video Journal of Education and Pedagogy, 1*(1), 6–12.

White, E. J. (2017). Heteroglossia as a dialogic route to metaphoricity in education. In I. Semetsky (Ed.), *Edusemiotics: A handbook* (pp. 207–220). Springer.

White, E. J., Peter, M. A., & Redder, B. (2015). The work of the eye in infant pedagogy: A dialogic encounter of "seeing" in an education and care setting. *International Journal of Early Childhood, 47*(2), 283–299.

White, E. J., & Redder, B. (2015). Infant and teacher dialogue in education and care: A pedagogical imperative. *Early Childhood Research Quarterly, 30*, 160–173.

CHAPTER 6

Deconstructing the Use of Video for Research with Children

A Methodology of 'Truth' and Meaning

Julie Carmel and Elizabeth Rouse

1 Introduction

This chapter poses a deconstructivist methodology for seeing and being seen in media – when young children are the research participants (Koch, 2019) or co-subjects (White, 2017). We focus less on video 'as research' and more on the increasing use of video 'for research'. We do so by drawing on Derrida's deconstruction approach as a frame of analysis to raise discussion and debate around the ethics of using publicly available videos as a means of collecting data in research. The chapter draws on a larger study by Julie Carmel in which the analysis of a publicly available video has been used as a tool of analysis to investigate how children with physical disabilities are portrayed as representative of the diversity in the society in which we live. Whilst this study draws on materials that can be accessed via public digital platforms such as YouTube, Derrida's notion of deconstruction calls for a critical lens on text that invites us to delve beyond the surface of what is being presented. We contend that visual images are a form of text and that they can be deconstructed and analysed accordingly. As such, we propose a critical reading of visual representations of children in popular culture – as forms of 'moving' text rather than 'truth' (Peters & White, 2018).

2 Derrida and Deconstruction

The premise of deconstruction is to 'work towards creating a different philosophy of truth and meaning' (Campbell, 2012, p. 107) that orients towards finding contradictions in what is being presented and what is actually occurring, and subsequently seeing the contradictions. Deconstructing images requires a critical lens and the ability to delve beyond the surface of what is being shown in order to discover what is being seen and to address questions that arise for understanding 'other' through different, often contradictory, non-traditional

© KONINKLIJKE BRILL NV, LEIDEN, 2020 | DOI: 10.1163/9789004433328_006

ways of interpreting the seen. Derrida's (1997) methodological route to seeing takes its point of departure from the deconstruction of linguistic signs. It requires questioning the accepted basis of the meaning of text and an inherent desire to place meaning at the centre of this presence. Close interrogation is achieved by deconstructing the concepts of the meaning of words and both how they are constructed within the writing itself and how they produce meaning.

Derrida (1997) suggests that meaning is not fixed and should not to be located outside the text but rather within it. By questioning the accepted basis of the meaning of text and an inherent desire to place meaning at the centre of this presence, Derrida orients towards a re-visioning of what is normalised as truth – using the concept of 'aporia' to explain any contradictions that might be present. Aporia, in a Derridean sense, is the moment where the text (image) may represent that which may be contrary to what was intended.

Seeing and interpreting using a deconstructive lens invites the researcher to look for that which runs *counter* to the intended meaning of the text by finding the interplay between language and the construction of its meaning – a concept Derrida calls 'grammatology' (Gaston, 2011; Norris, 1987), which invites the researcher to look beyond the surface of the meaning and find truth. This truth can be found by deconstructing text, piece by piece, which Derrida calls logocentrism. Gaston (2011), in his interpretation of Derrida's 'Of Grammatology' (1967), contends that 'logocentrism is inscribed ineluctably within all our western languages. As soon as you open your mouth or put pen to paper you are imperturbably repeating logocentric assumptions' (p. 39). According to Derrida (1978, 1997), logocentrism is the presence of the text that regards words and language as a fundamental expression of an external reality. When applying logocentrism to visual images, viewers interpret what they are seeing based on their own coherence of what is being presented.

Derrida (1976) further contends that reading any text with a deconstructive lens requires consideration of the author's *intention* behind the text's production. Reading the text in this way provides an opportunity to unearth the possibilities of the visual in diverse ways, which he describes as endless and subjective, 'enshrined in the orienting concept of difference' (Derrida, 1976, p. 62). Doing this requires looking using two lenses: first, drawing out the ideas of the text [image] and second, applying a critical eye to draw out the transformative understanding of what is being presented. This is achieved by deconstructing the text [image] into two separate categories: the signified, which relates to the idea or concept of the structure of the text (image), and the signifier, the idea associated with the linguistics of the text (image). With regard to the word disability (the signified), for example, the understanding of this concept is dependent upon the readers' interpretation of disability, and this may be contradictory to the writer's intention. It is not until the reader is provided with more information about disability (the signifier), such as impairment, that he or she may have the same understanding as what the writer intended when using disability as a concept. Derrida (1982) refers to this as *différance,* and it is this *différance* between what is being written (shown) and what is being intended that reduces the meaning of the text (vision) and captures opposition within the concept itself. This *différance* then leads to other ways of reading (seeing) and thinking, which may not be evident when first viewed.

3   Deconstructing the Visual as Text in Media

We contend that seeing through a deconstructive lens can also be applied to visual text. The location of visual texts, such as video in media, provides additional opportunities to encounter *différance* through polysemic interpretation. This is achieved by exploring the authors intentions and requires the reader to find any blind spots in the author's intention. It also requires the exploration of what the author is, or might be, attempting to convey to the reader (audience). Deconstructing visual images, as for written text, necessitates viewing what is included and, importantly, what is not included. It is also about seeing what may appear to be an innocuous image as having deeper meanings. Deconstructing the visual requires seeing how we see, how we are able to see and what we are allowed or made to see in the image (Foster, 1988, as cited in Rose, 2007, p. 2). This seeing is influenced by what the viewer gazes at and what he or she prioritises as significant or important.

Lenz Taguchi (2006), when discussing the application of deconstruction as a method of reconceptualising early childhood practices, suggests that when early childhood educators are undertaking any analysis of documentation, they should 'begin wherever we are ... in the text where we already believe ourselves to be' (Derrida, 1976, p. 162, as cited in Lenz Taguchi, 2006, p. 257) as a starting point. She also states that all educators must look beyond any assumptions they may have about children and learning because applying deconstruction is a 'process of redoing by undoing' (p. 276).

In her paper, "Deconstructing and transgressing the Theory-Practice dichotomy in early childhood education" (2007), Lenz Taguchi discusses how educators can apply Derridean concepts to children's visual representations of their ideas; she also mentions that doing so requires early childhood teachers to 'let go of taken-for-granted notions of children' (Lenz Taguchi, 2007, p. 277) and how they learn. Derrida (2003) claims that even though this can be one of the most difficult things for educators to do, applying deconstruction requires this of those educators. This is because applying a deconstructive lens is about 'redoing by undoing' (Lenz Taguchi, 2007, p. 276), thinking differently about what is being seen and going beyond the surface to find the 'truth'. In her 2006 chapter, "Reconceptualizing Early Childhood Education Childhood Education: Challenging taken-for-granted ideas", Lenz Taguchi explores the application of Derrida's deconstruction to the analysis of documentation and written, video, dialogue or work samples – undertaken on children in a preschool in Sweden, where they discussed setting arrangements at the lunch table – and the ways in which children documented their learning or discussion around this

Taguchi (2006, 2007) contends that applying a deconstructive lens can open up new levels of understanding and help all educators to go beyond 'shallow evaluations of the children' and come to 'more thoughtful analysis of the children's learning' (2006, p. 263). Deconstructing visual texts concerning children and their lives can therefore help educators to review what is really taking place.

4   Visual Data as Video for Research

Regarding the use of existing videos as data, it is increasingly common for research to be undertaken with videos that are readily available rather than videos generated by researchers for research. This ease of availability, on platforms such as YouTube, affords researchers the opportunity to collect data without the necessity of going out into the field. Using existing videos provides researchers with a framework of analysis to explore the narratives that reside within the video. However, in using existing videos, researchers should be aware that these videos are always constructed and must not be seen as a means of objectively documenting reality (Rose, 2006), because existing videos are subject to a variety of influences. More often than not, they have been produced under strict guidelines and present one point of view. Banks (2001) thus cautions researchers to look for and make a distinction between the internal and external narratives of images, and he states that researchers must make a clear distinction between the purpose of the video and the production thereof, and they should take these into account when using video as research.

When video is used 'as' a research tool, young children often have the opportunity and the level of involvement to be able share their thinking about the world as they see it. However, when video is used 'for' research, the assumption is that the extent to which the child was given an opportunity to participate in the video is often determined by the parent; moreover, when a researcher uses this video for a purpose other than the initial intent, it further removes the child's voice and opportunity to present the world as he or she sees it. When researchers use existing video for research, it is imperative to ask the following questions, among others: (1) 'is this in the best interests of the child?' and 'is it "entrenching a predominately paternalistic model of the best interests?"' (Brems, Desmet, & Vandehole, 2017, p. 4); (2) 'for how long should a video be available on platforms such as YouTube?' and 'where does a child's right to rescind the use of his or her image occur?'; and (3) "For how long a video should be made available as a research tool?' The list of questions goes on; therefore, the overarching question that must be asked of visual research concerning children remains: 'is it appropriate or ethical to use this video for research and, if so, then what meanings are produced as a consequence of its presence?' These are some of the many questions we might pose concerning visual research and the methodologies that orient its 'seeings'.

5   By Way of Example

The example we offer attempts to illuminate this concept. It is taken from a vignette aired as part of a popular children's television programme produced in 2012 and aired in 2013 that is still widely used in Australia today. The deconstruction of this video forms part of Author 1's larger doctoral thesis, which explores how children with disabilities are framed in a particular television programme made for preschool children. The programme chosen is held in high esteem in the Australian media, has won many awards for excellence in programming for preschool children and has been aired for over 50 years on Australian television. It strives to include contemporary issues that preschoolers face in their everyday lives. This video is an example of one of these contemporary issues – in this case, disability.

From the video, we can glean that at the time of production, Callaghan and Nate were approximately 5–6 and 3–4 years old respectively and most likely did not have the ability to provide informed consent. At the time of this analysis, in early 2020, Callaghan and his brother were approximately 13 and 11 years old respectively. Before proceeding, it is important to point out that deconstruction of visual images has a different purpose than other visual methodologies in that 'it does not seek to give an answer to an image' (Campbell, 2012,

p. 172); instead, it seeks to find and question the truth in the complexities within the image.

As mentioned above, this video is part of a made-for-preschoolers Australian television programme, and it forms part of a doctoral thesis that assesses this programme over a 7-years production period (Carmel, 2012–2018). The programme is aired in a 7-year cycle, and this video falls into this period, having been produced in 2012 and aired in 2013. Julie began collecting data in 2016, and despite her efforts to interview the producer and writer of this particular video, she was unable to do so because they are no longer part of the production team and could not be located. In the absence of dialogue with the production team, applying a Derridean lens to this video has allowed Julie to identify the dominant discourses and discursive practices therein. It is important to note that when applying a deconstructive lens to any text (image), what is revealed is dependent on the gaze of the person looking, and it inscribes his or her thinking.

The selected video involves what appears to be a family on a trip to the local library. We are introduced to two young children – one with a 'disability' (Callaghan) and one 'typically developing' (Nate) – accompanied by what the viewer can only assume is their family. The moment is not noteworthy; it is a typical everyday occurrence for the children – something that they most likely do on a regular basis. The following snapshot offers a brief glimpse of the scene that unfolds, and it is followed by a series of analytical processes for engaging critically with the visual text (see Figure 6.1).

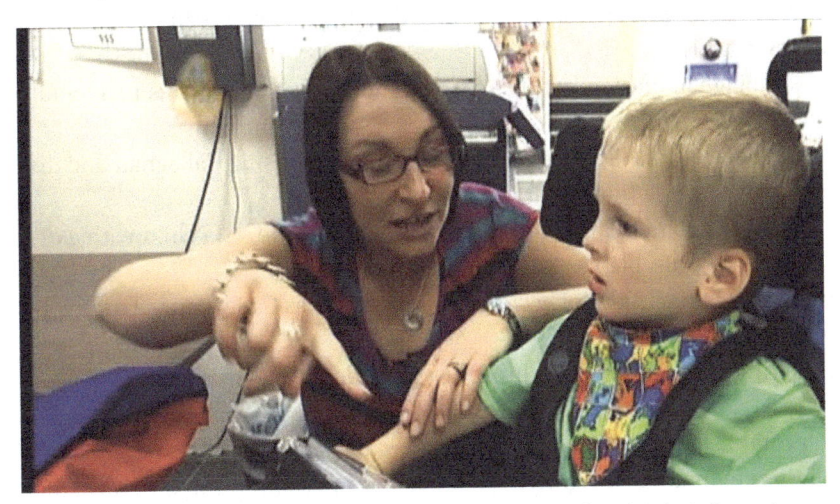

FIGURE 6.1   Snapshot: Callaghan visits the library (2013): ABC Playschool windows vignette. (Source: YouTube, downloaded June 27, 2019 from https://www.youtube.com/watch?v=J64r9MBRt4g)

5.1 *Look for Intent and Its Underlying 'Truth'*

Applying a deconstructive lens to this snapshot requires the viewer to question what is being seen upon first viewing. Derrida (1989) argues that this questioning should come from within the text and look 'at what the image includes and excludes, detecting the social roles it creates' and finding any 'hierarchies' that may appear natural in the image (Fyfe & Law, 1988, p. 1). When we deconstruct this viewing, we seek deeper meanings and contradictions (Aporia) that may be present. Derrida (1978) contends that when deconstructing any image, we must first look at the *intent*. By exploring the intent of those who were involved in the production of this vignette through a Derridean lens, the authors of this chapter may find 'truth'. However, according to Derrida, as cited in Culler (2008), one must acknowledge the possibility that this truth may be invalidated by future discoveries and consequently should be seen as a relational framework that may evolve. As this snapshot is from a vignette that was included in an Australian programme made for preschool children (Playschool, 1966-present), and in the absence of any direct knowledge from the production team, the authors can only assume that the purpose of this was to depict preschoolers in everyday situations in inclusive ways. According to Harrison (2013), the aim of Playschool vignettes is to provide an 'authentic reflection of this increasing diversity within the early childhood experience of family and community life' (p. 144).

Therefore, drawing on this concept and applying a Derridean lens, we must first ask, 'has this been achieved?' A series of questions then arise, as follows:

- How are the children, most especially Callaghan, being seen in relation to achieving this?
- Was Callaghan chosen because he had a disability, or was this incidental? Does it matter? If so, how?
- Is the focus of this vignette on including or normalising Callaghan and disability or on depicting children visiting the library?
- How is Callaghan being represented here – as a child, as a child with a disability or as a disabled specimen?
- Has Callaghan's disability become his identity? Has Callaghan become a living sign amongst other signs?

Considering these questions through a Derridean deconstructive lens, disability has now become the signified, and inclusion has become the signifier, which establishes assertions of the object/subject relationship. For the writers of this chapter, these signifying relationships pose powerful questions that compel them to explore further.

As previously stated, the objective of the producers of Playschool is to emphasise real-life experiences as a means of engaging the preschool audience and providing opportunities to see, in this instance, realistic representations of a child with a disability. Including marginalised groups, such as a child with a disability, can create an awareness of disability in society and provide opportunities to normalise differences. From a normative perspective, setting media attention on disability can be seen as an additionally important aspect of social integration and ultimately acceptance.

When marginalised groups, such as those with a disability, are included in the media, viewers are exposed to these differences, thus providing opportunities for quality discussion, and this may lead to a change in attitude. This is similarly to what Novak (Chapter 12, this volume) found in his research relating to immersive technology and changing teachers' attitudes.

As we do not know the complete 'truth' behind the producer's intent (and we might join with our post-truth colleagues to ask if truth is even possible to begin with), we may assume that it was perhaps an attempt to 'normalise' Callaghan and depict him in everyday happenings. The social model of disability, which lies within critical disability theory, emphasises that it is society that disables, not the disability. Therefore, it may not be a stretch to claim that the purpose of this vignette was to present Callaghan as a child participating in a visit to the library. With this in mind, when deconstructing the families' intent, we must focus on how the children, both Callahan and Nate, are being included and seen. In Figure 6.1, Callaghan can be seen with his 'mother', who is helping him to return library books, and presumably his father and siblings watch on. Nate is in the background, being held by his father, while the focus is placed on Callaghan and the borrowing of the books. Callaghan thus becomes the signified, and the books the signifier; they become dependent on each other, which is an important aspect of the 'story' being told: a child's visit to a library.

5.2   *Explore Counter-Intuitive Meanings or 'Truths'*

Derrida suggests that in the process of deconstructing any image (text), we must look for the counter-intuitive ways of analysis to find the 'truth'. When using a deconstructive lens, this means asking, 'what might the truth be?'

Actively finding the dissonance within the image leads the viewer to question, 'what is purpose of this?' and 'how is the presence of Callaghan being seen in relation to inclusion or normalisation?' By looking deeper at this image and its wider context within the video, one can see *what is not there*: other people. If the purpose of this vignette is about the inclusion and normalisation of Callaghan and about meeting the aim of the ABC, as stated earlier, to provide children with authentic views of their life worlds, then the fact that there are no other people in the library contradicts this purpose. In this instance, the

FIGURE 6.2   Snapshot: Callaghan visits the library (2013): ABC Playschool windows vignette. (Source: YouTube, downloaded June 27 2019, from https://www.youtube.com/watch?v=J64r9MBRt4g)

FIGURE 6.3   Snapshot: Callaghan visits the library (2013): ABC Playschool windows vignette. (Source: YouTube, downloaded June 27, 2019 from https://www.youtube.com/watch?v=J64r9MBRt4g)

signified in the image becomes inclusion, and the signifier is the absence of other people, which signifies inclusion. Derrida claims, 'there is nothing outside the text' (Derrida, 1997, p. 159). Based on this concept, we would argue that Callaghan, being a child with a disability, is seen as simply a means to an end.

Callaghan is seen as participating in an 'everyday' action – we can ask, however, 'how 'normal' is this?' Given the inclusion of books being returned, it can be assumed that this is not Callaghan's first time to the library; however, one must ask the following: (1) Does his family normally accompany him to the library? (2) Is this part of Callaghan's normal activities, or is this being 'staged' for the cameras? (3) How, then, is Callaghan being seen by his family? and, based on the fact that they have accompanied him on this occasion to the library, (4) Is their inclusion in this vignette an attempt by the family to demonstrate the inclusion or normalisation of Callaghan?

Callaghan has become the signified and his family the signifier in this video in that the families' inclusion in the video could be seen as a means to depict Callaghan participating in an everyday family outing.

Deconstructing this snapshot in this way helps the viewer to make visible that which might not be visible on the first viewing. When deconstructing any image, it is important to note that each 'reading' is influenced by the previous one and influences the next one. Further analysis of this video may reveal additional contradictions in the attempt to normalise disability.

Further into the video (see Figure 6.4), Callaghan and his mother can be seen at the book boxes. Callaghan's mother chooses the books for him, as the boxes are not designed for a child with a disability to access; however, in the background, we can see children's books displayed on a book case. The following question should be asked here: why was Callaghan not taken to this display and given the opportunity to choose his own books? Applying a Derridean lens to this question may aid in finding the answer. Here, we argue, is a further contradiction (aporia). The very nature of the setup of the library (signified) and how Callaghan was given the opportunity to choose books (the signifier) is evident here. The contradiction in this scene is the desire to demonstrate inclusive practices, when in fact the opposite has occurred. truth be?'

FIGURE 6.4   Snapshot: Callaghan visits the library (2013): ABC Playschool. (Source: YouTube, downloaded June 27, 2019; https://www.youtube.com/watch?v=J64r9MBRt4g)

Campbell (2012) claims that this very essence of deconstruction 'reinforces the playful, active and dangerous nature of deconstruction (p. 117). However, it is important to note that Derrida (1997) himself takes great pains to point out that when deconstructing any image (text), no simple interpretation can explain the totality of the image because the image (text) is subjective. This subjectivity is based on what the viewer is trying to find and on the purpose of the deconstruction. In this case, deconstructing the video 'Callaghan visits the library' has afforded the authors the opportunity to look beyond the surface of images that are produced with the intention to demonstrate inclusion and the normalisation of disability. This deconstructive analysis has been undertaken through a non-lived experience of disability, and we would contend that this viewpoint may influence our perceptions. We do, however, argue that when including any marginalised group in the media, producers have a duty to present realistic representations and are accountable for them. In this video, the way in which disability is represented can influence how the audience receives the underlying message, which might inscribe thinking.

6   Ethical Implications for the 'Video for Research' Approach

The repurposing of existing video data, whether it is from an archive, YouTube or an institution's video database, raises many issues that are key for video-based and visual research, including the need to understand the history of a video, its context of production, its original purpose and audience, and how these factors are embedded in the video as an artefact (Jewitt, 2012). When drawing from video available in the public domain, the following is of key consideration: although data or information may be publicly available, this does not automatically mean that the individuals with whom this data or information is associated have granted permission for its use in research (NHMRC, 2018) or for a purpose other than that for which original consent was granted.

The re-examination of video designed for young children raises several ethical considerations that are brought about via Derrida's theoretical lens. First, the video is produced with a particular goal and purpose in mind, namely, intent. Parents have generally consented to their children being included on this basis. It can be assumed that the consent process surrounding the inclusion of this family in this video was clear and legally contracted, and it is not the purpose of this paper to assume or suggest that the parents were doing anything other than acting in the best interests of their children and as legal guardians, making decisions for their children in this context. However, what can also be assumed and argued is that the parents, in consenting to involve their children in this film, did not necessarily consent to the video being later accessed from a public domain platform and used in this research. As White (2017) asks, 'did the parents understand that their faces would be used and potentially downloaded and used by people all over the world in ways that are not necessarily the intent for which consent was given?' In an era of big data, in addition to asking whether the children were afforded the opportunity to consent to the filming and whether they were aware that they were being filmed, we might also question the possibilities of subsequent invisibility.

In relation to a constructivist examination of video that features children, it can be argued that neither of these children, nor their parents or, indeed, the producers provided consent for this video to be later used in research. The way in which the representation is both de-constructed and re-constructed calls for researchers to be accountable not only for the integrity of their research but also an awareness of the influence this has on the lives of others (White, 2017). Looking deeply and critically into video as production to explore the depiction of diversity (or any other topic for that matter) will uncover different truths from those intended at the time of consent or production. It is therefore important to allow for discussion about the extent to which any discoveries can be claimed as truth. Indeed, a reflexive attitude on behalf of the researcher is not only desirable, but essential.

7   Conclusion

Seeing and being seen can be complex issues to explore, as they present many complexities. Furthermore, seeing and what is seen are related to the gaze of the viewer and what they bring to the viewing. The dynamic between what is seen and the unseen is always subjective and can be influenced by varying factors. To deconstruct any text, Culler (2008) claims that one must demonstrate how the text (video) undermines the key concepts that it is asserting by delving beyond the surface and see what is really there.

Using Derrida's deconstruction theory, this chapter examined and deconstructed a video/vignette from a popular Australian preschool children's television programme. This allowed the authors to unpack the layers of this video/vignette and discover what they saw when applying their own gaze and find their own 'truth'.

In this chapter, the 'truth' presented by the authors is their 'truth' alone. To another viewing the same video/vignette, another 'truth' may emerge and, in examining the same video through a different lens, may be just as valid as what has been argued here. The implications are that when we as researchers or as adults use existing videos/vignettes for our own research purposes, we must ask ourselves, would the child and the families be happy with how we are using it, how we are deconstructing it and the discourse used to describe what we see? As deconstructive researchers, we should always start from the position of this question as a methodological proposition that underpins our work. In consideration of young children and the (mis)representations of their lives (or in this case 'abilities'), we assert that researchers cannot do otherwise.

8   Summary Statements

– Video in social media concerning children is becoming more widespread. However, its unproblematic representation of children calls for more critical interrogation and accountability – thus positioning publicly available video as a site for research.
– Derrida presents a frame of analysis that enables researchers to look beneath the surface and deconstruct images to find a deeper or contradictory meaning.
– A number of ethical implications exist regarding the use of publicly available video images for research purposes; these implications go beneath the surface of those images being permitted 'just because' they are publicly available.
– Using a deconstruction lens as presented by Derrida, researchers should challenge and question the way they engage with publicly available visual images of children and families in research in order to reflect on how they may be representing or misrepresenting the voices of 'others' on their behalf.

Acknowledgements

We wish to thank Jayne White for her excellent feedback, editing and encouragement to persevere with us throughout the writing and publishing process.
    Images used in this chapter were downloaded from YouTube and are used under the Fair Use doctrine. The video does not contain copyright written on the YouTube site.

References

Australian Broadcasting Commission. (2013). *Playschool – Callaghan visits the library.* Retrieved from https://www.youtube.com/watch?v=J64r9MBRt4g&t=69s

Banks, M. (2001).*Visual methods in social research.* Sage.

Brems, E., Desmet, E., & Vandehole, W. (2017). *Children's rights law in the global human rights landscape: Isolation, inspiration, integration?* Routledge.

Campbell, N. (2012). Regarding Derrida: The tasks of visual deconstruction. *Qualitative Research in Organisation and Management: An International Journal, 7*(1), 106–124.

Culler, J. (2008). *On deconstruction. Theory and criticism after structuralism.* Routledge.

Derrida, J. (1977). *Of grammatology* (G. Spivak, Trans.). John Hopkins Press.

Derrida, J. (1978). *Writing and difference* (A. Bass, Trans.). Routledge and Kegan Paul.

Derrida, J. (1982). *Margins of philosophy* (A. Bass, Trans.). Chicago University Press.

Lenz Taguchi, H. (2006) Deconstructing and transgressing the theory-practice dichotomy in early childhood education. *Educational Philosophy and Theory, 39*(3), 275–290.

Lenz Taguchi, H. (2006). Reconceptualizing early childhood education: Challenging taken for granted ideas. In J. Einarsdottir & J. A. Wagner (Eds.), *Nordic childhoods and early education. Philosophy, research, policy and practice in Denmark, Finland, Iceland, Norway, and Sweden* (pp. 257–288). Information Age Publishing.

Farini, F. (2019). As a Conclusion, to the Future: A discussion on trust, agency and the semantics of rights in intergenerational relationships. In F. Farini & A. Scollan (Eds.), *Children's self-determination in the context of early childhood education and services discourses, policies and practices* (pp. 267–281). Springer.

Fyfe, G., & Law, J. (Eds.). (1988). *Picturing power: Visual defection and social relations, sociological review monograph.* Routledge Joy.

Gaston, S. (2011). Derrida and the end of the world. *New Literary History, 42*(3), 499–517.

Harrison, C. (2013). A look 'through the windows' at ABC play school: 45 years in a changing media landscape. *Early Child Development and Care, 183*(1), 137–148.

Jewitt, C. (2012). *National centre for research methods working paper 03/12: An introduction to using video for research.* National Centre for Research Methods. Retrieved from http://eprints.ncrm.ac.uk/2259/4/NCRM_workingpaper_0312.pdf

Koch, A. (2019). Children as participants in research. Playful interactions and negotiation of researcher–child relationships. *Early Years.* doi:10.1080/09575146.2019.1581730

National Health and Medical Research Council. (2007). *National statement on ethical conduct in human research. Australian Government* (updated 2018). Retrieved from https://www.nhmrc.gov.au/about-us/publications/national-statement-ethical-conduct-human-research-2007-updated-2018#block-views-block-file-attachments-content-block-1

Nutbrown, C. (2010). Naked by the pool? Blurring the Image? Ethical issues in the portrayal of young children in arts-based educational research. *Qualitative Inquiry, 17*(1), 3–14.

Rose, G. (2007). *Visual Methodologies. An introduction to interpretation of Visual materials* (2nd ed.). Sage Publications.

White, E. J. (2011). 'Seeing' the toddler: Voices or voiceless? In E. Johansson & E. J. White (Eds.), *Educational research with our youngest: Voices of infants and toddlers.* Springer.

White, E. J. (2017). Video ethics and young children: Video editorial. *Video Journal of Education and Pedagogy, 2*(2). doi:10.1186/s40990-017-0012-9

Winter, C. (2013). "Derrida applied": Derrida meets Dracula in the geography classroom. In M. Murphy (Ed.), *Social theory and education research: Understanding Foucault, Habermas. Bourdieu and Derrida* (pp. 184–199). Routledge.

White, E., & Peters, M. (2016). The video journal and visual pedagogies: In the age of visual cultures. *Video Journal of Education and Pedagogy, 1*(7). Retrieved from https://link.springer.com/article/10.1186/s40990-016-0008-x

CHAPTER 7

Visual Dialogic Self-Study in ECE
'Video-of-Video'

Bridgette Redder

1 Introduction

This chapter brings dialogic self-study in early childhood education (ECE) to the field of visual methodology. The *visual dialogic self-study methodology* emphasises not only what can be heard but also what can be seen in dialogue with others. This chapter considers how visual dialogic self-study, as a (visual) methodology in its own right, provides a way for the researcher to 'see' his or her 'self' through visual means in relationship with other – in other words, 'finding' self. The chapter explains the importance of a visual orientation to a dialogic self-study in making aspects of the self's encounters with others visible, in order to deeply understand the self's multiple accountabilities to self and others. Furthermore, the chapter introduces the potential of video-of-video as a method to visually capture how the self in relationship with others is revealed outwardly in dialogue. This introduction is made because in dialogue, a person 'becomes for the first time that which he is – not only for others but for himself as well' (Bakhtin, 1984, p. 252). In addition, to illustrate how the employment of a visual dialogic self-study methodology might be applied in practice, I reflect briefly on my own self-study as an ECE teacher. An example is subsequently presented from my research concerning how being accountable to infants, teachers and self means exposing the self in dialogue and being exposed by others. As a result, the following is illuminated: how the visual dialogic self-study methodology provides a way in which to make pedagogy visible, and hence accountable, because it is open to critique and scrutiny.

2 Dialogic Self-Study as a Visual Methodology in ECE

Hamilton and Pinnegar (1998) define self-study as 'the study of one's self, one's actions, one's ideas, ...' (p. 238). Self-study is oriented toward the exploration and immediate improvement of one's own professional practice (LaBoskey, 2004) and professional self-understanding as a teacher (Hamilton, 1998). It takes a self-reflective stance together with responsibility for the self and others

© KONINKLIJKE BRILL NV, LEIDEN, 2020 | DOI: 10.1163/9789004433328_007

(LaBoskey, 2004). Moreover, self-study places researchers at the centre of their own enquiries as the subjects being researched. It is also about the individual 'I' who lives in a world that is shared with other 'I's', and it strives to make one's practice explicit to the self and others.

A Bakhtinian (1993) dialogic approach to self-study further strengthens the view that a study of the self is never about the self in isolation from the other. This dialogic approach suggests a view of the self as one who is made up of multiple voices. From a Bakhtinian dialogic perspective, the self is never solely about the self: Bakhtin's self is not separated from other individuals; although unique, the self is always in relationship with others and therefore inextricably connected to the other (Bakhtin, 1993). Moreover, what the self says and does, is influenced by the person or people who are listening from the past, present and future; the self's response to another will shape not only the other but also the self – for which the self is accountable. A Bakhtinian dialogic approach thus recognises that people are accountable for the decisions they make in practice, actualised in concrete acts, in dialogue with others.

Visual methodologies enable an individual (the self) to make sense of his or her lived experience in everyday contexts through visual representation and visual voice. By introducing a dialogic self-study to the field of visual methodology, a visual representation of the self's pedagogical practice and an account thereof are made visible. In the past, self-study through visual representation and visual voice employed an array of visuals both as data and as provocations for reflection in the self-study process. Practice and professional experience is often documented using pictures, drawings, collages or videos, which are subsequently analysed for what they can glean about practice. For example, when working with the visual, self-study researchers have utilised participatory visual methodologies (PVMs) for social justice teaching in teacher education programmes, using methods such as photovoice, drawings, cellphilm production and participatory videos to explore the notion of 'seeing for ourselves' as a foundation for reflexivity (Mitchell, Moletsane, MacEntee, & de Lange, 2019, p. 4).

On the one hand, teacher self-study research and dialogic research studies, although fairly new, have been undertaken in ECE spaces. On the other hand, visual dialogic self-study research is a new methodological contribution to the ECE arena. This type of self-study is an empowering research methodology for ECE teachers, and it holds much potential for educational reform. As a visual methodology, visual dialogic self-study affords an individual (the self) a new way in which to visually explore his or her multiple accountabilities. As ECE teachers undertake visual dialogic self-study research, they make visible the role they play in addressing performance measures and improving the educational system. The visual account of their pedagogical encounters with others provides a means for ECE teachers to (i) interrogate their practice based on what they can see from their unique position in the world and in doing so, internally self-evaluate how they are accountable to self and others, and (ii) have their practice scrutinised by others based on what they can see from their unique positions in the world, providing an external evaluation of how the self is accountable. A visual dialogic self-study consequently provides a more meaningful way for an individual (the self) to make visible how he or she is accountable; this is because the way in which the self engages in everyday pedagogical experiences is open to scrutiny by the self and others based on what can be seen. It also provides transparency for a review process that brings pedagogical practice visually into the open and does not sweep it under the carpet, thereby providing opportunities for ECE teachers to uncover their practice and discover themselves.

2.1 Video-of-Video – The Orienting Method

The employment of video-of-video allows for a visual account of the subjective everyday lived experience between the self and others to be captured digitally. When self-study employs video-of-video, it provides layers of video of the self that are laid bare for all to see. The teacher is pedagogically exposed for public interrogation and analysis based on what can be seen inside and outside the dialogue. *Video-of-video* invites an individual's teacher colleagues to share their interpretations of the self's visual account of his or her practice, knowingly aware that they too are being videoed, and although not the subjects of research, they are also making visible what they value pedagogically as they scrutinise the pedagogy of the self being studied. Meaning-making together, through video-of-video as a method to study the self, allows for new ways of seeing to be born out of the exposure of values, feelings and emotions in dialogue, through the excess of seeing that is afforded to the knowledge created in dialogue, often in moments of struggle, challenge, vulnerability and discomfort. By visually making practice explicit, video-of-video, when combined with a dialogic self-study, enhances the transparency of the research process because the review offered by the self's teacher colleagues draws from a visual account of pedagogy as it actually played out in practice. Critical questions can then be asked of what can be seen' – inviting alternative perspectives and interpretations offered based on events that could actually be seen, not imagined.

Video-of-video provides a means of *stepping back* from the self, thereby providing a route to understanding how one is accountable to the self and others because the self as the teacher *inside* the event is able to *step back* as the teacher and/or researcher outside of the event. This means that the ECE teacher undertaking a visual dialogic self-study is able to study the self as the subject being researched from a visual vantage point that he or she would not have access to inside the event. As such, this visual perspective enables the self as the researcher outside of the event to see parts of the self as the teacher subject inside the event – a view that, without visual means, would be inaccessible to self. This unique outside position also enables seeing that captures the participation of self with multiple others in dialogue – seeing from the outside provides an expanded view of what could be seen from the inside. Visual methods have more generally been used as a means of fighting familiarity and as a tool of defamiliarisation (Mannay, 2010). In providing a way to step back from the self, video-of-video forges paths for the self to resist familiarity and be open to being confronted by what is uncovered in the process of interrogating the self. Video-of-video is key to analysing the self from multiple orientations. Furthermore, through visual means, video provides a way to ensure that an ECE teacher, as the self, is using his or her excess of seeing with responsibility and not using what he or she can see:

> as an ambush, as a chance to sneak up and attack from behind. This is an honest and open surplus, dialogically revealed to the other person, a surplus expressed by the addressed and not the second hand word. (Bakhtin, 1984, p. 299)

2.2 Application of Video-of-Video

This method requires visual dialogic self-study researchers to video themselves engaging with children in practice and then taking selected video events from the video data to 'critical inquiry meetings' with teacher colleagues (e.g., a staff meeting), where discussions about practice typically take place. The selected video events are then analysed and critiqued at these meetings, and the critical meeting itself is also video recorded, thus providing the video-of-video (video of the self in dialogue with teachers discussing video events taken to critical inquiry meetings). The employment of video technology innovations in research has made it possible for researchers to make valuable contributions to early years research (see, for example, Novak, Chapter 12, this volume; White, 2009). Participants in the critical inquiry meeting are able to co-experience what they say because of their insider view as teachers in the same ECE setting, and they are then able to return to their outside positions using their unique excess of seeing to offer their particular perspective on the pedagogical practice of the self who is being studied. The employment of video as a data collection tool, as a method of analysis and as a provocation for dialogues at critical inquiry meetings – to discuss and reflect in dialogue with self, based on what can be 'seen' – means that the particulars of context, time and space are able to be viewed in another context and space later in time (i.e., at critical inquiry meetings).

2.3   *Affordances and Limitations*

From their outside position, teachers in critical inquiry meetings are able to offer the individual being studied a view of his or her self that he or she cannot see because of the limitations imposed by the self's excess of seeing. Critical inquiry staff meetings thus provide a source of intersubjectivity as ECE teachers make meaning together, fuelled by video as a provocation, reflecting on what they see and how the video events speak to them. As the teacher and researcher inside the event, it is important to find a way to 'step back' and see the self from an outside position in order to give meaning through the self's excess of seeing later in time. Video-of-video enables this by providing a way for the self to contemplate self as another through visual means (initially inside the dialogue with teachers at the critical inquiry meetings AND then subsequently from an outside position). Moreover, a visual dialogic self-study methodology affords a way for ECE teachers to better understand how their practice implicates them in the lives of both the infants and the teachers to whom they are accountable. It makes the voice of the teacher visible, thereby providing a visual account of his or her own practice and making the self being researched less vulnerable to accusations that may arise when 'insiders' review one another. However, a limitation of a visual dialogic self-study is that the self as the primary research subject limits the extent to which discoveries can be generalised. A further limitation could be that teacher colleagues say what they think a person wants to hear. In addition, time restraints in terms of critical inquiry meetings may be viewed as a limitation. For example, a staff meeting may be 1 h in duration, and the video-of-video discussions may be required to extend beyond that.

2.4   *An Example of a Visual Dialogic Self-study Approach in Practice*

The visual landscape of a community-based ECE infant setting was the location for this study. While I, as the teacher self being studied, was the primary participant in this visual dialogic self-study, the infants attending the community-based infant setting and the teachers were also considered participants, even though they were not the subjects being researched. The infants' ages ranged from 3 months to 18 months. At the time of recording, a maximum of 16 infants could attend the infant unit in the ECE setting per day. Not all infants attended on a full-time basis; therefore, up to approximately 31 infants visited the centre at different times and on different days. In total, 31 parents or caregivers were approached in relation to their infant's participation, and one parent did not grant consent for her child to participate in the research. Six teachers, not including myself, made up the teaching team in the infant unit – four teachers were qualified with a Bachelor of Teaching degree, one had a Diploma in Teaching, and one was not qualified; teacher ratios were 1:4. The context of a staff meeting as a dialogic space to critique my pedagogical practice was chosen because staff meetings are generally a time when discussions about practice take place.

Figure 7.1 shows a screenshot from the video-of-video footage. Evident in the background is my laptop, which is playing one of the video events, watched by the teachers at this critical inquiry meeting. I am kneeling on the floor – closest to the laptop, which is positioned inside the dialogue circle – surrounded by my teacher colleagues who discussed and reflected on my pedagogical practice. This image demonstrates how the video-of-video, from its outside vantage point, provided a way for me to access parts of my body not accessible by my excess of seeing, when positioned as illustrated here, inside the dialogue circle with teachers. From the outside vantage point, the video-of-video made it possible for me to visually study the self later in time as I watched the video-of-video during the analysis process. Seeing myself as another in this way meant that in my 'stepping back', I could make a moral judgement about the self as other (in my authoring of me), thereby determining how I was morally answerable.

FIGURE 7.1   Seeing the 'self' inside the dialogue circle from an outside vantage point

2.4.1 Self-Analysis through Video-of-Video

I selected 3 of the 15 events presented to staff at the three critical inquiry meetings for in-depth self-analysis. These were selected because they represented events that held special meaning for me as an accountable teacher working with infants and seeking to better understand the pedagogical decision-making that informed my interactions (or in-actions). Watching a video of myself, in dialogue with my teacher colleagues critically analysing footage of my practice with infants, provided the visual data I required to analyse myself in dialogue with others. A dialogic orientation for my analytic frame meant I was able to capture and analyse the dialogue *within* me (inner dialogue) in relationship with the dialogue *without* (i.e., between the teachers and I [external dialogue]). This allowed for the development of an analytic framework that spoke to Bakhtin's 'I' as a plural voice and was attentive to the dialogic concept of *answerability* as the moral element of dialogue. Answerability is an attitude of consciousness – a term Bakhtin (1990, 1993) gives to individual (self) responsibility for decisions that are actualised in responses to and for others in concrete acts. Paying heed to answerability as the moral element of dialogue meant considering how participants in dialogue are personally responsible for the meanings that are created in dialogue with others.

TABLE 7.1 Answerable 'I' orientations

Answerable 'I' orientations	Definition
I for myself	How (my)self looks and feels to my own consciousness
I for you	How (my)self appears to others from the outside; how (my)selves are shaped from the outside by others
You for me	How others appear to (my)self; how (my)selves shape others
I for us	How I appear to others as a group (i.e., the teaching team); how (my)self is shaped by the team as a collective 'we'
I for thou	How form is given from external bodies of authority from the outside (i.e., the United Nations Convention on the Rights of the Child)

SOURCE: REDDER (2019)

2.4.2 Plural 'I', Answerable 'I'

As a plural voice, the I, for Bakhtin, is never solely about the self in isolation from the other. Instead, consideration is always given to how both the self and others shape one another in dialogue. I achieved this by developing an analytic framework based on the fundamental concrete moments that make up an answerable act: 'I for myself', 'the other for me' and 'I for the other'. I extended this further to include 'I for us' and 'I for thou', as the following table of *Answerable 'I' orientations* highlights:

The dialogic self-study method I employed to analyse the self through video-of-video was born out of this framework, which considered alternative methods of viewing the self from different answerable positions because of people's unique ways of seeing the world based on their particular position in it (physically, emotionally and morally).

Reflexive journal entries were additionally applied to represent inner dialogues (I for myself) and the staff inquiry meeting transcripts of the video-of-video represented the self's external dialogue with others. The transcripts of the dialogue during the critical inquiry meetings, entries from my reflexive journal and the video-of-video recording of the dialogue during the staff meeting were analysed simultaneously from (my) self's multiple viewpoints (I for me, I for you, you for me, I for us and I for thou). This meant I reflected on the reflexive journal, I for myself (inner dialogue), and the staff meeting, I for you, you for me, I for us and I for thou (external dialogue), from the multiple viewpoints that comprised the answerable act.

The following example is of one of the answerable acts that I analysed in more depth after multiple viewings of the video-of-video titled *Shock, Horror*.

2.4.3 Shock, Horror!

I played this event to teachers at the third critical inquiry meeting. The original data source event was not long in duration; however, it provoked much discussion about my practice. I chose this event because I valued infants having opportunities to engage with their peers in meaningful ways, which I saw as a means of them contributing to their own learning. Moral answerability was evident in the decision I made to not 'shut down' the 'cup banging' that was initiated by the three infants sitting at the table (Redder, 2019). A revised excerpt from the vignette follows:

> Vignette 1 Shock, Horror
> Sitting at the same table as three infants, I watch as they start to bang their cups on the table. Smiling, I say 'water is going everywhere', as cups are positioned at the ready for another round. Celine, who is writing on

the daily communication sheet, notices what is unfolding at the table and walks toward us. Leaning down, Celine takes a cup from one of the infants, then pauses and gives it back. Celine leaves. Moments later she returns, cloth in hand! Without saying a word, she wipes the water that has been spilt on the table.

Vignette 1 is drawn from footage that was played at the critical inquiry meeting. After the teachers viewed this event, I asked them to critique my practice based on what they could see in relation to moral answerability. Celine was the first person to speak. The following dialogue is an example from the critical staff inquiry meeting:

Celine: What did I come across to do?
SV: You took a cup away or something.
Celine: Emm because I am writing something at the bench. Aww am I coming to steal someone's cup.
SV: Yeah.
Celine: Shock, horror. [Teacher transcript, staff meeting 3]

My inner dialogue reflects how Celine's words of 'shock, horror' altered the way I looked at the original data source event:

> I felt your words trivialised my practice. I realised you said these words in jest, but they diminished the value I placed on infants having the opportunity to engage with one another in this way. [I for myself]
>
> Celine's words made me feel trivialised [I for me], as if my pedagogical practice could be dismissed, as if it didn't matter. The tone that Celine used was bordering on a 'big deal' tone with a touch of sarcasm (I for you). The irony of this event for me was that I perceived Celine to be poking fun by using a bit of carnivalesque (I for you), which I also perceived the infants were doing (I for you). I did not consider (my)self to be a voice of authority (I for you) in the infant unit as I held a part-time position, so I waited before responding in the staff meeting dialogue because 'I did not want to sound like the voice of authority, that's me in life' (I for myself). In this moment, I wondered if I was being dethroned. (see Redder, 2019, p. 101)

Being accountable to the infants potentially meant not being accountable to a colleague because of the struggle between what was valued amongst answerable agents in the dialogue. This discovery highlighted for me how my moral position in relation to what I valued, such as fostering infants' contributions to their own learning through their engagement with one another, was seen differently when viewed through the eyes of another (I for you).

2.4.3.1   Self-Discoveries

A self-analysis through video-of-video revealed that I am made up of multiple selves, each with numerous accountabilities to different other selves. With a focus on multiple selves, my analysis concluded that to be answerable to myself, my colleagues and the infants with whom I worked simultaneously meant the following:

– having the courage to expose my feelings and values in dialogue with others – when this occurred, opportunities were opened up for voices to be heard in the dialogue;
– actively participating in the dialogue, not passively agreeing;
– celebrating the act of people challenging my practice, since it opens up opportunities to voice my perspective when it takes place in an environment where we are not being subsumed by the voices of others.

Engaging with the self in this way can be challenging and confronting; it can make a person feel highly vulnerable and uncomfortable with what he or she discovers about the answerable self. However, through a dialogic self-study and what is afforded through video-of-video, I remain convinced that ECE teachers can be more self-aware about their answerable acts and how they engage in dialogue with others – infants and teachers.

The video data generated – in terms of the pedagogical events and the critical friend meetings – was the catalyst for rich dialogues about pedagogy that would not have taken place had the visual in the form of video not been available. In critically analysing my practice, the teachers at times critically reviewed their own practice through reflection that was based on what they could see through their analysis of me, as the following excerpt reveals:

In the dialogue during the staff meeting, Sandy acknowledged that one of the originally viewed data source events was an answerable act for her too:

> ... Like the fact I've had to hand you Lucia while she's having a bottle just to cope. Bryn was overdue to bed to go to sleep so. I felt quite bad doing that. (Sandy)

Although the teachers critiqued my practice, the dialogue also opened up opportunities for them to reflect on their practice and sense of morality, based on the meanings they ascribed to what they could see in terms of their pedagogy – evidenced in the way Sandy said she 'felt quite bad for doing that'. This example highlights how values shaped in dialogue between answerable selves can take on new meaning and, furthermore, how a dialogic self-study as a visual methodology is never just about the individual 'I' – although I was studying (my) self, other teachers queried their practices. This example also demonstrates that Sandy was faced with a moral choice in relation to which infant to share herself with, thus highlighting the interconnectedness of answerable acts. Another member of the team queried whether the answerable act in that moment was 'having to pass her while she's having a bottle'. This excerpt illuminates how having access to the video provided multiple interpretations of an answerable act. It also illustrates that what I considered to be answerable was different to what other teachers considered to be answerable – different but connected – highlighting infant teachers' different pedagogical priorities.

2.4.4 'How to' Guidelines

The video-of-video approach is comprised of layers upon layers of video i) as a source of data and ii) as a source of analysis. Self-analysis through video-of-video involves the following:

- *Phase 1: Data Collection.* The researcher initially video records his or her practice engaging with children in an ECE setting.
- *Phase 1: Original Data Source Analysis.* Video events from the initial data set are selected to take to separate critical inquiry meetings (see image 1 for an illustration of one of these meetings) in order for the researcher's teacher colleagues to critique his or her practice.
- *Phase 2: Data Collection.* The dialogues during the critical inquiry meeting (second phase of data collection) are video recorded.
- *Phase 2: Data Analysis of Critical Inquiry Meeting Dialogue.* This second phase of data analysis involves the researcher as the self being studied analysing the critical inquiry meeting's video-of-video data from Phase 2 using an analytic framework.
- *Phase 3: Data Collection Reflexive Journaling.* The researcher keeps a reflexive journal, which is considered to be another form of dialogue. It provides a space to capture the voice of the self – inner dialogue with the self in tandem with external dialogue with the self, shaped by the self's excess of seeing from his or her vantage point inside the dialogue (Phase 1 data analysis and Phase 2 data collection), as well as from the excess of seeing afforded through the lens of the recording device from an outside vantage point.

3 Ethical Issues

When undertaking a visual dialogic self-study research project, the self is the primary subject being researched; however, consent from teachers, children's parents and, where possible, children themselves is required for their participation in the study. If consent is not given by a teacher or child in the research, then the filming of one's practice can only occur when the teacher or parent is not present (i.e., at home; off the floor; or, in the case of a child, present but asleep). The visual nature of this methodology means that although family are not recruited as participants, consent is also obtained from the family members of children who featured in the video footage when they were present during the process of recording interactions with children. Furthermore, ethical issues concerning positions of power are important to consider when carrying out a self-study in the ECE service that one works to provide assurance that abuse of power will not occur. In addition, if the ECE teacher undertaking a study of the self is a key teacher, and if consent is not obtained for an infant in his or her care, then it is imperative to ensure that the infants concerned are not harmed or disadvantaged in any way by the teacher not being their key teacher while recording is taking place. It is of utmost importance that infant assent be monitored and evident throughout the video data collection process. It is the researcher's responsibility to ensure ongoing monitoring of the infant/s for evidence that agreement throughout the research process has occurred. Therefore, dissent on the part of infants, toddlers and young children themselves is monitored by the researcher; however, it is also advisable to seek another person to monitor this (e.g., the centre co-ordinator and parents or caregivers) and to immediately cease video recording on that day if a child is distressed. Cessation of video recording is also the case for teachers who may become distressed at critical inquiry meetings. Given the visual nature of the data, it is not possible to assure confidentiality. This should be clearly expressed in participant information letters and consent forms.

4 Future Research Possibilities

Considering a collaborative visual dialogic self-study approach would be valuable for future research in order to analyse the pedagogical practices of multiple teachers from various plural 'I' perspectives (I for myself, I for you, you for me, I for us and I for thou). A collaborative dialogic self-study would provide insight into the form-shaping potential of the self's practice to alter the practices of teacher colleagues.

5 Summary Statements

– A visual dialogic self-study methodology is about making pedagogy visible and hence accountable because it is open for scrutiny.

- As a (visual) methodology, a dialogic self-study provides a way for an individual (the self) to better understand how he or she is accountable for the decisions that are made in practice and that affect infants' learning and how they are understood.
- Video-of-video provides an approach to peel back the layers upon layers of video, in order for the self to discover the self.
- To find the self, it is important to lose layers and layers of the self. Conversely, the layers and layers of video and video-of-video are central to a dialogic self-study.
- As a (visual) methodology in its own right, a visual dialogic self-study has the potential to make an important, previously unexplored contribution as a formal dialogic self-study methodology.
- By employing video-of-video as a means of 'stepping back' from the self provided a route to overcoming the limitations of the self's excess of seeing.
- A visual dialogic self-study provides a means for ECE teachers to be open about their pedagogy by making it visible to teacher colleagues, thereby holding them accountable for their ways of being and becoming in the everyday lives of infants, toddlers and young children so that authentic understanding can be achieved based on what can be seen.

Acknowledgements

I wish to thank the teachers and infants who participated in my doctoral self-study that informs this chapter. I will always appreciate your openness and support. I would also like to thank the University of Waikato for awarding me a PhD scholarship which recognised the value of research that encompasses infants, video and the visual. To the reviewers of this chapter – Dawn Mannay, Sheena Elwick and Jayne White – thank you for the edits that lifted the chapter to a higher level. Finally, I would like to acknowledge the exemplary leadership of Professor Jayne White as editor of this book and Chief Supervisor of the PhD that informs these ideas – thank you for your honesty, integrity and for granting me access to parts of me through your seeing.

References

Bakhtin, M. M. (1984). *Problems of Dostoyevsky's poetics* (C. Emerson, Trans.). University of Minnesota Press.

Bakhtin, M. M. (1990). *Art and answerability: Early philosophical essays by M. M. Bakhtin* (V. Liapunov & M. Holquist, Eds., V. Liapunov & K. Brostrom, Trans.). University of Texas Press.

Bakhtin, M. M. (1993). *Toward a philosophy of the act* (V. Liapunov & M. Holquist, Eds., V. Liapunov, Trans.). University of Texas Press.

Hamilton, M. L. (1998). *Reconceptualizing teaching practice: Self-study in teacher education*. Falmer Press.

Hamilton, M. L., & Pinnegar, S. (1998). Conclusion: The value and the promise of self-study. In M. L. Hamilton (Ed.), *Reconceptualizing teacher practice: Self-study for teacher education* (pp. 235–246). Falmer Press.

LaBoskey, V. K. (2004). The methodology of self-study and its theoretical underpinnings. In J. J. Loughran, M. L. Hamilton, V. K. LaBoskey, & T. Russell (Eds.), *International handbook of self-study of teaching and teacher education practices* (Vol. 1, pp. 817–869). Kluwer Academic Publishers.

Mannay, D. (2010). Making the familiar strange: Can visual research methods render the familiar setting more perceptible? *Qualitative Research, 10*(1), 91–111.

Mitchell, C., Moletsane, R., MacEntee, K., & de Lange, N. (2019). Participatory visual methodologies in self-study for social justice teaching. In J. Kitchen (Ed.), *2nd International handbook of self-study of teaching and teacher education*. Springer.

Redder, B. (2019). *Teacher pedagogy as an act of moral answerability: A self-study of an infant teacher's answerable acts in infant pedagogy in New Zealand ECEC* (Unpublished doctoral thesis). University of Waikato, Hamilton, New Zealand.

White, E. J. (2009). *Assessment in New Zealand early childhood education: A Bakhtinian analysis of toddler metaphoricity* (Unpublished PhD thesis). University of Monash, Melbourne, Australia.

CHAPTER 8

But Where Is the Child?

Using Digital Documentation in Pedagogical Practice with Parents and Practitioners

Amanda Crow

1   Introduction

This chapter elaborates the potential of a phenomenographic methodological approach for understanding pedagogical practices in early childhood education (ECE). Within this framework, digital pedagogical documentation (comprising of photographs, videos and observations of children) are explored through a conversational interview as a means of understanding how early childhood practitioners and parents see the child and childhood. The method offers the potential to explore how parents and ECE practitioners 'see' the world through children's eyes. Phenomenography is an under-explored methodology in ECE, and it is offered as a way to develop pedagogical practice and reinforce collaborative relationships through shared experiences (Marton, 1988).

An interpretive framework is presented through which to consider the potential of the phenomenographic method and to enable a richer understanding of pedagogy. Within this framework, pedagogical documentation in digital format is used as a prompt to provoke conversation, thus enabling practitioners and parents to work collaboratively and engage in shared discussion about the everyday experiences of children. The method is therefore twofold, using the digital documentation as a visual tool to explore shared meanings through a conversational, phenomenographic interview.

The chapter begins by discussing the theoretical origins of pedagogical practice and the development and uses of documentation in ECE. The rationale for using phenomenography is explored, and examples from the authors' research in an English preschool are presented to illustrate the way in which the method can be used to highlight the dilemmas surrounding research on and with children. Although the children were not active participants in the research, their visibility – albeit interpreted by the adults – was clearly evident. The chapter explores a number of ethical dilemmas that can occur when using the method, influenced by political policy, the nature of power and the consideration of researcher positionality. Finally, the chapter concludes with suggestions to inform future research involving children and families.

2   Theoretical Orientations: Pedagogy and Documentation

Pedagogical practices in early childhood have seen a surge in interest in recent years (Carr, 2001; Clark, 2011; Merewether & Fleet, 2014), and research in the field has focused on a range of factors, including (i) respect for children's rights, (ii) the view of children as active rather than passive citizens and (iii) political influences. Studies attempting to understand children's everyday lives have become more prevalent, as preschool children are spending more time in ECE settings. Merewether and Fleet (2014) propose that this has led to changes in pedagogical practices and the way in which childhood is constructed and reconstructed, particularly the recognition of child-friendly methods that seek to understand children's perspectives. This important contribution has helped to inform the transition from research 'on' children to research 'with' children (Chesworth, 2018, p. 2).

Socioculturalism offers a theoretical perspective for understanding childhood; it focuses on the importance of respecting children as individuals and is associated with the way in which children learn through their social interactions in partnership with others (McDowall-Clark, 2013; Merewether & Fleet, 2014). In terms of pedagogical practice, this view is helpful because children are seen as social beings with agency, capable of being involved in matters that relate to them. Rogoff's work here is particularly informative when exploring pedagogy, as she suggests that a shared history can help to make sense of new situations (1990). This is a view supported by Dahlberg, Moss and Pence (2007, p. 143), who explored the possibilities that can be gained when pedagogical practices are shaped by practitioners, children and families (see also Carr, 2001).

Pedagogy in ECE has different interpretations; one simplistic definition is 'interactive processes between teacher and learner' (Siraj-Blatchford, Sylva, Muttock, Gildon, & Bell, 2002, p. 10). Furthermore, Oliveira-Formosinho (2009, p. 234) includes the importance of democracy and partnership in pedagogical practices, suggesting that 'pedagogy in participation' is a process that promotes ethical research and practice. This holistic view takes into account the development of safe places for children to play and learn and to grow and develop. Supported by adults who respect and value children's needs, that is used to situate the theoretical orientation of the method explored in this chapter, further strengthened to include the opportunities that can be gained when the relationships between parents, educators and children are also considered (Formosinho & Passos, 2019).

Pedagogy that encompasses the importance of historical and cultural influences on childhood (Rogoff, 1990), and that views childhood through a sociocultural lens, provides a theoretical construct in relation to children, constructing meaning alongside others (Oliveira-Formosinho, 2009, p. 234). This concept is a central theme in this chapter, as the explored visual method frames the importance of pedagogical practices through collaborative conversations and pedagogical documentation. In England, over the past two decades, pedagogical practice has been influenced by developments in childhood studies, and research has encouraged a commitment to listen to both children and parents (Brooker, 2011; Merewether & Fleet, 2014). Furthermore, the Early Years Foundation Stage (EYFS) – the legislative framework, that all English ECE settings must follow when providing education and care for children – details partnership and equality of opportunity as central principles (Department for Education, 2017, p. 3).

International policy and research have had an impact on the EYFS and pedagogical practice in England, particularly the child-centred philosophy of Reggio Emilia in Italy (Kinney and Wharton, 2015) and the early-years curricula of New Zealand and the Netherlands – countries in which the developing child is valued as a competent, capable and resourceful individual (Dahlberg et al., 2007). The EYFS framework places emphasis on the development of positive relationships between practitioners and parents whilst valuing children as unique individuals who are capable of benefiting from the experiences available to them (DfE, 2017, p. 7). This view of the child as an individual reinforces the debate about pedagogical practice being centred on the rights of children (Alasuutari, 2014; Palailogou, 2014).

3   Pedagogical Documentation as Teacher-Research

Lomax (2012) explored the way in which research has influenced and conceptualised childhood, highlighting the work of James, Jenks and Prout, and Morrow in relation to child-centred practices and the shift in perspective from a passive to an active child. Lomax (2012) suggests that this perspective describes the increase in participatory work with children, which has led to a shift in the way children are 'seen'. Pedagogical documentation is one such way in which children are represented. It is a familiar term used in ECE across the world (Alasuutari, 2014), and it describes the practice of collecting artefacts and documenting information to understand the experiences of children. When used in partnership, it is a tool that provides an opportunity to see children through different lenses – individually and culturally as well as with others – as in sociocultural theory (Rogoff, 1990). According to Merewether (2018), the term 'pedagogical documentation' was coined by Dahlberg, Moss and Pence to describe the tools used to explore how practitioners [pedagogues] use 'reflection and democracy' when listening to children (p. 260). Furthermore, documentation in digital format is increasingly being used in ECE; access to mobile technology is improving the way in which visual biographies are increasingly being utilised in a variety of ways to record, reflect, act on and react to children's interests and ultimately to document and assess children's learning (Sparrman & Lindgren, 2010, p. 249).

Nevertheless, documentation should be more than just a way to record what children do. Although pedagogical practices have used documentation to inform practice for a number of years, it has often been interpreted differently depending on the research discipline (Merewether, 2018, p 260). For example, in developmental psychology, the approach has been used to assess children against 'predetermined categories', thus missing the potential to see what they are capable of doing (Dahlberg et al., 1999, as cited in Merewether, 2018, p. 260). According to Fleet (2017, p. 11), different interpretations of pedagogical documentation continue to exist in practice, making the defining of pedagogical documentation challenging. Therefore, it is important to take into consideration the 'geographical and socio-political' contexts of documentation, rather than it being a 'catch-all' description for a collection of artefacts or narrative about the child.

Lenz Taguchi (2010, p. 8) advocates for the use of documentation in creative ways to enhance rather than normalise children's learning. This approach recognises the potential to explore shared spaces and develop new ways of thinking and learning together (Merewether, 2018), further supporting the benefits of documentation as a tool to enhance pedagogy. Documentation in England appears to serve many different purposes. Although the EYFS highlights the importance of encouraging children to be active and think critically, it also emphasises documenting learning to inform assessment (DfE, 2017). This ambiguity between being creative and being bound by assessment targets often leads to practice being misunderstood, hence missing the potential to enhance ECE practice and make learning visible (Fleet, 2017; Kinney & Wharton, 2015).

Moreover, this misunderstanding could be related to political expectations, as practitioners utilise documentation both to understand children's levels of achievement and as a medium to assess children's progress in readiness for school (Department for Education, 2017, p. 13); this is an indication that the staged approach to child development is still influential in English practice. Parents and practitioners share information and record children's development and learning to inform assessment practices (described as children's 'next steps') and ultimately 'school readiness' (DfE, 2017, pp. 7, 13). Fleet (2017) proposes that this is one of the many complex layers when using pedagogical documentation, highlighting the potential for superficial recording of assessment practices in order to meet political expectations. These layers are explored further during the chapter, using examples from the authors' research generated through the use of pedagogical documentation and collaborative pedagogy.

4 Applying Phenomenography in an English ECE Setting

The research method and the theory associated with the authors' study used an interpretative framework to explore phenomenography as a way of seeing the world through the shared experiences of parents, practitioners and children. Although the children were not direct participants in the research process, their presence in the documentation, photographs, videos and written observational stories meant that their involvement, although indirect, could not and would not be ignored. Phenomenography seemed fitting as the chosen research approach, as it offered the potential for parents and practitioners to characterise their perceptions about their everyday experiences and the experiences of the children, both at home and in the preschool.

Marton (1988) suggests that phenomenography as a research approach considers how relationships are connected by thought, action and feeling, and according to Larsson and Hölmstrom (2007, p. 56), it provides a methodology that allows research to consider participants' experiences and how they create meaning in different ways (see also Nicola Firth, Chapter 10, this volume). In ECE, this explanation offers the opportunity to observe how relationships between the adults – the parents and practitioners – consider not only what children need but also how they tune in and listen. According to Merewether and Fleet (2014), the concept of listening can be illustrated through the work of Rinaldi in Reggio Emilia; it is suggested that listening can make children's voices visible (p. 899). Pedagogical documentation, within this context, can offer the potential to enrich pedagogical practice. As suggested by Dahlberg et al. (2007), it is also about 'seeing and understanding' (p. 143). Indeed, the present study utilises documentation as a talking point, allowing parents and practitioners to discuss what they could see and understand in the observations and pictorial representations.

Furthermore, the documentation process itself has the potential to open up discussions about shared experiences, observations and videos clips, and it included detailed descriptions of parents and practitioners sharing experiences together with the children. Dahlberg et al. (2007) argue that this approach to discussing documentation can help adults to respect and listen to children and inform practice, but only if the process is transparent. This means acknowledging the subjective nature of documentation, particularly when discussing the way in which observations are interpreted, as they are often used primarily to assess rather than explore new possibilities with children (Dahlberg et al., 2007). Therefore, it is important to not take what is seen for granted and to challenge preconceived assumptions; as Brooker (2011) argues, discussing what children can do must be recognised, as failure to be open and transparent can lead to tokenistic practices; this view is supported by Fleet (2017).

Phenomenography is not a familiar research methodology associated with ECE; its potential lies in the opportunity to focus on shared experiences and to create or co-construct meaning. In relation to collaborative pedagogy, phenomenography can aid in understanding the 'what and the how' in research (Larsson & Holmstrom, 2007). That is, it has the potential to explore what pedagogy is and how it is understood, with pedagogical documentation being the means through which to do this. Open-ended interviews comprise the favoured method for collecting data when using phenomenography, since this method encourages participants to engage in collaborative conversations. The conversation evolves and does not rely on predetermined questions, meaning that the interviewer is also a participant and involved in the collective experience (Zhang, 2017).

In summary, phenomenography, using the collaborative interview method prompted by the pedagogical documentation, offers the potential to understand the collective experiences of parents, practitioners and, primarily, children. According to Zhang (2017, p. 258), this collaborative approach allows participants to jointly constitute understanding, as prompts are used, rather than predetermined questions, and the interviewer and interviewees jointly explore and develop the conversation. The method is therefore participatory and illuminative, and it allows for an exploration of what pedagogy is and how parents and practitioners interpret what they see when viewing the everyday lives of children. The following sub-section describes the research setting and explores the development and application of the method, highlighting the dilemmas surrounding research on and with children.

5   The Method in Practice: The Context and Conduct

A preschool in the north of England was the setting for the overarching research study. Based in a community building, the preschool conforms to the requirements of the Office for Standards in Education (Ofsted) – the regulatory body in England that inspects childcare and education – and follows the

EYFS framework. Each child was assigned a key person on admission to help build a relationship between the child, parent and practitioner; this is also a requirement of the EYFS (DfE, 2017, p. 22). Seven children aged between 2 and 3 years, their mothers and their respective key people were recruited to the main study. This chapter focuses on two of the phenomenographic interviews – with participants Pearl and Zack.

Zhang (2016) suggests that this conversational method can be used to explore the importance of relationships and the way in which parents and practitioners view and share information about the child. As explained previously, the use of prompts rather than pre-determined or prescribed questions is unique to the method, allowing the conversation to develop in a less formal way. Using pedagogical documentation as the visual prompt enabled engagement with the participants in conversations about what they could see the child doing in the images; it also encouraged the sharing of information about different cultures, values and routines at home and in preschool.

Focusing on pedagogical documentation ensured that the approach was participatory, as phenomenography takes into account the various ways of seeing (Larsson & Holmström, 2007) and the way in which individuals experience, conceptualise, perceive and understand (Marton, 1988). The participatory aspect of the method, however, raised questions about the children, who were visibly present in the documentation, but not physically present in the interviews. This aspect is explored further in the following section using excerpts from the study.

5.1 The Method in Practice: What Happened?

Each interview took place in a familiar room in the preschool and lasted approximately 45 minutes. The interview started with a review of the consent process, followed by the practitioner opening the digital documentation. In each interview, the practitioner began the conversation by inviting the mother to look at the child's first day, and both participants reminisced about the process of settling in. They then narrated the annotations as they talked about their perceptions of what they could see. Although I was clearly the interviewer, the collaborative nature of the conversation meant that I was invited to join in, comment and engage in the discussions. This does raise ethical questions about positionality and researcher bias, which are discussed later in the chapter.

6 Pearl and Zack's Stories

The interviews with both Pearl and Zack's (names have been substituted) mothers generated rich narrative data, prompted by the visual pedagogical documentation. Pearl's mother had initially talked about the importance of regular meetings with her daughter's key person and the benefits they offered her. This respectful relationship became even more evident during the interview; observations of Pearl at home and in preschool were discussed, and a narrative evolved that included discussions about Pearl's speech and communication and the two-year development check, which is a requirement of the EYFS (Department for Education, 2017, p. 130).

The way in which the documentation prompted discussion about Pearl at home and in preschool became clear, and Pearl's presence also emerged. The narrative explored how Pearl had been observed by the practitioner playing with other children in the photograph titled 'making relationships'. The description of Pearl running outside to play with her friend developed into a story of friendship and co-operation, and while it was still an interpretation by the adults, Pearl was clearly constructing her play with others.

Zack's interview followed the same pattern, with the conversation quickly focusing on a discussion about Zack's language development and how his mother felt it had improved since starting preschool. As his mother explains:

> He's started to join words, and he's sort of pointing; he's demanding things from me now, so he's like, 'mummy come here'.

The practitioner talked through the story of Zack's first day, and his mother spoke of her trust in the setting and in Zack's key person in particular. Trust seemed to feature a great deal, especially as the practitioner had been the key person for Zack's sister when she attended the preschool.

Trust also featured highly in regard to Zack settling into the preschool. The practitioner talked about Zack needing to keep his backpack on; 'for the first week or two, he just used to leave it on', and his mother commented on his reluctance to take it off, suggesting that Zack was unsure and wondering, 'should I trust them with my things?' Zack's mother seemed pleased that his key person did not insist that he take his backpack off but was happy to let him keep something that was familiar and comforting to him. His mum laughed as she explained that she knew when he felt settled, as he gave her his backpack: 'He runs in now and shouts, "mummy bag off"'. She also shared that he takes his 'shoes off' when he arrives, commenting that he does that at grandma's; this, she said, helped her to see that he was 'fine'.

Phenomenographic research calls for an approach to analysis that considers the 'what and how' questions (Larson & Holmström, 2007). When analysing the data from the interviews, it was important to listen to what the participants said and how they discussed what they could see each child doing in photographs and videos. The fact that both Pearl and Zack had a presence, even though they were not involved in the interviews, became apparent during the interview conversations. Pearl's mother mentioned that the documentation enabled her to see that Pearl was happy and playing; she spoke about sitting at home with Pearl and looking at the photographs together and noticing the way Pearl led the conversation.

> Like if I say, 'oh what are you doing there? Are you pouring the water?' And she will go, 'no I wasn't', you know she will tell me and then go into more detail. Or if I get somebody's name wrong.

This description of Pearl correcting her mother as they looked through the digital documentation, although construed by the adults, adds an interesting and rich aspect to the data. The pedagogical documentation generated by the key adults for and with the children appeared to have depth and meaning for the parents, practitioners and indeed the children.

7   Affordances and Limitations

The visual methodology discussed in this chapter can be viewed in a number of ways: first, as a visual account of the children engaged in their everyday worlds, and second, when used in phenomenographic interviews with others, the visual prompts provided an insight into the interests and experiences of the children and their lives at home and in preschool. The methodology therefore generated data from two perspectives, one that involved the parent, practitioner and child (present virtually), and the second between each of the adults, including me as the researcher. This section of the chapter not only discusses what the methodology can offer but also explores the implications and limitations.

The phenomenographic interview appeared to confirm the importance of respectful partnerships in ECE. Trusting relationships between parents and practitioners were evident during the interviews and appeared to be strengthened through their reciprocal approach to the pedagogical documentation; this trust seemed important to all participants. The interviews created opportunities to share information and discuss children's learning; the presence of each child was acknowledged, their voices interpreted, and, interestingly, the way each child made their needs and wants known. However, the collaborative nature of the interview and the involvement of the researcher raise questions in relation to researcher bias and positionality – aspects that are considered in the ethics section.

The digital documentation provided a visual opportunity to see the children as individuals and to observe how they interacted with other children in the setting and their siblings and how the environment and their cultural experiences were important to them, as perceived by Rogoff (1990). Zack taking his shoes off because 'he does that at grandma's' endorsed this point well and is an example of the sociocultural concept that social and everyday experiences can enhance development (Rogoff, 1990; Hedegaard, 2012).

A methodology of this nature requires researchers to be flexible and open their minds to the various ways of seeing, and the need to engage in ethical research rather than being swayed by ideological trends became apparent (Oliveira-Formosinho, 2009, Palaiologou, 2014). If pedagogical practice is to be child-centred and position children at the centre of their social worlds, then it could be argued that any method of engaging in research with and for children should respect rather than diminish their agency (McDowall Clark, 2013). However, observing children does not mean that they are fully participating, and as the EYFS states, observation should be used by practitioners to understand [children's] levels of achievement, interest and learning (Department for Education, 2017, p. 13); this firmly places observation in the frame of assessment. Both mothers talked about wanting to be sure that their children were *learning* whilst at preschool, and even though they did not use the word 'assessment', once this was shared with the practitioners, the interview conversation quickly focused on levels of development and attainment.

Sparrman and Lindgren (2010, p. 250) discussed the need to recognise the work of Michael Foucault and the 'power of gaze' in relation to pedagogical documentation and particularly the use of observation of children in ECE. They suggest that although observation is a recognised and accepted pedagogical practice, it also subjects children to being looked at, thus making them subjects rather than partners (Sparrman & Lindgren, 2010). Recognising this further supports the need to conduct research following clear ethical guidelines (Gallacher & Gallaher, 2008; Oliveira-Formosinho, 2009; Palaiologou, 2014). Acknowledging the inequity of power is also necessary when scrutinising the fact that the phenomenographic interview conversations included aspects of noticing children's developments and achievements, as the practitioners often steered the conversation to the topic of assessment.

McDowall Clark (2013) proposes that collaboration in this way can reinforce the political activity of expecting parents to conform to set expectations – a nod here to the EYFS and the notion of assessment and measuring progress. The interview enabled the discussion to centre on the child both at home and in the setting. Furthermore, whilst this aspect appears to be collaborative, it has the potential to introduce tension and conflict in relation to the differences between the perceptions and expectations of the parent and practitioner, thus reinforcing the need to acknowledge the potential imbalance of power between the adults and their perception and interpretation of each child (BERA, 2018; Sparrman & Lindgren, 2010).

In summary, pedagogical documentation can provoke and prompt collaborative pedagogy. It requires honesty and an acknowledgement that relationships are complex. The methodology explored the way in which the children were seen by the adults and as individuals with agency; however, it also highlighted that their actions were sometimes used to inform assessments against politically driven targets – reinforcing the argument by White (2011) that ECE teachers need to work ethically, reflexively and lingeringly with pedagogical documentation practices, 'attempting to understand richly, rather than obediently seeking outcomes through isolated frameworks that ignore complexity' (p. 63).

8   Ethical Considerations

When conducting research in ECE settings, researchers must take into account the potential ethical issues that can arise. Research on, with and for children supposes that researchers have considered their best interests and comply with the United Nations Convention on the Rights of the Child (UNCRC) (United Nations, 1989; BERA, 2018). The method of using pedagogical documentation as a prompt to engage parents and practitioners in the phenomenographic interviews discussed in this chapter, offered a way of seeing children. They were captured interacting and playing with others in the observations, photographs and videos, and the discussions between the participants developed into stories relating to family and culture and conversations about how best to support the children. However, whilst offering creative methods to inform ECE practice, everyday research should be conducted carefully and ethically, as research conducted in this way is still managed and interpreted by adults (Gallacher & Gallaher, 2008, p. 505; Lomax, 2012, p. 106). Furthermore, Palailogou (2014) states that ethical dilemmas and challenges must be considered when engaging in research in ECE settings, especially when considering the way children are represented.

Consent to participate was gained from each of the adults; however, the documentation contained artefacts captured over time, and on reflection, consent or assent from the children was less obvious. Sparrman and Lindgren (2010) discuss that, in documentation, children are often captured from above – a birds-eye view (p. 255). This places the adults as onlookers; therefore, being open and transparent is essential in any study that involves observation and documentation. Researchers contemplating following this method must consider and acknowledge that this visual approach is not one of giving children their own audible voice, but one interpreted and filtered by the adults in their lives.

That said, the method offered opportunities for the practitioners and mothers to share important information relating to the preferences and needs of each individual child. The phenomenographic approach enabled conversations to develop about the children's cultural experiences, their developmental needs and ways to support their early learning experiences. The digital aspect of the documentation captured experiences at home and in preschool, offering different perspectives regarding the lives of the children and their families.

Focusing on the pedagogical documentation highlighted the importance of a trusting relationship between the mothers and practitioners, and the conversational nature of the phenomenographic interview offered the space for the participants to explore and reflect. It should be acknowledged, however, that this interview style also has the potential for an imbalance of power between i) the adults and ii) their perception and interpretation of each child (BERA, 2018; Sparrman & Lindgren, 2010). Murray (2015) suggests that professionals should be viewed as the 'empowered partner' (p. 1720), since their familiarity with the child can be a hindrance, and professional experience can seem threatening to others. Tensions can arise between parents and practitioners based on the political pressure to assess and prepare children for school, especially if the practitioner is perceived to be the expert (Sparrman & Lindgren, 2010). When engaging in pedagogical research with parents and children, being aware of emotions and unconscious processes is thus key.

Furthermore, the participatory nature of the phenomenographic interview necessitated the involvement of the researcher in the data collection process, meaning that the conversations that developed during the interview included all who were present. Therefore, the researcher had a dual and potentially contentious role. This is especially the case if researchers have experience of ECE practice, as is often the case. Being aware of one's positionality is crucial because, according to Mannay (2016), it requires the researcher to explore both the practical and moral aspects of any given situation. This could mean being open and transparent about professional heritage and not taking knowledge of ECE practice for granted. To mitigate positionality, adopting a reflexive approach is recommended, since it offers the possibility to examine assumptions. However, researching familiar territory has its advantages, as it enables a greater understanding of the context (Mannay, 2016, p. 30).

Ethical research with children can be ambiguous; it is often influenced by the various participatory and creative methods featured in contemporary debates (Clark, 2011; Merewether & Fleet, 2014; Palaiologou, 2014; Merewether, 2018) and in the various applications of visual participatory methods used to understand the perspectives of children (Clark, 2011). The current discussion that exists around participatory methods is heavily influenced by literature that explores the everyday experiences of children; nevertheless, it can also lead to the illusion of participation, particularly in relation to whether children are seen or not seen (Palailogou, 2014, p. 690). In relation to using the phenomenographic interview and documentation to explore pedagogy, embracing the method as a way to help adults respect children, to value their capabilities and to see the world through their eyes is possible, but with the caveat that this approach is interpretative and subjective.

9   Concluding Thoughts and Future Possibilities

Highlighting the potential of phenomenography, this chapter has explored the theoretical orientations and methodological principles that might be used to provoke conversations with ECE teachers and parents using visual documentation. Documentation in a digital format was used as a visual provocation to engage parents and teachers in a phenomenographic interview which invited them to share their understandings of children's everyday experiences. The collaborative nature of the interview enabled participants to utilise existing video, photograph and narrative observations of children to discuss (i) what they were seeing and (ii) their relationships. Rich data was generated which highlighted the importance of adult relationships with children as an orienting source of seeing, the purpose of pedagogical documentation, and the ethical dilemmas that arise as a consequence concerning children's agency and visibility under surveillance of this nature.

This chapter has also considered some of the tensions that arise for visual researchers in conducting research on and/or with children. Future research using this methodology and associated methods could explore some alternative ways visual provocations may inform pedagogical practice in new ways. Involving children at earlier phases of the research project as well as involving them in the narrative that are generated out of phenomenographic interviews could be a useful beginning in this regard.

10   Summary Statements

- Relationships are important but must not be taken for granted – successful partnerships in early-years practice (and research) between children, parents and ECE teachers are built on positive relationships.
- Phenomenography as a methodology in ECE has the potential to help parents and teachers to understand pedagogy because it offers insight into the way they 'see' the child.
- Being open and honest about one's role as a researcher or teacher-researcher is important because during the pedagogical interview, the conversation will move and shift in different directions. The tendency to want to lead the conversation will sometimes take over, and acknowledging this is necessary at the outset.
- When engaging in pedagogical research with parents and children, the researcher should also be aware of emotions and unconscious processes; in particular, acknowledging that power has the potential to disrupt relationships is key.
- Observations have a place in ECE research practice because they offer the observer/s – in this case, parent and teacher alike – a window into the child's world. In phenomenography, they are a tool to elicit understanding, a way of encouraging an open-ended discussion about pedagogical practices rather than focusing on assessment practices.

References

Alasuutari, M. (2014). Voicing the child? A case study in Finnish early childhood education. *Childhood, 21*(2), 242–259. doi:10.1177/0907568213490295

British Educational Research Association (BERA). (2018). *Ethical guidelines for educational research*. Retrieved from https://www.bera.ac.uk/researchers-resources/publications/ethical-guidelines-for-educational-research-2018

Brooker, L. (2011). Taking children seriously: An agenda for research? *Journal of Early Childhood Research, 9*(2) 137–149. doi:10.1177/1476718X10387897

Carr, M. (2001). *Assessment in early childhood settings: Learning stories*. Sage.

Chesworth, L. (2018). Embracing uncertainty in research with young children. *International Journal of Qualitative Studies in Education, 31*(9), 251–309. doi:1080/09518398.2018.1499982

Clark, A. (2011). Breaking methodological boundaries? Exploring visual, participatory methods with adults and young children. *European Early Childhood Education Research Journal, 19*(3), 321–330. doi:10.1080/1350293X.597964

Dahlberg, G., Moss, P., & Pence, A. (2007). *Beyond quality in early childhood education and care: Languages of evaluation* (2nd ed.). Routledge. doi:10.4324/9780203966150

Department for Education. (2017). *Statutory framework for the early years foundation stage*. Retrieved from https://assets.publishing.service.gov.uk/government/uploads/system/uploads/attachment_data/file/596629/EYFS_STATUTORY_FRAMEWORK_2017.pdf

Fleet, A. (2017). The landscape of pedagogical documentation. In A. Fleet, C. Patterson, & J. Robertson (Eds.), *Pedagogical documentation in early years practice: Seeing through multiple perspectives* (pp. 11–26). Sage.

Formosinho, J., & Passos, F. (2019). The development of a rights-based approach to participation: From peripheral involvement to central participation of children, parents and professionals. *European Early Childhood Research Journal, 27*(3), 305–317. doi:10.1080/1350293X.2019.1600801

Gallacher, L., & Gallagher, M. (2008). Methodological immaturity in childhood research? Thinking through 'participatory methods'. *Childhood, 15*(4), 499–516. doi:10.1177/0907568208091672

Hedegaard, M. (2012). Analysing children's learning and development in everyday settings from a cultural historical wholeness approach. *Mind Culture and Activity, 19*(2), 127–138. doi:10.1080/10749039.2012.665560

Kinney, L., & Wharton, P. (2015). *An encounter with Reggio Emilia. Children and adults in transformation* (2nd ed.). Routledge.

Larsson, J., & Holmström, I. (2007). Phenomenographic or phenomenological analysis: Does it matter? Examples from a study on anaesthesiologists' work. *International Journal of Qualitative Studies on Health and Wellbeing, 2*(1), 55–64. doi:10.1080/17482620601068105

Lenz Taguchi, H. (2010). *Going beyond the theory practice divide in early childhood education introducing an intra-active pedagogy*. Routledge.

Lomax, H. (2012). Contested voices? Methodological tensions in creative research with children. *International Journal of Social Research Methodology, 15*(2), 105–117. doi:10.1080/13645579.2012.649408

Mannay, D. (2016). *Visual, narrative and creative research methods. Application, reflection and ethics*. Routledge.

Marton, F. (1988). Phenomenography: A research approach to investigating different understandings of reality. In R. R. Sherman & R. B. Webb (Eds.), *Qualitative research in education: Focus and methods*. Falmer.

McDowall Clark, R. (2013). *Is there space in partnership with families?* Reflections Paper. Retrieved from http://www.tactyc.org.uk/pdfs/Reflection-McDowall-Clark.pdf

Merewether, J. (2018). Listening to young children outdoors with pedagogical documentation. *International Journal of Early Years Education, 26*(3), 259–277. doi:10.1080/09669760.2017.1421525

Merewether, J., & Fleet, A. (2014). Seeking children's perspectives: A respectful layered approach. *Early Child Development and Care, 184*(6), 897–914. doi:10.1080/03004430.2013.829821

Murray, J. (2015). Early childhood Pedagogies: Spaces for young children to flourish. *Early Child Development and Care, 185*(11–12), 1715–1732. doi:10.1080/03004430.2015.1029245

Oliveira-Formosinho, J. (2009). Togetherness and play under the same roof: Children's perceptions about families. *European Early Childhood Education Research Journal, 17*(2), 233–248. doi:10.1080/13502930902951478

Palaiologou, I. (2014). 'Do we hear what children want to say?' Ethical praxis when choosing research tools with children under five. *Early Child Development and Care, 184*(5), 689–705. doi:10.1080/03004430.2013.809341

Rogoff, B. (1990). *Apprenticeships in thinking: Cognitive development in social context.* Oxford University Press.

Siraj-Blatchford, I., Sylva, K., Muttock, S., Gilden, R., & Bell, D. (2002). *Researching effective pedagogy in the early years.* Research report RR356. Department for Education and Skills, University of Oxford. Retrieved from https://dera.ioe.ac.uk/4650/1/RR356.pdf

Sparrman, A., & Lindgren, A. L. (2010). Visual documentation as a normalizing practice: A new discourse of visibility in preschool. *Surveillance & Society, 7*(3–4), 248–261. Retrieved from http://liu.diva-portal.org/smash/get/diva2:329330/FULLTEXT01.pdf

United Nations. (1989). *The United Nations convention on the rights of the child.* UN. Retrieved from https://www.unicef.org.uk/what-we-do/un-convention-child-rights/

White, E. J. (2011). Aesthetics of the beautiful: Ideologic tensions in contemporary assessment. In E. J. White & M. A. Peters (Eds.), *Bakhtinian pedagogy: Opportunities and challenges for research, policy and practice in education across the globe* (pp. 47–68). Peter Lang.

Zhang, Q. (2016). Do learning stories tell the whole story of children's learning? A phenomenographic enquiry. *Early Years, 37*(3), 255–267. doi:10.1080/09575146.2016.1151403

CHAPTER 9

Cameras and Carnivals

A Visual Dialogic Route to Young Children's Humour

Laura Jennings-Tallant

1 Introduction

This chapter focuses on how Bakhtin's dialogic theory of carnivalesque was utilised within a visual dialogic methodology, operationalising a range of concepts, including his theory concerning time and space or 'chronotope' (Bakhtin, 1984a), and using White's (2009b) polyphonic video technique. Sullivan argues that a dialogic approach to data analysis offers methodological tools for the analysis of participant subjectivity (Sullivan, 2012), as he suggests that subjectivity, in this instance, changes and responds to others, and if a researcher wishes to focus on subjectivity within data, then it may be fruitful to adopt a dialogical methodology (ibid.). For this reason, and given that the concept of carnivalesque is in itself dialogic and cannot be discussed without reference to Bakhtin's theory of dialogism more broadly, this chapter combines the discussion of the operationalisation of carnivalesque theory as part of a dialogic methodology. Bakhtinian conceptual and theoretical thinking weaves into practice in two ways: to privilege ways of 'seeing' the subjective voices of those involved and to explore the relationship between young children's humorous behaviours and Bakhtin's study of carnivalesque folk humour in the middle ages.

2 Dialogic Methodology

While numerous social researchers have operationalised Bakhtinian dialogism as a methodology, both in and out of the education field, concerns over the misappropriation of Bakhtin's ideas have been raised:

> ... unless we try to understand how Bakhtin came to assemble his potent analytical instruments, we cannot achieve more than an approximate calibration of their true usefulness, and their application may become somewhat mechanical and unsubtle. (Matusov, 2007, p. 216)

© KONINKLIJKE BRILL NV, LEIDEN, 2020 | DOI: 10.1163/9789004433328_009

Therefore, it is important to clarify how Bakhtinian thinking might be utilised to facilitate novel ways of seeing young children's interactions in an early childhood setting, particularly in relation to the Bakhtinian concept of carnivalesque Bakhtin (1984a).

3   Grounding Dialogic Assumptions

Many approaches to, and interpretations of, dialogue exist, such as those of Buber, Habermas and Gadamer (Sullivan, 2012). Clarification of a Bakhtinian approach to dialogue is therefore needed. An apt definition is offered by Sullivan (2012, p. 212), who suggests that dialogue is a vehicle for the exchange of lived experiences that are brimming with 'personal values and judgments', and this definition has been adopted here. This is particularly relevant for the analysis of the data, as well as for the focus on visual methods throughout this study, which places emphasis on the participants' subjective points of view. First, the distinction between conceptual and visceral understandings must be made clear. For example, we can abstractly understand the concept of love as a strong feeling of affection; however, we acquire a different understanding of the sensation of love through experiencing and feeling it viscerally (Sullivan, 2012). The Russian language has two distinct words that describe abstract and lived truth: *istina* and *pravda*; Bakhtin often depicts them as representing contrasting sides of a single idea (Bakhtin, 1993). Furthermore, Sullivan (2012) argues that to experience another person as humorous involves both an abstract understanding of what it means to be humorous (istina) and the instant sensation of it in a specific encounter with another person; for example, if we make another person laugh, we may *feel* humorous (pravda).

For Bakhtin (1990), this type of lived experience is only available to us via someone else. He describes the act of seeing a part of someone that they cannot see as 'authorial surplus', and he suggests that in authoring another, we 'gift' them the opportunity to experience something in a way that would be impossible otherwise. White explains further that it '[r]epresents the visual and discursive horizon of social partners who, as a result of their unique line of vision, are each privy to privileges and constraints which will influence their interpretations of other – literally and figuratively drawn from their unique ideological horizon' (White, 2009a, p. 58). Sullivan proposes that this horizon affords power to authorship, granting it the capacity to shape others, and that the intonation and emotional register of language are two important factors in this process (Sullivan, 2012).

The orienting frame of this study is chronotope which Bakhtin (1981) refers to as the '… intrinsic connectedness of temporal and spatial relationships …' (p. 167). In this social research context the concept is used metaphorically to highlight both the children's carnivalesque scenes as socially constructed time-space patterns, and the adults' responses to these. White (2017c, para. 20) indicates that in early childhood environments the carnivalesque chronotope can denote a 'revised kind of democracy – one that is much needed in our societies or systems where individualism and obedience reign supreme'. This offers rationalisation for the use of chronotope as an analytic frame as this study operated within such an early childhood 'system'.

4   Bakhtinian Carnivalesque and Young Children's Humour: Carnivality

This chapter presents data from a 6-year study (2012–2018) that introduces young children's humour as 'carnivality' using Bakhtin's (1984a) theory of carnivalesque to construct an image of children's humour as a carnival that celebrates the border between art and life, subversion, misalliances, excess and grotesqueness (Jennings-Tallant, 2018). A carnivalesque scene involving 3- and 4-year-olds in a nursery is analysed later in the chapter to illustrate the nature of the data collected and analysed via visual dialogic, including White's (2009b) polyphonic video technique.

4.1   *Young Children's Carnivality*

The study in this chapter investigates the potential benefits of framing children's humour in early childhood education (ECE) settings and laughter outside the popular paradigm of developmental psychology. Given the popularity of developmental psychology both in children's humour research (Tallant, 2015) and in early childhood research, and in practice more widely (Cohen, 2011; Dahlberg, 2005; Taylor; 2015; White, 2017a), the project aimed to use a complimentary theoretical approach that helps to explain why humour is not highly valued, pedagogically speaking, within ECE. Bakhtin's carnivalesque theory of folk humour in the middle ages offers a fitting lens through which to examine notions of humour as trivial; in opposition to the statelier 'seriousness'; potentially disruptive; and, at times, subversive (White, 2014; Tallant, 2015, 2017). The study found that young children's humour can be framed beneficially as carnivalesque (Jennings-Tallant, 2018) and that it can present as a challenge for early childhood practitioners. This suggestion of young children's humour posing a challenge was examined in detail and ultimately led to the use of Bakhtin's analysis of medieval carnival in reframing children's humour in ECE settings as 'carnivality' (Jennings-Tallant, 2018). Carnivality refers to a set of behaviours and a state that children enter that is driven by positive laughter and 'presents all children with an outlet, a chance to escape their lived experience of pressure, momentarily' (Jennings-Tallant, 2018). The findings indicate that conceptualising children's humour in ECEC settings as 'carnivality' can encourage a better understanding of the significance of their humour within their early pedagogical experiences (Jennings-Tallant, 2018).

5   Visual Surplus – A Route to Seeing Polyphonically

The fundamental interest in visually exploring children's experiences of carnivalesque rests on the Bakhtinian concept of polyphony, which was inspired by Bakhtin's interest in Dostoevsky's novelistic approach – first operationalised in the context of early childhood research by White (2009a). A polyphonic approach requires the researcher to consider the nature and position of the multiple voices and perspectives present (Sullivan, 2012). In an act of operationalising Bakhtin's previously mentioned concept of 'authorial surplus', White (2014) furthered the concept for research purposes to focus on the aspect of seeing, coining the term 'visual surplus'. Related to polyphony, visual surplus explains that individuals have a unique field of vision, allowing them to see and interpret the world in a way that is inaccessible to others (White, 2016). To further explain this moulding of others, Bakhtin uses art as an analogy, suggesting that during encounters, we offer one another a form that may be received willingly or resisted. Furthermore, we have the capacity to shape our worlds as a work of art may be shaped, transforming our lives according to the social values we hold in esteem, such as to be humorous or to be a generous friend, and dialogue can be a means of 'feeling the different shapes and sounds' of these 'idea[s] [... intonation ...] through life' (Sullivan, 2012, p. 4). The distinction Bakhtin makes between abstract and lived experiences has direct implications for the analysis of data collected in this study. Significantly, this study's focus is on the lived experiences of children and practitioner participants, rather than the abstract, in an attempt to gain better access to the subjectivity of the participants who are 'changing and respon[ding] to others' (Sullivan, 2012, p. 1). I viewed this approach as deeply aligned with the Currere (Pinaar, 2004) method: an influential theory in duo-ethnographical approaches to research, which are also concerned with subjectivity and intersubjectivity (Sawyer & Norris, 2013). Adopting this Currere-inspired approach offered the practitioners an opportunity to reflect on the relationship between their own life stories and the subjectivity of their perspectives. In turn, this facilitated for them a deeper understanding of the significance of subjectivity and inter-subjectivity when analysing their own and the children's lived experiences.

6 Unpacking the Method

A number of early childhood research projects utilise video in an attempt to make sense of the visual qualities of the situations they seek to explore. A range of these studies adopt interpretivist approaches using static video cameras to record participants behaviours (for example, see Cohen, 2007, 2015; Loizou, 2005, 2007, 2012). The use of head cameras in social research with young children is less common. White's (2009a) polyphonic approach to video involving the use of head cameras is the most documented method and can be explored further in a range of papers (for example, White, 2009b; 2016). White's work informed the development of the visual dialogic methods used in this study.

6.1 *'Visualising' Young Children's Carnivalesque Humour*

The collection of data for this study involved several interconnected methods, including observations, filming, dialogic encounters as interviews with the researcher and children, research journals and analysis journals, in line with the complexity of a Bakhtinian dialogic approach to research and the need to be faithful to Bakhtinian ideology. As the 'work of the eye/I' (White, 2017b, 2017c) is at the centre of the project, all of the utilised methods spiralled out from this concept.

The research study was small-scale, carried out in England, and it explored children's humour in an urban, private nursery setting (Tallant, 2015, 2017). The study required careful ethical consideration – an idea that is discussed in more detail later. An example of data generated by eight 3- and 4-year-olds of British and Eurasian extraction (three girls and four boys) and by me (as the researcher) is considered here. All of the children (whose names are pseudonyms) attend the same nursery and had known each other for at least a year.

7 *Data Analysis: Underpinning Theory and Methods*

The analysis of the data from multiple perspectives reflected the intersubjective and polyphonic nature of the interactions presented and considered by all participants in the study. Salient and pertinent utterances from the data, or 'key moments', were chosen after reading through the entire data set in search of utterances that were rich with examples of carnivalesque. The key moment presented below appears in this chapter in the centre of the page. This for-matting represents the central role that the participant researchers' voices have within the analysis. Their voices were privileged throughout this study, as significant potential exists for their voices to be undermined or over-ridden by an authoritative researcher voice and the authoritative voices within the literature and theory (Sullivan, 2012). This would neglect the polyphonic, het-eroglot context in which the 'heroes' are being authored within this research and hence become monologic: the antithesis of dialogism (Bakhtin, 1984b). In addition to being presented as key moments, in the wider project, utterances from the data also appeared via a variety of other dialogic methodological devices that embodied the visual emphasis of the project throughout the anal-ysis – soundbites or smaller selections of data brought together – as they speak to a pertinent theme in an interesting way: created dialogues and created dia-logues with an invisible other, both detailed in the methodology, and both of which highlight the dialogic nature of the utterances by decontextualising and then re-contextualising them to provide a fresh perspective (Sullivan, 2012).

Throughout the analysis, the children's experiences of, and thoughts about, humour were focused on closely, as were the practitioners' professional reflec-tions and analysis of these, coupled with my own analysis guided by a Bakhtin-ian dialogic lens. All of the presented data were framed within a carnivalesque genre and chronotope, or time/space, thereby addressing the nature and mani-festations of young children's humour in a nursery setting and adult reactions and responses. Framing the data in this way also provided the beginnings of a justification for reflecting upon young children's humour using a Bakhtinian carnivalesque lens.

8   Data Collection and Analysis Methods

The data collection and overall analysis were organised into two rounds, and data from both feature below. Each analysis round required the participants to analyse both spoken and written utterances under the premise that the tran-scription process transforms utterances via their passage through time and space (or through chronotopes [Bakhtin, 1984a]), resulting in a potential dif-ference between an utterance's spoken and written form. Both utterance forms consequently required analytic attention from the researcher and participants, as outlined later in the chapter, in Figure 9.1. The following steps were included in both rounds of data collection and analysis:

– The children's everyday encounters were filmed via the use of head cameras worn by all participants and the researcher. Examples of humour (classified

by the presence of laughter and/or smiling cues [Provine, 2001]) were collected and transcribed into key moments, which were then analysed and
discussed in the dialogic encounters with the practitioners and children.

– The practitioners and I engaged in biographical dialogic encounters (BDES),
which were all filmed. These initial encounters were designed to understand
the practitioners' experiences with and perceptions of humour throughout
their childhoods and adult lives, as well as their thoughts about the nature
and significance of humour and laughter inside and outside of ECE, and to
discuss how they came to be ECE practitioners. This initial encounter was
an important start to the data collection process and was designed to set the
scene for the practitioners and I to explore the children's humour and their
responses to humour via the Akin to the Currere method, which involves
autobiographical reflection on experiences with education that shape our
understanding of self in society (Pinaar, 2004). The BDES were designed
as an opportunity for the practitioners to reflect on their experiences of
humour throughout their lives, explore their personal relationships with
humour and begin to link these to their views on young children's humour
and its place within ECEC culture and pedagogy.

– Dialogic Encounter 1 (DE1) took place after the observations and after
the first analysis, which was conducted by me as the lead researcher, during which I scanned the videos for examples of humour and created key
moments (KMs) from that process. During this encounter, the practitioners
and I watched the collection of KMs on the video and analysed what was
occurring and whether there was anything we deemed significant.

– The purpose of Dialogic Encounter 2 (DE2) was to revisitDE1, sometime
after it had taken place, to check whether any thoughts had changed or
whether the practitioners or I believed that our ideas had been misrepresented inDE1. In a sense, it was a form of member checking, which Sullivan
suggests has an important role within dialogic research because of the recognition of the presence of multiple voices and their hierarchical positions
in relation to one another (Sullivan, 2012).

– Lastly, the practitioners had access to a dialogic analysis journal, which
included transcripts of all the encounters we had shared, alongside data
from the children. The idea was to provide them with a further opportunity
to ensure that their voices were being represented in a way that they were
comfortable with, and that meant they could do this at their own pace.

With the adoption of key moments, the study utilised an 'utterance' as the unit
of analysis. As Sullivan states, 'Key Moments are an utterance of significance'
(2012, p. 72), and utterances differ from a sentence or word via their addressiv-
ity and answerability (Bakhtin, 1986). Helin (2013) suggests that using an

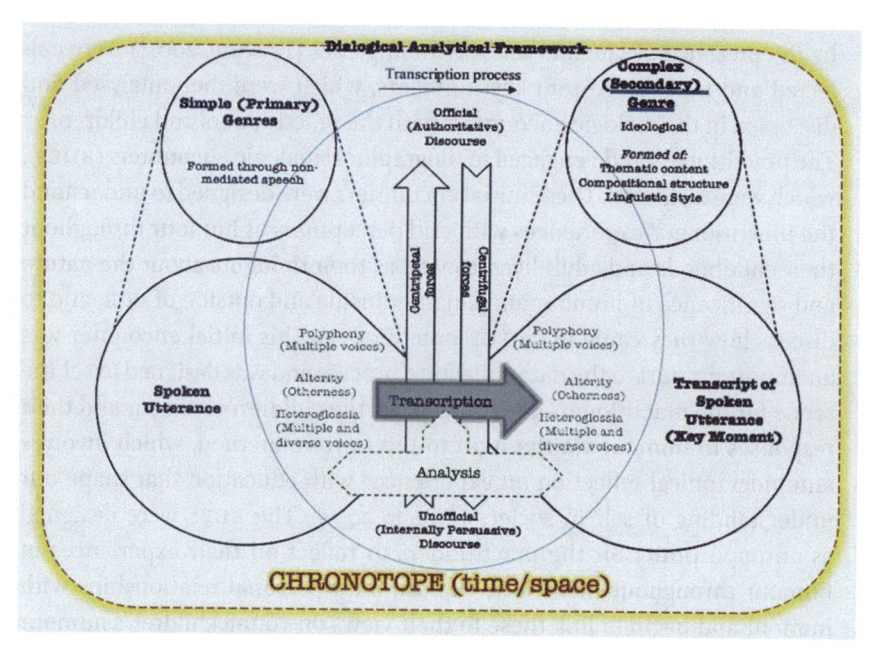

FIGURE 9.1   Analytic framework

utterance as a unit of analysis provides an opportunity to heed 'Bakhtin's suggestion for approaching relationality ... through paying attention to utterance chains in the unfolding' (2013, p. 226). This is possible because 'an utterance ends when the speaker makes room for an active responsive understanding to be developed', meaning that 'a response does not necessarily need to be in the form of spoken words; it can be silence, or something else that passes as an appropriate response in the dialogic moment' (2013, p. 226). In addition, given their flexible parameters, it is possible that a word imbued with intention and reactivity can be an utterance, as can a chapter in a book (Bakhtin, 1986). Further support for an utterance being a fitting unit of analysis within dialogic research comes from Wertsch (1998, p. 50), who argues that it is the 'real unit of speech'. The dialogical approach to analysing utterances adopted in this study is encapsulated in the framework shown in Figure 9.1.

8.1   An Illustration of the Analytical Process

Data were analysed, drawing on the wide range of ideas that comprise Bakhtin's broader theory of dialogism. An example of the data and the way in which some of the analysis manifested through a dialogue between the researcher and the adult participants – an integral feature of the visual dialogic approach – follows to illustrate how encountering the camera footage facilitated integral analytical dialogues among the children, practitioners and me.

FIGURE 9.2   Example of the polyphonic video technique with two viewpoints displayed

The scene below, Key Moment Dialogic Encounter 1 (KM DE1), is taken from the children's dialogic encounter: an event intended to offer them a chance to react to the video footage of themselves. The scene script is presented in the centre of the page to denote the central role that the participants' voices played within the study. In addition, the participants within the scene are represented by the character stickers they chose to personalise their head cameras. Moreover, the images next to the title were used throughout the writing up of the project. The presence of a key denotes a 'key moment', and the 'carnivalesque fool' indicates carnivalesque genre. Figure 9.2 is a cartoonised (the cartooning of the videos as an ethical response is discussed in more detail later in the chapter) screenshot of the polyphonic screening of the key moment, which was screened during the children's dialogic encounter, and illustrates the scene from the perspective of two of the practitioners involved.

KM DE1 'I fell on my bottom'

The children are sitting around a laptop waiting to watch films of themselves, captured from the head cameras worn during the observation process. The films are made up of more than one screen, each of which displays the images from an individual head camera or from one of the static cameras – see the screenshot in Figure 9.2.

Imogen: Oliver's on it. [*In the video, Oliver is dancing and then slips, falling onto the floor*]

Video: Oliver: 'I fell on my bottom!' [*smiles*]

Elsa: You fell on your bottom? Oooooh.

[*Sebastian laughs, and Oliver, Imogen and Annabelle smile; then, Oliver looks at Laura*]

Laura: [*With a neutral facial expression*] You fell on your bottom, Oliver.

[*Oliver smiles, walks away from the laptop and falls over exaggeratedly, whilst laughing. Annabelle watches him and then exaggeratedly falls off the child-sized sofa*]

Laura: [*Now smiling*] Are you falling again?

Oliver: Yeah [*Smiles and comes back and sits down in front of the screen*] I want to see me again.

Laura: You want to see you again? [*The other children do not seem keen to do as Oliver suggests*] Well, we've got another one here, and I think Nathaniel is in this one ...

[*The video continues to play, and all of the children watch the screen as Nathaniel is singing in the video. Oliver then jumps up and falls onto the floor, exaggeratedly, once again. He turns back to the screen smiling. Oliver laughs and Sebastian laughs, too. Sebastian jumps up and falls onto the floor*]

OLIVER

ANNABELLE

SEBASTIAN

IMOGEN

NATHANIAL

FIGURE 9.3   Overt voices present in utterance represented by individuals' head camera stickers

Imogen: It goes like this [*falls on to the floor*], buuurrrr [*smiles*].

Below is the analysis of 'I fell on my bottom' that the practitioner participants and I engaged in. Once again, this is presented in the centre of the page to represent the central role of the voices within the encounter.

I fell on my bottom' – a practitioner perspective
KM from Ana and Bulda's DE1

Laura:	Oliver laughs when he says, 'I fell on my bottom'. Why is that funny in your opinion?
Bulda:	Well, it's almost like adults watching ... You've Been Framed ... it's that, that, slapstick humour isn't it ...
Ana:	Energetic ... not necessarily based on language ...
Bulda:	No, no ...
Ana:	It's more of a ...
Bulda:	It's more of an active-y thing, isn't it?
Ana:	Yeah.
Bulda:	Yeah ... laughing at each other WITH each other, 'cause obviously he wasn't hurt because he'd have been upset ...
Laura:	Yeah, that's interesting, because Oliver laughed as well, didn't he?
Bulda:	Yeah.
Laura:	But sometimes I think if people hurt themselves ...
Bulda:	He might have got cross if they'd have laughed.
Laura:	People might laugh but the person themself isn't laughing.
Bulda:	Yeah.
Ana:	Yeah. Yeah. And whether they'd have laughed if he had hurt himself ... it would have been different. If he hadn't have laughed as well ... and then, you know, he would have been upset, it would have been interesting to see if they'd have laughed or not.
Bulda:	Yeah.
Ana:	Whether they'd have found it funny ...
Bulda:	Yeah.
Laura:	Yeah, that would have been interesting ... and how do you think ... how do you think you might have reacted if ...?
Ana:	The same, I think ...
Bulda:	Yeah, might have said, 'oo are you alright?' but then ...
Ana:	If he'd have laughed ... but if he didn't laugh then I might have said "ooo, never mind, up you jump" and all those kinda ...

Bulda: Shivying him up kinda ...
Ana: Yeah. Yeah.
Bulda: [*quietly*] getting on with it.
Ana: But then maybe be careful just in case it did go wrong ... BECAUSE they kind of have to learn that, yeah, those things can be funny but obviously try not to do it too much because you could hurt yourself. [*laughs ... B smiles*]

The joint exploration and analysis of this key moment seen here influenced the creation of a summary table of key moment 1 (see Table 9.1). It maps out an overview of the key moment in relation to the dialogic concepts of genre and discourse, the emotional register of learning or truth, the time-space elaboration of genre (or chronotope) and context, from a Bakhtinian perspective (Sullivan, 2013). This analysis was only made possible as a result of the visual dialogic approach employed in the study. Table 9.1 thus demonstrates how this study used visuality to develop a shared understanding of the children's experiences.

TABLE 9.1   Summary of key moment 1 from 'Embracing the Carnivalesque: Young Children's Humour as Performance and Communication'

Participants	Key moment	Genres and discourse	Emotional register of learning or truth	Time-space elaboration (chronotope)	Context
Imogen, Annabelle, Alice, Oliver, Sebastian, Dave, Nathaniel, Yanto and Laura (me)	Dialogic Encounter 1 (DE1) child participants	Carnivalesque – performance, free communication between unlikely individuals, clowning, mimicry	Humour – the comic, joy, denial, uncertainty, togetherness	Reflecting on the past, time as full of potential	Organised dialogic encounter – the children watched the video of their own volition and were free to stop watching at any point

SOURCE: TALLANT (2017, P. 76)

9 Affordances and Limitations

A key requirement for the success of authentic dialogic analysis of polyphonic video is arguably having the time available to engage in dialogue about the data. Throughout the project, I gained the impression that it was extremely difficult for the practitioners to find time for this research as a result of their busy working lives, which is reflective of the involved nature of ECEC practice, generally. This presented some issues, particularly with respect to needing to end dialogic encounters prematurely. This potentially meant that not only was possible data missed, but I also sensed that the practitioners were often clock-watching, and this affected their ability to focus. Nevertheless, the dialogic approach seen in this study is rich in potential; however, the need to devote time to it may be problematic. Having sufficient time to devote to the approach is imperative to ensure that the dialogues that take place are not rushed and that participants have the opportunity to become accustomed to the potentially discombobulating nature of watching multiple videos playing simultaneously and alongside one another.

Another possible limitation of the polyphonic video technique was that it proved challenging for some of the participants. They said that they had difficulty finding a point of focus when watching the multiple videos playing simultaneously and that it made them feel somewhat dizzy. This could have been addressed by having an opportunity to spend a significant amount of time watching and re-watching these polyphonic videos, so that the practitioners could acclimatise to the novel sight of multiple screens. Unfortunately, as previously mentioned, we did not have the luxury of time, given the practitioners work schedules. I am consequently uncertain about whether the practitioners were ever able to totally overcome their adverse feelings about the polyphonic approach. Research participants' time availability is thus an important consideration for researchers who intend to adopt this approach.

After having considered potential limitations, we now explore what the approach affords researchers. This study found that it is important to consider Bakhtin's theory of carnivalesque when encountering and observing young children's humour; therefore, we briefly consider why, here.

The grotesque realism aspect of Bakhtin's carnivalesque, which places positive, liberating, energised emphasis on the lower bodily strata (essentially, our physical bodies from the waist down) focuses on areas of our bodies' that, particularly when considered in any way connected with young children, are often considered taboo, risqué, forbidden, out-of-bounds and to-be-hidden. For this reason, it is especially important for us to recognise children's affinity with and enjoyment of ideas that relate to this area of the body highlighted via the visual methods used in this research study. The detailed reasons for children's interest must be left for another time and place, as they are outside the scope of this chapter; however, the research evidence does exist (see White, 2015; Tallant, 2015). In answer to the question, then, of how this fervent interest that children have in the lower bodily strata reconciles with adult sensibilities and their potential discomfort (arguably, a trait often associated with British culture – Ogden, 2013) in paying close attention to this area of the body, I suggest the following: early childhood professionals can learn to become more at home in interacting with, and responding to, this area of children's interest by becoming more familiar with why and how children are interested in this bodily area and by adopting the help of Bakhtinian carnivalesque theory to frame and inform this new understanding.

10   Information about the Transana Data Analysis Software

The Transana analysis software was utilised in the research project. It is primarily a multimedia transcription and analysis tool that allows researchers to combine mixed-media data for analysis in a more streamlined and coherent fashion. The primary reason for choosing this software was its capacity to house multiple video clips alongside one another, as this facilitated the polyphonic video method.

I encountered technical difficulties with the Transana software and saving of data. This issue impacted on the data collection process when Transana crashed and I lost data that had taken a significant amount of time to piece together for us to watch and respond to in the dialogic encounters. While I was eventually able to overcome the issue, it took away valuable time from the dialogic encounters – time that was already in short supply. I was able to seek help from the Transana support team and discovered how to ensure that the issue did not repeat itself in future – perhaps a useful note for researchers contemplating using the Transana software.

11   Technical Challenges and Ethical Considerations

The employment of head cameras and the involvement of young children in this project afforded particular ethical considerations that must be discussed. As White (2011) points out, many people may argue against asking a young child to wear a camera on his or her head. Those people will likely have concerns about adult-child power differentials or perhaps worry about the potential danger of the proximity of electrical equipment to the body (ibid.). There may also be scepticism concerning the capacity of the camera to 'capture' meaning. Moreover, it is a challenge to know how to respond to Sumsion et al.'s (2011) posed quandary: do any possible advantages of potentially learning more about young children's lives 'outweigh the possibility that we may ... be invading their worlds'? Indeed, a wide range of ethical questions are raise in relation to the use of head cameras in research with young children; however, what appears to be vital is that researchers are able to employ the sensitive, organic approach to research necessary to ensure that children's rights and needs take precedence over any perceived research priorities (White, 2011).

11.1   Technical Challenges

When considering using head cameras, I would urge researchers to take into account the quality of the equipment they use. Sumsion et al. (2011) mentioned the difficulties they encountered in obtaining an appropriate camera for their *Infants Lives in Childcare* project and noted that a considerable amount of trial and error was required before landing on the most effective camera. I experienced a similar challenge but eventually sourced a number of compact cameras from a well-known online retailer, chosen for the simple reasons that the cameras appeared to do what was required, were relatively inexpensive and were convenient to acquire. For the most part, the cameras were a success; however, they were not without their flaws, possibly because of their low cost. One flaw was that the cameras' instructions were sparse, and troubleshooting information was non-existent. On several occasions, filming took place, and on inspecting the video footage, the cameras were found to have failed to save footage despite them appearing to work at the time of recording. As researchers, we should not be under any illusions that the quality of the tools we use, regardless of whether this is dictated by a lack of available funding, can make a significant difference to the outcomes of the research. It is perhaps useful to raise an obvious but easily overlooked reminder for researchers to consider the potential limitations of certain visual tools and thus to have contingencies available, wherever possible.

11.2   Ethical Locational Considerations

The use of head cameras in research with young children requires careful consideration of the location in which filming is taking place, particularly for reasons of privacy and protection of personal space. It is important to note that head cameras record everything in the field of vision of the wearer. In this project, the door to the outside space consequently remained closed for the duration of the observations to prevent children's head cameras from inadvertently filming anyone who had not granted consent for this – a salient consideration for any study employing head cameras. In addition, a large photograph of a head camera and an arrow pointing to a cardboard box was placed in front of the door to the children's toilets. It was consequently not possible for children to walk into the toilets without circumnavigating the box. The children were asked to place their head cameras into the box before going into the toilets to prevent inadvertent filming whilst the children were in a situation requiring physical privacy. An adult also monitored the door to the toilets during filming to ensure that children did not forget to take off their cameras before entering the toilets.

11.3   *An 'Animated' Ethical Conundrum*

Significantly, the university ethical clearance stipulations placed upon the project meant that the videos had to remain confidential and anonymous throughout the project. As a result, if the videos were to be seen by anyone outside of the project, they needed to be 'cartoonised' using software to ensure that the people in the videos were not identifiable. Figure 9.3, presented earlier in this chapter, is a still image taken from a video I cartoonised for trial purposes. It is possible to see, here, that the image is blurred, changing the way the physical environment is seen, axiomatically. This raises questions about the authenticity of the identities and voices of those in the videos and prompts us to ask whether it is possible to turn an image of someone or something into a cartoon version without affecting the way in which they are perceived and 'authored' by others. We can argue that video images offer a visual form of dialogical access to events of being. They allow us to 'see' a version of the video participants' reality for our subjective interpretation. By committing events to video, we create a record of them, available to be authored through dialogue between the images and the viewer/s. Moreover, if we accept Stadler's (2000, p. 55, as cited in Elwick et al., 2014) view that, in encountering video, '[t] he construction of meaning requires the mutual involvement of [the video] and its [spectator]' and that video 'relocate[s] what can be seen as a mutually animating event' (White, 2016, n.p.), then we could ask whether 'cartoonising' recorded images, which thus alters and distorts them, serves to fabricate an inauthentic dimension, thereby adversely affecting anyone's ability to understand, interpret or 'author' the participants seen in the video. The lack of clarity regarding this issue informed my decision not to cartoonise other videos of the data and hence not to allow them to be seen outside of the project. This decision raises further questions, however, about what everyone involved or interested in the research may be missing out on as a result of the video images being unavailable for viewing after the project.

12   Future Possibilities

Many possibilities exist for using visual dialogic methods, particularly those looking to operationalise polyphony to facilitate ways of seeing. The idea that using video, especially through the employment of head cameras, complicates participatory relations between the viewers and the children in the films (Elwick, 2015) arguably only presents an opportunity for richer dialogues and more complex shared understandings of young children's experiences. Furthermore, a head camera's capacity to 'defamiliarise the 'mundanely visible' (ibid., p. 336) and prompt adults to consider the ways in which we 'see' young children is potentially reductive (ibid.) could help us to reflect and adapt our practice to the benefit of children. This potential can bring us into what Elwick describes as 'uncharted areas' that facilitate debates between participatory researchers that may well be contentious and difficult. However, it is precisely this that may lead us to develop 'a fuller appreciation of [children's] capacities to exceed epistemic boundaries created by "adult" perception and ways of knowing' (Elwick, 2015, p. 336).

13   Conclusion

This chapter illustrated that it is possible to take the Bakhtinian concept of carnivalesque and create a visual methodology around it in order to identify where it could be seen within children's humorous behaviours and encounters. We observed how Bakhtinian carnivalesque can be used to develop a visual, polyphonic (White, 2009a) method that privileges the voices of participants in order to explore young children's humorous encounters and actions as carnivality (Jennings-Tallant, 2018). The chapter also considered how video has been used in a range of contexts to operationalise various visual methodologies, but it noted that White's (2009a) polyphonic video technique is still relatively new and offers rich opportunities for researchers intending to adopt visual methods. From an ethical perspective, video in general and White's (2009a) polyphonic method present a number of potential challenges that must be considered before deciding to adopt these approaches. This should not act as a barrier, however, as the possibilities engendered by adopting polyphonic methods arguably outweigh any challenges.

Given the plethora of other theoretical approaches to analysing young children's humour that dominate the research and literature overall and, in particular, the pedagogical significance of young children's humour, it is imperative that the significance of carnivalesque readings are not overlooked or ignored. As highlighted above in the analysis sections, the importance for children, of professionals' understanding how the carnivalesque provides us with a helpful elucidation of what underpins children's humorous actions and behaviours, cannot be underestimated.

Professionals' consideration of how Bakhtin's theory of carnivalesque can enhance our understanding and awareness of children's intentions, motivations and humorous behaviours is extremely important and useful. This study demonstrates that young children's carnivality (Jennings-Tallant, 2018) is woven throughout early childhood practice and needs to become part of the 'furniture' in everyday ECEC practice if children are to be afforded the opportunity to have their expressions intricately recognised and both empathised and sympathised with. Furthermore, additional studies are necessary that employ similar visual methods to those used here if we are to enjoy the full potential they can offer us in our endeavour to gain helpful shared understandings that may enrich young children's worlds.

13   Summary Statements

- This chapter focused on a research project that explored young children's humour using a Bakhtinian carnivalesque lens.
- To achieve this, a visual dialogic methodology was employed, utilising Whites (2009a) polyphonic videoing technique.
- This approach facilitated the analysis of the data by allowing the emphasis to be on the participants and researcher's points of view.
- Transana data analysis software was utilised to facilitate the polyphonic video technique.
- The chapter argued that the adoption of polyphonic methods offers a fresh way for researchers to focus on visual data, which affords new opportunities in terms of 'seeing' young children as carnivalesque participants in ECE settings.

References

Bakhtin, M. M. (1981). *The dialogic imagination: Four essays*. University of Texas Press.

Bakhtin, M. M. (1984a). *Problems of Dostoevsky's poetics*. University of Minnesota Press.

Bakhtin, M. M. (1984b). *Rabelais and his world*. Indiana University Press.

Cohen, L. (2011). Bakhtin's carnival and pretend role-play: A comparison of social contexts. *American Journal of Play, 4*, 176–203.

Dahlberg, G. (2000). Everything is a beginning, and everything is dangerous: Some reflections of the Reggio Emilia experience. In H. Penn (Ed.), *Early childhood services: Theory, policy and practice*. Open University.

Elwick, S. (2015). 'Baby-cam' and researching with infants: Viewer, image and (not) knowing. *Contemporary Issues in Early Childhood, 16*(4), 322–338.

Grace, D., & Tobin, J. (2002). Pleasure, creativity, and the carnivalesque in children's video production. In L. Bressler & C. Thompson (Eds.), *The arts in children's lives* (pp. 195–215). Springer.

Jennings-Tallant, L. (2018). *Children and their underworld: An exploration of young children's humour as Bakhtinian carnivalesque* (Unpublished PhD thesis). University of East Anglia, Norwich.

Jennings-Tallant, L. (2019). 'Let the wild rumpus start!' Using carnival as a metaphor to highlight the pedagogical significance of young children's humor. In E. Loizou & S. Recchia (Eds.), *Research on young children's humor* (pp. 203–221). Springer.

Loizou, E. (2004). Humorous bodies and humorous minds: Humour within the social context of an infant childcare setting. *European Early Childhood Education Research Journal, 12*(1), 15–28. doi:10.1080/13502930485209281

Loizou, E. (2005). Humour: A different kind of play. *European Early Childhood Education Research Journal, 13*(2), 97–109. https://doi.org/10.1080/13502930585209701

Loizou, E. (2007). Humour as a means of regulating one's social self: Two infants with unique humorous personas. *Early Childhood Development and Care, 177*(2), 195–205.

Loizou, E., Kiriakides, E., & Hadjicharalambous, M. (2011). Constructing stories in kindergarten: Children's knowledge of genre. *European Early Childhood Education Research Journal, 19*(1), 63–78.

Matusov, E. (2007). Applying Bakhtin scholarship on discourse in education. *Education Theory, 57*(2), 215–238.

Ogden, C. (2013). Surveillance of the leaky child: No-body's normal but that doesn't stop us trying. In C. Ogden & S. Wakeman (Eds.), *Corporeality: The body and society* (pp. 80–98). University of Chester Press.

Piaget, J. (1953). *The origin of intelligence in the child*. Routledge & Kegan Paul.

Provine, R. (2001). *Laughter: A scientific investigation*. Penguin.

Qvortup, J. (2005). *Studies in modern childhood: Society, agency and culture*. Palgrave Macmillan.

Sawyer, R. D., & Norris, J. (2013). *Duoethnography: Understanding qualitative research*. Oxford University Press.

Sullivan, P. (2012). *Qualitative data analysis using a dialogical approach*. Sage.

Sumsion, J., Harrison, L., Press, F., Mcleod, S., Goodfellow, J., & Bradley, B. (2011). Researching infants' experiences of early childhood education and care. In D. Harcourt, B. Perry, & T. Waller (Eds.), *Researching young children's perspectives: Debating the ethics and dilemmas of educational research with children* (pp. 113–127). Brunner-Routledge.

Tallant, L. (2015). Framing young children's humour and practitioner responses to it using a Bakhtinian carnivalesque lens. *International Journal of Early Childhood, 47*(2), 251–266. doi:10.1007/s13158-015-0134-0

Tallant, L. (2017). Embracing the carnivalesque: Young children' humour as performance and communication. *Knowledge Cultures, 5*(3), 71–84. doi:10.22381/KC5320176

Taylor, A. (2013). *Reconfiguring the natures of childhood*. Routledge.

White, E. J. (2009a). *Assessment in New Zealand early childhood education: A Bakhtinian analysis of toddler metaphoricity* (Unpublished PhD thesis). Monash University, Melbourne.

White, E. J. (2009b). *Bakhtinian dialogism: A philosophical and methodological route to dialogue and difference?* Annual Conference of the Philosophy of Education Society of Australasia. Retrieved from http://www2.hawaii.edu/~pesaconf/zpdfs/16white.pdf

White, E. J. (2010). Polyphonic portrayals: A Dostoevskian dream or a researcher's reality? In *Proceedings from the Second International Interdisciplinary Conference on Perspectives and Limits of Dialogism in Mikhail Bakhtin* (pp. 87–96). Stockholm University. Retrieved from http://www.su.se/polopoly_fs/1.30109.1344252792!/menu/standard/file/publication_2 010_bakhtin_con f_sthlm_2009_correct_ISBN.pdf

White, E. J. (2011). 'Seeing' the toddler: Voices or voiceless'. In E. Johansson, & E. J. White (Eds.), *Educational research with our youngest: Voices of infants and toddlers* (pp. 63–86). Springer.

White, E. J. (2014). 'Are you 'avin a laff?': A pedagogical response to Bakhtinian carnivalesque in early childhood education. *Educational Philosophy & Theory, 46*(8), 898–913.

White, E. J. (2016). A philosophy of seeing: The work of the eye/'I' in early years educational practice. *Journal of Philosophy of Education, 50*(3), 474–490.

White, E. J. (2017a). The 'work of the eye' in infant research: A visual encounter. In L. Li, G. Quinones, & A. Ridgway (Eds.), *Studying babies and toddlers: Relationships in cultural contexts* (pp. 123–136). Springer. Retrieved from http://link.springer.com/book/10.1007%2F978-981-10-3197-7

White, E. J. (2017b). Video ethics and young children. *Video Journal of Education and Pedagogy, 2*(2). Retrieved from https://videoeducationjournal.springeropen.com/articles/10.1186/s40990-017-0012-9

White, E. J. (2017c). A feast of fools: Mealtimes as democratic acts of resistance and collusion in early childhood education. *Knowledge Cultures, 5*(3). http://dx.doi.org.bathspa.idm.oclc.org/10.22381/KC5320177

CHAPTER 10

Phenomenological Participatory Research
Opportunities for 'Seeing' and Producing Meaning

Nicola Firth

1 Introduction

The methodological approach explored throughout this chapter is interpretative hermeneutic phenomenology, which seeks to make meaning out of everyday phenomena in the world (Willig, 2013). I yolk this approach with participatory research methods (Green, 2016). The chapter demonstrates how these methods were employed in order to study 3- to 6-year-old boys' experiences in their early childhood education (ECE) environment. Using a visual approach to 'make meaning from visual representations' (White & Murray, 2016, p. 506), a range of visual data collection methods were utilised, including walking tours, cameras or iPads, and photo-production focus groups, with the aim of engaging boys in participatory research

I explore how the use of visual data collection methods can enhance engagement and the power of children's voice in research through verbal and non-verbal interactions. Capturing young children's voices is not always easy to achieve, and creative participatory research with children is often unavailable and missing in literature; therefore, children's own experiences are being 'marginalised' (Lomax, 2012, p. 106). It is also recognised that adults are not always best positioned to represent a child's viewpoint. The use of visual data collection methods thus assisted in engaging participant boys in data collection activities and capturing their conceptions of their own learning environment (Einarsdottir, 2005). These visual methods seek to understand the child's world and own unique perspective, as it is understood that research involving young children is imperative for understanding their lives (Clark & Statham, 2005; Graham et al., 2013).

The rationale behind the research is that boys' educational underachievement has been an international concern for some time (see Gurian & Stevens, 2005; Marshall, 2014; Weaver-Hightower, 2009). Much data relating to boys' underachievement has been taken from quantitative data sets with older boys in upper primary and high schools. In contrast, little focus has been placed on young boys in their early learning environments (Warrington & Younger, 2006). Hence, I argue that the experiences of these boys represent an encounter with power that has been previously silenced. The visual data collection methods aimed to capture children's verbal and non-verbal voices, through discussion about the images the children had caught on camera. The utilised methods allowed for a 'child-friendly' approach which seeks to make children will feel more at ease with an adult researcher when these types of data collection activities are deployed (Einarsdottir, 2005, p. 525). Reichart et al.'s (2009) imperative – 'If you want to tell it like it is, you have to hear it like is' (p. 60) – informed the interpretative phenomenological approach accordingly. It is important to remember though, that it is the researcher's own interpretations of the children's experiences and what has been seen and heard. Researchers need a set of skills and practices to use visual creative methods, and careful observation and listening skills are needed.

2   Interpretative Phenomenological Methodology

An interpretative phenomenological approach was adopted with the intention to interpret and analyse how boys view their 'world as it is experienced' (Willig, 2013, p. 83) by them, in particular contexts and at particular times, relating directly to the qualitative epistemological stance. The aim of such an approach is to develop 'a better understanding of the nature of the phenomena as they present themselves ... does not separate description and interpretation' (Willig, 2013, p. 86). Seeing and hearing the direct experiences in the boys' own learning environment, alongside them, provided the opportunity to observe the 'qualities of an experience as it is lived' (Willig & Rogers, 2017, p. 194) and experienced by them. Hermeneutic phenomenology sits within the interpretative phenomenology methodology, relating to spoken accounts of the experiences of participants. Sloan and Bowe (2013, p. 1292) cite van Manen (1997), explaining that the researcher must 'examine the text to reflect on the content and discover something 'telling', something 'meaningful', 'while interpreting the meaning of the phenomenon or lived experience' of the participant.

The term 'life-world' relates to the underpinning philosophy of phenomenology that I employ, arising from Husserl's stance on descriptive phenomenology. It is considered to be a way of 'reaching true meaning' (Sloan & Bowe, 2013, p. 1294) and engaging with the relationship between consciousness and engagement in the world around us (Willig, 2013). Relating to the life-world, Philosopher Merleau-Ponty, who was interested in Husserl's stance on phenomenology, also stated that a person and his or her world are inextricably entwined (Diprose & Reynolds, 2014; Willig & Rogers, 2017). Nevertheless, he paid more attention to the latent content of experience and called for 'hyper-reflection', concerning the 'incompleteness of consciousness, and hence of, phenomenology' (Diprose & Reynolds, 2014, p. 10). Husserl was mainly concerned that the world could be known only through a person's thoughts and consciousness, and outside of that, there was no real existence (Dowling & Cooney, 2012), whereas Merleau-Ponty took Husserl's philosophy forward and developed it to include subjectivity within the real-life world, moving outside of the consciousness.

Similar views from Heidegger, a student of Husserl's, relate to the phenomenological approach, but with a stronger interpretive stance (Dowling & Cooney, 2012; Sloan & Bowe, 2013). Heidegger argued that Husserl had an objectivist stance within his philosophy of phenomenology because he settled for 'generic descriptions' rather than delving deeper into the 'fine-grained' view of the phenomena under investigation, and Heidegger contended that the observer could not detach him- or herself from the phenomena taking place, as Husserl would (Sloan & Bowe, 2013, p. 1294). The fundamental role for Heidegger within his philosophy was that 'modes of understanding attunement and language are the essence' (von Eckartsberg, 1998, p. 148) of being human, and the observer must become involved in the everyday activities of the world (von Eckartsberg, 1998). The attribution of the use of language and interpretation is key to Heidegger's interpretative phenomenology (Sloan & Bowe, 2013) and hermeneutics. Through verbally recorded photo-production focus group discussions with the boys, immediately after the walking tours had taken place, I was able to make an attempt at interpreting what they were saying relating to the visual cues (i.e., the photographs). Interpretative phenomenology is concerned with how research participants 'see meaning in their experience' (Smith, Flowers, & Larkin, 2009, p. 187), and the photographs supported the participant boys not only to engage in the activity, but also to actually 'see' and prompt the memory of their experiences and learning environment during the photo-production focus group discussions. It must be noted that, on the one hand, Husserl's descriptive phenomenology and Heidegger's view of interpretative phenomenology have similarities; each of these philosophies seeks to 'uncover the life-world' and 'human existence as it is lived' (Sloan & Bowe, 2013, p. 1295). On the other hand, a significant difference is that interpretative phenomenology does not attempt to separate description and interpretation; in fact, Willig (2013) argues that description is rather a form of interpretation.

Through regular observation and dialogue with the participant boys in part of their real 'life-world' (Sloan & Bowe, 2013; von Eckartsberg, 1989) – that is, a preschool private day nursery and a mainstream school – I had the opportunity to interpret what they were 'saying' through language and 'see', through their actions, what they were 'doing' and what images they photographed. This supported my understanding of the phenomena taking place. It is understood from the outset that there are criticisms of the interpretative phenomenological approach and the way in which meaning is interpreted; however, I argue that the phenomenological approach does offer epistemology that has scientific strength for human scientific research, with educational research used as an example of its strength (Dahlberg & Dahlberg, 2003). The use of visual data collection methods is seen as a tool to understand how a person views his or her world at a particular moment in time (Silver, 2013), relating directly to the phenomenological approach.

3   Participatory Research

A participatory research framework was adopted with the participating boys during the data collection period. The objective of this approach was that they became active participants during the data collection period, and together we developed opportunities for shared agency, which supported making their views and opinions visible, relating to the interpretative phenomenological approach. Reavy and Johnson (2017) consider visual methods to be a strength in enhancing agency, and they suggest that photographs taken by participants that are discussed between participants and researchers engage both parties. It was also recognised that, as an adult, I perceive the world differently to children; therefore, adopting a participatory approach was integral to the research study in order to capture the children's experiences by engaging with them and using child-friendly data collection methods (Green, 2016).

The term 'participation' is generally used in a positive manner, and this type of approach can provide the opportunity to empower children. However, methods of data collection are normally designed by adult researchers, not children, even though children are expected to engage in them (Gallacher & Gallagher, 2008). This arguably disempowers them to some extent and takes away opportunities for 'shared agency', as they are not involved in the whole process of the research design. Since participant children may become passive rather than active participants, the researcher must question whether the children are actively engaging or passively responding during data collection (Gallacher & Gallagher, 2008). Nevertheless, I argue that using a child-friendly visual component as a tool to engage participation aids in shifting the child from a passive participant to an active one. This is a view supported by Del Busso (2011, cited by Silver, 2013), who state that photo-production methods support the active engagement and involvement of participants, as they offer additional thoughts about what they want to photograph and why, thus leading to the participants feeling empowered.

There has been a growing shift towards participatory methods (Gallacher & Gallagher, 2008) and the use of visually orientated data collection methods with children (Lomax, 2012). Children should be seen as participants involved in the research process, and they should also be seen as subjects, not objects (Gallacher & Gallagher, 2008; Lomax, 2012). Green (2012) refers to photography as a child-friendly method and considers walking tours to be a successful data collection tool to use with children; it helps the researcher to understand the children's experiences and perspectives in their particular environment, namely, their learning environment. This type of approach relates to 'participatory phenomenological' (Green, 2016, p. 280), as the aim was to engage the participant boys as active researchers; therefore, it aligned with the already chosen approach of interpretative phenomenology.

4 Orienting Methods in Participatory Research with the Visual

Participatory methods relating to the social study of childhood trace back to the early 1990s when a paradigm shift occurred to reposition children as being competent, rather than incompetent (Gallacher & Gallagher, 2008), unreliable and incomplete (Lomax, 2012), as they had largely been understood until then. Adopting visually orientated methods within a phenomenological frame that sought to examine experiences with the participants made it possible to grant them authority over their experiences. Through a range of methods, including walking tours, cameras or iPads, and photo-production focus groups, young children's experiences were captured through visual expressions.

Visually orientated data collection tools such as wearable cameras, video cameras, art-based approaches, walking tours, and mapping are increasingly being recognised as creative and participatory child-centred methods (see Arnott, Robinson, & Wall, 2018; Clark, 2011; Green, 2012, 2016; Lomax, 2012). It was essential that the chosen data collection methods were creative and child-friendly, with the intention to engage the participant boys in the activities and include their views, opinions and voices during the research study. Walking tours and photo-production were the ultimate chosen methods, with the aim that the boys would participate and engage in the activities, thereby affording them opportunities to 'see' and 'talk' about their ECE learning environment.

4.1 Walking Tours as a Method

Walking tours are traditionally used as a data collection tool in educational research that seeks to involve children in research related to children's geographies and environmental spaces and places (Lomax, 2012; Green, 2012, 2016). It is argued that walking tours provide children with the opportunity to 'show and tell' their experiences of 'familiar and naturalistic' environments (Green,

2016, p. 281). With this in mind, the intention was to promote and encourage discussion relating to the participant boys' views and opinions of their learning environment.

4.2   *Photo Production*

Photo-production is defined as the use of photographs that have been produced during the actual research process (Silver, 2013) – in this case, during the walking tours. Photographs can aid in establishing rapport between participants and researchers more than a traditional face-to-face interview (Collier, 1957, as cited by Silver, 2013). Research methods involving children should adopt innovative approaches, and the use of photographs to capture children's conceptions of their world supports this type of creative visual approach (Einarsdottir, 2005). Photographs can evoke deeper feelings and thoughts and 'deeper layers of human consciousness than words' alone (Silver, 2013, p. 157).

The focus group that underscored this method provided the opportunity to ask probing questions, whilst viewing the boys' photographs, in order to attempt to extract meaning from the spoken language of the boys relating to the images they had taken. This is considered a strength of the focus group approach (Gray, 2014).

5   How to Use the Data Collection Methods in the Real World

Prior to starting the walking tours and photo-production focus groups, I spent approximately six half days in the selected private ECE preschool and three full days in the selected maintained schools' Early Years Foundation Stage unit (nursery and reception class). The aim was to build up rapport and trusting relationships with the participant boys. It was essential that we established trust in order to address the potential power imbalance between myself, the adult and the boys (Green, 2016). During this period, I spent time working

TABLE 10.1   Sample of participant boys

Age	Number of participants	Place
3–4 years	3	Preschool, private day nursery
3–4 years	3	Mainstream school nursey
4–5 years	3	Mainstream school reception class
5–6 years	3[a]	Mainstream school Year 1

a Same boys as above, transitioned into Year 1

alongside the boys in their learning environments, so they felt comfortable in my presence.

The data collection activities all took place within the participant boys' natural environment, which is inevitable in the phenomenological approach. This brought about challenges, such as background noise and the presence of other children and adults who were not part of the data collection process. I underestimated these challenges, so it is important that the researcher considers the environment and environmental practices prior to data collection. Lomax (2012) advises that encounters between researchers and children, when using creative participatory methods, require high levels of management and are reliant on 'institutionalised educational practices' (p. 106). The activities took place during the daily routine of the school and preschool private day nursery.

The aim was for participatory research to conduct research '*with*' children, not '*on*' children, in order to hear their voices and experiences. St. Pierre and Jackson discuss qualitative data collection methods and suggest that the authentic voices of participants can be heard and produce 'uncontaminated theoretical interpretation' (2014, p. 715). This was the case during most of the data collection activity, as the children tended to lead the activities; however, this was not the case upon transcribing and analysing the data and findings, as I did this independently. It could be said that, because of this approach, the boys were semi-participants rather than full participants in the study (Gallacher & Gallagher, 2008). Children are also seen as a minority group, and regardless of a trend towards inclusive research working '*with*' rather *than* '*on*' minority groups in society, children's voices are still often absent or even silenced (Denzin & Lincoln, 2013; Sargeant & Harcourt, 2012). As Sargeant and Harcourt (2012, p. 2) point out, 'children's views are often perceived as a simply learned or parroted response', and they argue that 'adult-centred assumptions' of children must be challenged, and their views and opinions must be made visible. Relating to the interpretative phenomenological approach, it is argued that children's accounts of their experiences are pivotal to understanding their life worlds (Sargeant & Harcourt, 2012). By applying child-friendly data collection methods and encouraging the boys' active participation (Green, 2016) throughout this period, I believed that I was researching '*with*' them. Nonetheless, this is an assumption that I cannot truly say was the case, as it was me leading some of the activity and prompting questions.

6   Boys' on Walking Tours

The intention behind the walking tours activity was for the participant boys to show me around their learning environment in their pre-selected groups, talking about the likes, dislikes and experiences they wanted to share, whilst taking photographs on iPads. I initially sat with the small group of participant boys (three per group) and explained the activity I wished for them to take part in, ensuring that they wanted to participate. The use of iPads appeared to draw them in, and they displayed excitement at the opportunity to use the iPads to take photographs. I demonstrated how to use the iPads to take the photographs, and then we started the walking tour; I followed the boys, attempting to record their voices. The walking tours lasted as long as the boys were interested in the activity, whilst freely exploring their learning environment; they tended to lead this part of the data collection. Most of the boys were enthusiastic about participating, with examples such as the following present in the data:

> The boys were laughing and giggling, shouting 'cheese' to one another. More giggling and laughing, talking in excited voices. I asked, 'Are you enjoying doing this, taking pictures'? The boys all responded 'yeah', in animated voices whilst laughing.

One participant boy in the preschool private day nursery expressed that he did not want to participate, and unfortunately, one other participant boy was ill. Therefore, the walking tours were undertaken with one boy, Lee, who was keen to participate.

The following is an excerpt from field notes on the second walking tour with Lee:

> We went back inside preschool, and Lee went to the construction area (he spent all of his time in this area during the previous walking tour).
>   Lee asked me to hold the grasshopper; I did so.
>   He held the grasshopper in position and photographed.
>   Lee said 'like this', moved the grasshopper into position and took 11 more photographs, nearly all identical ...
>   Lee passed the iPad to me and said, 'you take picture of me and my dinosaur'.

Here, Lee can be seen leading the data collection activity, supporting the aim of walking tours to engage children in research. Lee was 'showing' and 'telling' (Green, 2016) what was important to him in his real life-world (Sloan & Bowe, 2013; von Eckartsberg, 1989), relating to the phenomenological approach. Upon completion of the walking tours with the mainstream nursery and reception class participant boys, we immediately moved into the photo-production focus group.

7   Boys' Participation in Photo-Production Focus Groups

The focus groups continued to take place within the boys' learning environment, so they felt at ease in an environment they knew. We sat around a cir-
cular table on child-sized furniture and placed each iPad on the table, so we
could view and discuss the photographs together. The use of the photographs
and the availability of visual cues to prompt discussion proved to be valuable in engaging and maintaining the boys' concentration during both of the
data collection activities, but particularly during the photo-production focus
groups. Both focus groups took place in the cloakrooms where children freely
moved indoors and outdoors. This brought about a challenge, as other children
were, on occasion, present, and they distracted both me and the boys from
the discussions taking place. Examples of distractions are evident in the field
notes:

> A child entered and needed some help putting her coat on, so I helped
> her and then continued with the focus group.
>   Had to direct another child outside and help with opening the door.
>   A child came inside (girl), and one of the boys said, 'you're not joining
> us'.

Nevertheless, we quickly picked up where we had left off with discussions and
viewing the photographs. I had pre-empted this issue, and I was thus able to
manage the children on the occasions when these distractions occurred.

Together, we viewed the photographs the boys had taken on the iPads and
talked about them. I tended to prompt the discussion and questions, although
the boys generally spoke freely. However, they did sometimes digress from
questions and prompts. Nevertheless, I encouraged them to do so, as I could
not assume what they were going to talk about or say next; it was therefore
important to allow the discussions to flow.

8   How the Walking Tours and Photo-Production Focus Groups
       Interrelated

It is suggested that photographs represent the 'real world', in the same way
that voice does, and images and pictures are interrelated (Denzin & Lincoln,
2013); this directly links to the visual data collection methods used with the
participant boys and clearly relates to the phenomenological approach. I voice
recorded both the walking tours and photo-production focus groups, with the

expectation that I would be able to link the boys' voices to the photographs they had taken individually. While this proved challenging upon transcription because I could not always decipher which boy was talking, this was not integral to the research, as I was not analysing each individual participant's thoughts and perceptions, but rather a collective response.

Throughout both data collection activities, the boys were actively engaged. Gallacher and Gallagher (2008, p. 506) mention 'active participation' and state that children should actively 'do' something and be 'handling things', and this is exactly what the boys were 'doing' throughout. The participant boys were engaged and being active in their learning environment, handling the iPad's, taking photographs and viewing and discussing images they had photographed themselves. At intervals, they became 'over-excited'; however, this was anticipated with a type of activity that they do not normally perform in school. When two of the boys went to show the class teacher the iPads during the walking tour, the teacher said, 'Oh wow, my goodness, that's special' to the participant boys. The teacher then stated to me, 'They've never touched an iPad in school'.

I was open to this and wanted them to freely participate in the activity together, but I did need to use behaviour management strategies to regain their focus at times, such as reminding them of the task.

Carrying out walking tours and photo-production focus groups worked well in practice, in correlation with each other, and the participant boys were engaged in both activities. Throughout the data collection activities, they were vocal and freely chose the photographs they took and where to go in their environment. The photographs they viewed during the photo-production focus groups provided the boys with the opportunity to voice their experiences within their ECE environment. These everyday experiences prompted meaningful discussions and interactions among the boys and between them and myself, enabling the boys to have a voice and offer a better understanding of their experiences in comparison to data collected mainly by me, as the adult researcher (Gallacher & Gallagher, 2008; Lomax, 2012).

9   Challenges during Early Data Analysis

A significant challenge in the early data analysis was deciphering the voices of the participants from background noise on the audio recorder. There were difficulties actually distinguishing what the 3-year-old participant boys were saying, particularly one boy whose speech was unclear. This resulted in 'messy' and 'chaotic' transcription of the data that I had to listen to many times over.

During transcription, I acknowledged where I was unable to decipher or distinguish what was being said; for example,

> Colin named something but I couldn't work the full words out. He said 'power' ...? I asked, 'Power what'? Colin said, 'Power' ...? I took a guess and said, 'Power supercharge?' Colin said, 'yeah'.
>
> Me: 'When you play outside, what do you like to play with?' Colin: 'We play ??? outside'. (Could not work out what he said)
>
> Colin: C: 'Cos it's ..., cos it's ...' (cannot decipher rest of what C said).

It is crucial to recognise challenges when adopting the visual methods that can be used in phenomenology, such as the examples provided. There are affordances and limitations with using a visual pedagogies approach, and this is, in reality, made more challenging with the young ages of the participant boys. It should not, however, be discarded by the researcher as a viable approach. The participant boys were well engaged in the data collection activity, and rich and meaningful data were collected. While 'digging' down into the data takes time, the views and opinions of the boys and researching 'with' them are of high importance. As Reichert et al. (2009, p. 60) state, 'If you want to tell it like it is, you have to hear it like is'. It is also essential, however, to be able to 'see it like it is' and observe the non-verbal through the visual images the participants have photographed and discussed; the images cannot be discarded for spoken language only.

10 Affordances and Limitations of Using Visual Data Collection Methods with Young Children: Methodology and Visual Methods

An interpretative qualitative epistemological positioning asks the researcher to recognises the subjective nature of their work, as are all participatory methods (Gallacher & Gallagher, 2008). The phenomenological approach is positioned with the aim of knowledge production through the subjective experiences of the participant boys (Willig, 2012). The boys can therefore be described as semi-participants rather than full participants (Gallacher & Gallagher, 2008) throughout the research period, as it was me who designed the visual data collection methods and the power of interpretative voice returned back to me – particularly during design, analysis and representation of the data. Throughout the data analysis, there was no consultation with any of the participants, and given the subjective nature of the interpretative approach, this could be seen as a flaw in the methodological approach. To minimise this, I used direct quotes from participants; Chandler, Ansty, and Ross (2015) consider this as a way to acknowledge the voices of participants. It is with a view this will maintain acknowledgement of the importance of what the participant boys said and demonstrate how I have interpreted and made judgements upon analysis of the data. I also used examples of images photographed by the boys to link what they did and said to the visual (Denzin & Lincoln, 2013). Mannay (2013, p. 138) refers to the 'auteur theory', which relates directly to the interpretative model and makes connections between the visual and the narrative data. The photo-production focus groups supported this approach because together we were able to discuss the photographs, and the boys verbally discusses and shared their thoughts and opinions. It is with warning that Reiger (2011) argues, 'pictures alone ... are hazardous to interpret without the reinforcement of other information gathered' (cited in Mannay, 2013, p. 138). The 'other information' supporting the visual images comprises the voices of the participant boys upon discussing their images.

Upon reflection, I could have involved the boys in choosing data collection methods by providing options for visual data collection, for example wearable cameras, which are considered to be a research tool for children to watch the footage after they have worn the cameras and to have discussions about their experiences (Green, 2012; Jennings-Tallant, Chapter 9, this volume). Though this tool is closely linked to the photo-production walking tours and focus groups, it may have provided more choice for the children. As Lomax (2012) suggests, providing children with choices generates more meaningful experiences than those generated solely by adults. I also attempted to re-visit the ECE settings upon data analysis, speak to the boys about my findings and have discussions with them. However, I was unable to carry out the latter, as the school setting had various staff changes soon after I completed my main data collection period. I contacted them to re-visit, but I was unable to do so because of hierarchal decisions that it may be too disruptive to the newly employed teachers. These are strategies to consider when designing such data collection techniques, to ensure children are involved as full participants in contrast to semi-participants.

11   Ethical Considerations

Ethical approval was authorised by the university ethics panel prior to any data collection. Nevertheless, ethical practice was persistently deliberated and reflected upon to ensure that participants and ECE settings were safeguarded. Using cameras and photographs where other children are present, and from whom ethical consent may not have been requested, brings ethical challenges, as it is inevitable that some will be in the photographed images. The researcher is responsible for considering how others who have not been asked for nor agreed to consent, but may be captured in images, will have their identities protected (Reavey & Johnson, 2017). To protect other children and adults in this research, no images will be used in the public domain that show those from whom consent has not been approved. In the case that any of these types of images are pertinent to the findings, Reavey and Johnson (2017) advise that the content of the image can be described verbally or facial images can be disguised through the use of digital media techniques, for example Photoshop software, to blur the image.

Ethically, when researching with children in participatory terms, the adult researcher needs to be aware of power relationships, which are understood to be unavoidable in social research. It is generally seen that within the child-adult relationship, the adult holds the power (Einarsdottir, 2005). Nevertheless, because of the chosen innovative research method of producing images and using photographs, Einarsdottir (2005) argues that this type of 'child-friendly' approach will allow the child to feel more at ease with the adult researcher. Nevertheless, Gallacher and Gallagher (2008) argue that 'child-friendly' methods are frequently claimed to empower children; however, participatory research can actually disempower them. As stated previously, I designed the data collection methods and analysed the data; therefore, it can be disputed that the participant boys were unable to fully exercise their agency, consequently partially disempowering the boys. I do, however, contend that using a child-friendly visual component as a tool to engage participation actively engaged the boys, leading to empowerment, as supported by Del Busso (2011, cited by Silver, 2013).

12 Future Possibilities for Visual Data Collection Methods with Young Children

Visual methods, whether they are photo-production or photo-elicitation (Silver, 2013) methods, wearable cameras (Green, 2016) or different forms of visual media, are undoubtedly becoming popular data collection tools to engage children in the research process. Digital media and the production of photographs have become increasingly popular and represent how we interact with the world around us (Reavey & Johnson, 2017), relating directly to the phenomenological approach in this study.

Visual methods support children in becoming participatory in the research process and active agents relating to the world around them, and through images, they are able to voice – both verbally and non-verbally – their own thoughts and perceptions of their experiences. For researchers using qualitative research methodologies such as phenomenology, the use of the visual and imagery can enhance and provide rich data directly from those they are researching with – in this case children. It is well-known that research involving young children is imperative for understanding their lives (Clark & Statham, 2005; Graham et al., 2013); therefore, more needs to be made of child-friendly data collection tools. We must advocate for different types of visual data collection tools to continue to grow in popularity and move away from traditional methods, such as observing children or collecting data from adults' perspectives. Whilst these data collection tools still have their place, new and innovative visual methodologies should be considered in the world of research. I argue that additional literature is needed in the movement for researchers to engage in the visual and feel confident in this approach.

13   Summary Statements

– Walking tours and photo-production focus groups are undeniably valuable and form a rich data collection tool when conducting research with young children in the real-life world. While such a tool presents challenges,. the researcher needs to see past them and find solutions.
– The participatory research framework and the adoption of visually oriented data collection methods provide opportunities to research 'with' and not 'on' children, where they can participate in research and become active agents.
– The researcher must be aware of children's positions and consider the research design from initial design to data analysis and findings, with acknowledgement of the young children's positions as semi or full participants.

14   Conclusion

It is acknowledged that adults recognise that children perceive the world differently, so when designing and deploying data collection methods aimed at uncovering phenomenological meaning, creative participatory methods must be highly considered (Green, 2016). The use of creative visual data collection methods in this study unquestionably supported the creation of meaning from young boys' perspectives of their ECE learning environment and pedagogical experiences. The walking tours and photo-production focus groups engaged them in the data collection activities and yielded rich data from the images that were generated and the discussions that took place. It is recognised that the boys were not full participants throughout the research and were in fact semi-participants; I recommend that researchers consider ways in which to include children from the initial research design of child-led visual methods through to the analysis of the data and findings. Representation of children's voices is crucial if we, as adults, are to attempt to understand and interpret their lived experiences. Building visual data collection tools into research design has the potential to contribute to knowledge; the researcher can not only interpret verbal meaning, but also develop opportunities to analyse the 'seeing'. Despite the challenges, I argue that visual approaches when researching with young children are particularly valuable methods for gaining insight into those children's views, perceptions and opinions of their environments.

References

Chandler, R., Ansty, E., & Ross, H. (2015). Listening to voices and visualizing data in qualitative research. *SAGE Open, 5*(2), 1–8.

Clark, A., & Statham, J. (2005). Listening to young children: Experts in their own lives. *Adoption and Fostering, 29*(1), 45–56.

Dahlberg, H., & Dahlberg, K. (2003). To not make definite what is indefinite: A phenomenological analysis of perception and its epistemological consequences in human science research. *The Humanistic Psychologist, 31*(4), 34–50.

Denzin, N., & Lincoln, Y. (2013). *The landscape of qualitative research.* Sage.

Diprose, R., & Reynolds, J. (2014). *Merleau-Ponty: Key concepts.* Routledge.

Dowling, M., & Cooney, A. (2012). Research approaches related to phenomenology: Negotiating a complex landscape. *Nurse Researcher, 20*(2), 21–27.

Einarsdottir, J. (2005). Playschool in pictures: Children's photographs as a research method. *Early Child Development and Care, 175*(6), 523–541.

ESRC. (2012). *ESRC Framework for Research Ethics (FRE) 2010: Updated September 2012.* Retrieved from http://www.esrc.ac.uk/files/funding/guidance-for-applicants/ esrc-framework-for-research-ethics-2010/

Gallacher, L., & Gallagher, M. (2008). Methodological immaturity in childhood research? Thinking through 'participatory methods'. *Childhood, 15*(4), 499–516.

Graham, A., Powell, M., Taylor, N., Anderson, D., & Fitzgerald, R. (2013). *Ethical research involving children.* UNICEF Office of Research – Innocenti.

Gray, D. (2014). *Doing research in the real world* (3rd ed.). Sage.

Green, C. (2016). Sensory tours as a method for engaging children as active researchers: Exploring the use of wearable cameras in early childhood research. *International Journal of Early Childhood, 48,* 277–294.

Gurian, M., & Stevens, K. (2005). *The minds of boys: Saving our sons from falling behind in school and life.* Jossey-Bass.

Lomax, H. (2012). Contested voices? Methodological tensions in creative visual research with children. *International Journal of Social Research Methodology, 15*(2), 105–117.

Mannay, D. (2013). 'Who put that on there ... why why why?' Power games and participatory techniques of visual data production. *Visual Studies, 28*(2), 136–146.

Marshall, J. (2014). *Introduction to comparative and international education.* Sage.

Reavey, P., & Johnson, K. (2017). Visual approaches: Using and interpreting images. In C. Willig & W. Rogers (Eds.), *The Sage handbook of qualitative research in psychology* (2nd ed.). Sage.

Reichart, M., Kuriloff, P., & Stoudt, B. (2009). What can we expect? A strategy to help schools hoping for virtue. In W. Martino, M. Kehler, & M. Weaver-Hightower (Eds.), *The problem with boys' education: Beyond the backlash* (pp. 56–81). Routledge.

Sargeant, J., & Harcourt, D. (2012). *Doing ethical research with children.* McGraw-Hill Education.

Silver, J. (2013). Visual methods. In C. Willig (Ed.), *Introducing qualitative research in psychology* (3rd ed.). McGraw-Hill Education.

Sloan, A., & Bowe, B. (2013). Phenomenology and hermeneutic phenomenology: The philosophy. The methodologies, and using hermeneutic phenomenology to investigate lecturers' experiences of curriculum design. *Quality & Quantity, 48*, 1291–1303.

Smith, J., Flowers, P., & Larkin, M. (2009). *Interpretative phenomenological analysis: Theory, method and research.* Sage.

St. Pierre, E., & Jackson, A. (2014). Qualitative data analysis after coding. *Qualitative Inquiry, 20*(6), 715–719.

von Eckartsberg, R. (1989). The unfolding meaning of intentionality and horizon in phenomenology. *The Humanistic Psychologist, 17*(2), 146–160.

Warrington, M., & Younger, M. (2006). *Raising boys' achievement in primary schools.* McGraw-Hill Education.

Weaver-Hightower, M. (2009). Issues of boy's education in the United States. In W. Martino, M. Kehler, & M. Weaver-Hightower (Eds.), *The problem with boys' education: Beyond the backlash* (pp. 1–35). Routledge.

White, M., & Murray, J. (2016). Seeing disadvantage in schools: Exploring student teachers' perceptions of poverty and disadvantage using visual pedagogy. *Journal of Education for Teaching, 42*(4), 500–515.

Willig, C. (2013). *Introducing qualitative research in psychology* (3rd ed.). McGraw-Hill Education.

Willig, C., & Rogers, W. (2017). *The Sage handbook of qualitative research in psychology* (2nd ed.). Sage.

CHAPTER 11

Visual Methodology
Processing Relational Pedagogy

Avis Ridgway, Gloria Quinones and Liang Li

1 Introduction

This chapter draws upon the wholeness approach, advanced by Hedegaard (2008), to exemplify the use of a visual research methodology for processing relational pedagogy in early childhood education (ECE). Through the dialectic formed, researchers illuminate the wholistic process of research collaboration for toddlers (two-year-olds). They identified a video clip to analyse ball play with two-year-olds from one long-day care (LDC) centre in Australia. Analysis of the selected video clip provided multiple perspectives for processing relational pedagogy and generating wholistic knowledge about educational research with two-year-olds.

The focus of this chapter is on the dialectical perspectives used to process a video that creates meta-awareness for three culturally diverse researchers and participants. Researchers purposefully viewed, reviewed and discussed a short video clip, thus creating a shared metanarrative. The conception of shared and rich intercultural dialogue amongst those three researchers mediated a meta awareness of the video. Furthermore, researchers generated a visual metanarrative methodology using a complex, expansive method of our own making that can capture nuanced moments of toddlers, educators and researchers' responses. Encountering different, all-embracing perspectives, the researchers use of one video clip provokes mutual dialogue around the action and meaning present in processing relational pedagogy.

The research question we explore is twofold: *How does visual methodology illuminate a wholistic process of generating metanarratives, and how does the creation of a metanarrative enrich understandings of relational pedagogy?*

2 Cultural-Historical Theoretical Framework

The chapter takes a cultural-historical theoretical approach in order to unpack the complex narrative process of researching relational pedagogy. Taking this perspective supports diversity and contradiction, which are viewed as opportunities for illuminating existing ideas and generating new ones.

3   A Wholeness Approach and Dialectical Process to Research

Hedegaard's (2008) wholeness approach encompasses different institutional settings, including three perspectives – societal, institutional and personal – all of which must be considered when studying children. In this chapter, we expand this view by including the researcher's perspective in order to process relational pedagogy in ECE. The societal perspective involves traditions and values specific to a society – in this case, Australian society – and the practice tradition of play-based learning. The institutional perspective involves everyday practices in day care, where we pay attention to the interactions between educators and toddlers in an activity, to process relational pedagogy. The personal or individual perspective involves the participation of individuals in the institution; for example, the child and the educator have their own personal motives and intentions.

Hedegaard's wholeness cultural-historical approach aims to frame the child's development as a dialectical and dynamic process: 'a recursive intertwining of person and society' (Edwards, Fleer, & Bøttcher, 2019, p. 3). The research questions are driven by practice and by the activity setting of the person being studied (Hedegaard, 2008). The concept of dialectic is taken as a dynamic movement among individuals, institutions and society. The adult-child relation also needs to be treated as a dialectical movement. As Rainio and Hilppö (2017) discuss, dialectical movement and contradictions are seen as negotiated activities that invite different forms of participation between the adult and children. The need to identify these contradictions is important for educators' work; an example in the intersection of adults' control and children's initiative to have freedom and be independent and creative (Rainio & Hilppö, 2017).

In this chapter, our focus is on the analysis of a video clip of play activity between toddlers and educators, with the purpose of enriching understandings of relational pedagogy. A wholeness and dynamic approach includes varied perspectives realised through mutual dialogue.

4   Mutual Dialogue

Gonzalez Rey's (2016) proposal that 'our relationship with our surroundings always implies that living activities existing within the intertwined flow of many unfolding avenues, open themselves during the course of activity' (p. 179) encourages our active use of mutual dialogue. We argue that mutual dialogue enables wholistic research and, in turn, through joint actions undertaken with shared intention, each participant can be consciously oriented to the others' presence (Bruner, 1991; El'konin & Vygotsky, 1987). In joint action, we purposefully engage with the process of mutual dialogue that has possibilities for uniting our varied narrative interpretations of the visual data (Ridgway, Li, & Quinones, 2016). Gonzalez Rey (2017) argues, 'dialogue is only possible between subjects, between persons empowered by their capacity of assuming singular positions in the relations with others' (p. 188). Dialogue is a valuable research tool in this study, as researchers and participants are active subjects in creating expression within dialogue, rather than exhausting it.

Elsewhere, visual methodology (without the metanarrative) is defined as offering a post-developmental methodology (beyond ages and stages thinking) for our research into very young children's pedagogical play practices (Fleer & Ridgway, 2014). In terms of practice, visual methodology uses video to instantly capture moments of change or transformation that may hold conceptual and contextual interest for researchers. However, this chapter aims to highlight the extended use of visual narrative methodology through mutual dialogue between researchers and participants. Researchers extend mutual dialogue by placing emphasis on the articulation of communicative, interactive, living practices, viewed in the context of one video clip.

The term visual metanarrative acknowledges that by extending the research process to see beyond visual narrative methodology, greater emphasis is placed on the need for awareness of the wholistic characteristics of mutual dialogue. On closer inspection of visual data, and through continued collaborative writing, we realise that a sustained, shared and co-constructed mutual dialogue starts forming. As self-observers and observers of the video clip (Hakkarainen, Bredikyte, Jakkula, & Munter, 2013), our collective effort to extend the understandings and meanings of relational pedagogy becomes a space of relational complexity.

5 Visual Methodology

In video clip usage, Pink (2001) challenges the authenticity and validity of researchers' visual narratives. Pink argues that visual narratives can be edited and re-organised to represent multiple perspectives. In this research, one video clip is interrogated, and the context of its creation from a larger video data set reflects our extended project: *Educators of babies and toddlers*: *developing a culture of critical reflection* (Quinones, Li, & Ridgway, 2016).

In the larger project, researchers generated 44 h (8 h for five educators and 4 h for one educator) of video observations of everyday practices in visits to three LDC centres. Generating video of toddlers supports the production of screenshot capture images for visual narrative methodologies that can reflect, image-by-image, 'the collective, imaginary, and emotional nature of participatory action' of educators and toddlers (Ridgway, Li, & Quinones, 2016, p. 4) and affective moments of everyday life (Quinones, 2016). After videoing educators and toddlers' practices at three different LDC centres, three collaborative forums with six educators were held over 6 months (Quinones, Li & Ridgway, 2018). A total of 17 h and 3 h of paired interviews were recorded in the collaborative forums. Educators were expected to generate an understanding of specialised pedagogy in toddler education through mutual dialogue, and selected video clips were viewed in those forums to prompt educators' personal perspectives of pedagogical practices.

In this chapter, we particularly focus on the participating educator, Jo, from one of the LDC centres. Jo's ball play with a small group of toddlers, discussed in the third collaborative forum, elicited participants' mutual dialogue. Jo and her colleague, Peta, who participated in the project, worked in adjoining infant-toddler rooms.

6   Creation of Metanarrative Taking Different Perspectives

Our shared video clip research discussion was audio recorded whilst we simultaneously wrote notes of what we saw, felt and thought. We took turns reading those notes to one another, thereby enacting a listening pedagogy (Dahlberg & Moss, 2005; Rinaldi, 2006). In these moments of listening and dialogue exchange, dramatic complexity and contradictions are produced. In triadic trust, we each elaborate and encounter one another's ideas as ontological enrichment. The creation of a metanarrative is configured within this complex mutual dialogue of articulated, interactive and subjective expression (Gonzalez Rey, 2017). This might reveal relational and pedagogical processes seen, or perceived, in the visual data.

7   Case Example: 'Ball Play' Processing Relational Pedagogy

An example of meta-analytical work within the scope of cultural-historical research is presented. LDC educators Jo and Peta's joint conversation illuminates educators' perspectives. Furthermore, their responses to a given video clip extend mutual dialogue with the researcher to build on 'dialogue commentary', used by Ridgway, Li and Quinones (2016). Dialogue commentary brings a first perspective of interpretative analysis and synthesis to video clip data, and by extending the discussion through mutual dialogue, researchers' subjective gaze provokes different perspectives. These involve educator Jo's holistic use of communication and space, found in her improvised, imaginative and specialised pedagogical practice. A synthesis of findings from toddlers and educators' perspectives brings conceptualised knowledge of relational pedagogy, which develops the researcher's perspectives for interpretative analysis to address our research questions holistically.

7.1 *Dynamic Perspectives of Analytical Framework*

Dawn (2016) argues, 'There is often an over-investment in visual and narrative techniques that fails to recognise the holistic process of fieldwork' (p. 87). To achieve research aims in identifying toddlers' specialised relational pedagogy, we use a holistic process of data generation and analysis. Our research efforts suggest that through trust and mutual dialogue, using a holistic process of data generation can reveal the images and perspectives of children in LDC, as well as those of the educators and researchers.

8   Case Example: Toddlers' Ball Play with Educator

Holistic views of toddlers, educators and researchers in the LDC centre were captured using two video recorders that filmed children's interactions with peers and educators. One camera focused on toddlers' movements and interactions, and another on educators' working social environment. The case example captured and synthesised a short visual narrative of processing relational methodology. Moreover, still shots from a video clip (see Figures 11.1–11.4) were used to create a metanarrative.

8.1 *Toddler's Perspective*

The following visual narrative focuses on children's participation in ball play.

Toddler educator Jo participator in outdoor ball play (Figure 11.1).

Jo participates in an imaginary situation of ball play that appears, to her, to be filled with the promise of playful throwing and catching of the red ball.

Four two-year-old toddlers, Gen, Sam, Isa and Tim (pseudonyms), engage with Jo (Figure 11.2).

FIGURE 11.1
Ball play starts
randomly (still from
video)

FIGURE 11.2
Ball clutched close to
body (still from video)

Educator Jo: 'Gen has got it! Yah Gen, catch Sam!'
Isa holds tightly onto the ball.

Toddlers' spontaneous activity flows around the movement of the red ball,
guided at times by Jo, who names different toddlers to indicate whose turn it is
to throw or catch the ball (Figure 11.3).

FIGURE 11.3
Jo catches ball (still from video)

Educator Jo: 'Oooh oh Sam. You throw big throws. Stand back a little bit, stand back, ready one two yeah'.

Ball play becomes a semi-formalised game, as toddlers take turns to catch and throw. Jo positions the toddlers for collective play, and issuing on-going dialogue commentary, Jo's expressive language flows. Her affective intentionality and expectations for ball play result in keeping the red ball in action as toddlers hold out their arms and point to the person whose turn is next (Figure 11.4).

FIGURE 11.4
Toddlers form ball play group (still from video)

8.2   *Revealing Holistic Process in Mutual Dialogue*

The initial analysis begins by taking a wholeness approach to mutual dialogue between toddlers' educators and researchers, and a metanarrative is achieved when researchers and participants engage in communicative exchanges. Mutual dialogue could be defined as a psychological tool for extending thinking (Hakkarainen & Bredikyte, 2014). The social environment and the way in which visual data are interrogated merge during researchers' mutual dialogue around the ball play video clip. This process symbolises the emergence of an affective, relational dimension where the dynamics of subjective sense are configured through the different expressions of the subjects (toddlers, educators Jo and Peta, and the researcher) in mutual dialogue (Gonzalez Rey, 2017).

The interactions between Jo and the toddlers demonstrate different forms of participating. For example, one child is observing, while another one is looking at the red ball, and the toddler in the middle looks at the educator (see Figure 11.3). All the toddlers have different forms of participation (Rainio & Hilppö, 2017). A relational pedagogy also involves a balance of dialectical contradictions, such as the educator's engagement in the ball play and the children's freedom to participate. The visual narrative provides a dialectical and dynamic process to study toddlers in play and to process the relational pedagogy of educator Jo.

8.3   Educators' Perspective

Educators' Jo and Peta, who work in adjoining LDC rooms, were paired in this dialogue. The researcher shared Jo's ball play video clip with the educators in the final collaborative forum and recorded their comments. The below transcript of Jo and Peta's mutual dialogue demonstrates that they actively and subjectively reveal their positions in relational pedagogy (Gonzalez Rey, 2017).

Researcher:	So, the question, I guess, is how are you part of the children's world, after seeing that video?
Jo:	Suggestions, again I knew what I was doing when I went in doing it, but I guess you don't see the importance of it all, or what you're doing until you see it like this. (As shown in video clip of ball play)
Researcher:	What do you notice about yourself, Jo?
Jo:	Talking a lot, questioning, asking them, giving turns, like ... his turn, naming. Waiting a little bit. I thought that I waited a fair bit. Not a fair bit, but I waited a little bit in between to see what they'd do ...
Peta:	[*often finishes Jo's sentences*] ... To decide what she wanted to do when she came over with the ball, and you said to Gen, 'no Gen you've got to wait. She's got the ball; let's see what she wants to do' sort of thing, and then you sort of, well, 'do you want to throw it to here', and then that's where it sort of escalated, but then Isa sort of came in, and I liked that you gave the option as well.
Jo:	It was up to Isa if she wanted to play with other people or if she wanted to go off on her own, but yeah, and then as you engaged them, yeah it was questioning, 'oh, who's going to get the ball?' and 'who are you going to throw it to?' and then also that genuine excitement of 'wow that was a big throw' and yeah. Just really just allowing the children to decide.
Peta:	No, just aware, aware of what's going on with the children and your language. Involved, because you (Jo) involved yourself with them. Encouraged taking turns and sharing, supporting children's developing relationships. Giving time for them to respond. I had ... yeah observing.

Researcher: So, you were watching everything that was going on, your genuine excitement for when they were actually taking turns and throwing it to each other and catching it ...

Jo and Peta's mutual dialogue acknowledges the importance of Jo's affective engagement with toddlers' group ball play. Affective engagement, an important dimension of play, 'consists of the child's agentic capabilities to jointly engage with the educator' (Ridgway, Quinones, & Li, 2015, p. 48). Furthermore, Jo creates an affective and intentional relational approach to play that extends to a metanarrative when ideas are shared, and Jo's colleague, Peta, extends the pedagogical narrative of ball play by emphasising the importance of giving toddlers choices in play. The researcher re-confirms the educator's effectiveness and affectiveness in the ball play video. In addition, educator Jo creates 'an affective attitude on how their joint play might be imagined' (2015, p. 48). Furthermore, the dialogical space is structured to capture each subjective sense that emerges in the research process, and a metanarrative of relational pedagogy eventually forms. Jo explains her relational pedagogy in giving toddlers waiting time, displaying genuine excitement and respecting toddlers' agentic capabilities by offering choices. Peta extends this metanarrative by generating a relational pedagogy in mutual dialogue that supports toddlers' relationships.

8.4   *Director's Perspective*

For the final stages of data collection, the researchers shared preliminary findings with the LDC centre directors, delivering oral presentations and discussions at each centre. The whole process reminds us of the importance of capturing institutional perspectives in educators' pedagogical practices, as evident in the LDC director's response after watching Jo's ball play video. The LDC director stated that

> the video just highlights her (Jo) overarching principles and values and what she does, and that is in her promise ... It really shows the best practices with children ... she and Peta, really acknowledge each other's work in the shared space.

The LDC director continued, thinking about other best practices in the centre:

> The milk time is quite busy ... I always suggest to the educators 'could anyone step back and watch what is happening?', and you could see and feel the absolute change because they stop running. It is a good example.

The LDC director reflects the philosophy and values of best practices in response to toddler's activities by inviting educators to stop roaming in a shared space with children and colleagues to more carefully observe and watch. This brings the institutional voice to our attention and offers meaningful reflection on institutional practices.

The institutional voice was extended by the director:

> Jo and I have recently joined the project related to the language we used and the distance of our position to the children's position ... how we can be at the children's level ... give me different positions, approximately 3–4 cm. That is what we learned. We are so conscious about this now. We always watch out going to children's level and different positions in her level.

Institutional practices from the perspective of the LDC director reflect dialogical comments on educators' physical positioning with toddlers. Jo's kneeling in visual snapshots of ball play (Figures 11.1–11.4) illustrates close proximity to toddlers and exemplifies the director's philosophy.

Overall, mutual dialogue with educators, the educational leader and the LDC director enriches the researchers' understandings of Jo's specialised pedagogical practices in toddler play. We can generalise the relational pedagogy of infant-toddler education by acknowledging different perspectives. The toddler's perspectives in the video clip analysis demonstrate the importance of the dialogical and opening character of this research in qualitative epistemology, as the dialogical process stimulates 'the reflections and interest of the participants in the investigation' (Gonzalez Rey & Martinez, 2017).

8.5　*Researchers' Perspective: Dialogue Commentary*

We engaged with this experimental research method with the aim of seeking new, theoretically significant insight into how a metanarrative is formed. The process of participating in mutual dialogue around the video clip, choosing concise words and writing synthesised summaries demonstrates the dialectical perspectives for analysis. Experimenting and playing with words, there emerges anticipation of processing new knowledge about how multiple perspectives enrich the politics of seeing. Acknowledging what each of us gave focus to drove the visualisation and production of a metanarrative. In mutual dialogue, researchers wrote down initial responses to the video clip, later summarising them with independent syntheses. Summaries read to one another bring heightened awareness of the perspectives of analysis afforded by using mutual dialogue as a research tool. In mutual dialogue, we assume similar and singular positions. Gonzalez Rey (2017) argues, 'dialogue is a powerful and valuable tool in our research as the researchers and participants are both as active subjects to create the expression within the dialogue rather than exhaust itself in the dialogue' (p. 188).

Gloria: It was interesting to pay attention to Jo's unspoken intentional pedagogy. Relational pedagogy – almost unseen but important to notice for an affective pedagogy –was found in Jo's touch, voice and the silence that gave flow to the playful event. A sophisticated game emerged with a common purpose and group collaboration with multiple playful exchanges for toddlers. The body was important, as participants pointed, gesturing to one another, to communicate the presence of the red ball. There was waiting time for the interactions to flow that formed part of the relational pedagogy of researchers, who witnessed the toddler group's interaction with the educator. The red ball and the space were important for researchers and educators, immersed in a relational pedagogy, to pay attention to. A game such as catch and throw involved many perspectives that the eye could pay attention to overall; however, it was Jo's delicate, soft voice that provoked the eyes of toddlers, who observed, listened and used their many senses to perceive Jo's metanarrative.

Liang: The relational pedagogical moments were present. Jo's pedagogical positioning can be noticed. She was at child-level and showed her interest in toddler-initiated ball play. She was not only an observer and resource provider, but also a player with the toddlers. Jo's affective engagement attracted more children to join in the play, and being a player allowed her to use simple and clear language, gesture and gaze to communicate with the children. She supported the children's learning about throwing the ball, counting, gaining new vocabulary and turn-taking, among other things. This can also be explained by the shared intention and relational interaction between Jo and the toddlers.

Avis: Relational pedagogy is found in the combination of educator Jo's effective and affective interactions, achieved through the intentional use of pedagogical positioning. As an affective player, Jo kneels at the toddlers' eye level whilst also effectively choosing a playground corner where a thrown ball cannot roll too far. Positioning maximises affective opportunities for Jo and the toddler's mutual participation and dialogue. Jo eagerly gazes at eye level with toddlers, enticing their gathering together as individuals to intentionally form a collective ball-play game. Affective pedagogy is achieved when Jo uses names for toddler turn-taking for inclusion in their catching and throwing. She personalises ball play through the use of 'me' words. Furthermore, her instructive support *effectively* frames the ball game, and *affective pedagogy* resides in Jo's positioning, tone of voice, touch, gesture, comments on action and offers of encouraging responses to toddlers.

As researchers, we created our own process of relational pedagogy. We discussed ideas first, and we then offered our responses and shared ideas for theoretical framing of the video clip data regarding toddlers' ball play. We expressed a shared understanding that all opinions were valuable, and being open-minded in this way would serve to bring richness and validity to our research approach. Each researcher wrote down, using bullet points, his or her immediate thoughts about the video clip. Next, a shared intention was built by listening to one another's ideas, by contributing further ideas and by having courage to disagree and offer other opinions. This required a level of trust and friendship: a 'give and take'; a 'toss and catch'; a 'taking of turns'; and the use of a set of rules, invisible yet still present, as in the video clip. The three researchers' dialogue commentary brought new possibilities for conceptualisation of relational pedagogy. Our metanarrative helped us to locate new knowledge through different ways of 'seeing'.

9   Discussion

For better understanding of educators' specialised relational pedagogy, the holistic process of analysis is framed. According to Li (2014), the holistic approach requires researchers to achieve different perspectives in visual narrative research. A wholeness approach included different perspectives – those of the toddlers, educators, director and researchers – for holistic mutual dialogue. This created the metanarratives of ball play that exemplify processes within relational pedagogy. By having these perspectives, we can now focus on conceptualised knowledge of pedagogy through the process of synthesis of all participants, including the researchers.

Using a visual metanarrative methodology provides researchers with the opportunity for deep analysis to achieve a richer understanding of the interaction, as well as the affective and relational pedagogy, practised with toddlers in LDC and with one another. Table 11.1 illustrates the multiple perspectives of toddlers, educators, LDC directors, and researchers, acknowledged when taking a wholeness approach.

TABLE 11.1   Relational pedagogy achieved in visual metanarrative through mutual dialogue

Metanarratives	Relational pedagogy
Toddlers' perspective	– Interest in group ball play with educator-gesture movement, language
	– Take turns, name peers
Educator's perspective	– Allows toddlers to make decisions and choices in ball play
	– Affective vocal and physical engagement
	– Close positioning at ground level for joint play
	– Wait time allows for flow of ball play
	– Naming toddlers and using gaze and gesture
LDC director's perspective	– Relates closely to educators and toddlers
	– Participates playfully in close proximity to toddlers
Researchers' perspective	– Affective engagement
	– Mutual dialogue
	– Soft voices
	– Written response summaries of video clip action

Through visual metanarrative methodology, it becomes possible for researchers to capture special and particular relational moments of affective engagement. Visual data analysis and development of mutual dialogue among participants and researchers, generates meta narrative understanding of joint play. Identification of multiple perspectives in affective and relational pedagogy illustrated through educators positioning and use of soft voices, shows how intimacy develops in joint play through affective engagement.

10   Conclusion

This chapter aimed to better understand the visual research methodology by illuminating a holistic process for generating metanarratives that unpack educators and toddlers' relational pedagogy. In answering how a small video clip can create a metanarrative, we used a wholeness approach prompted by one small video clip (Figures 11.1–11.4). These perspectives of complex and dialectical relationships, formed in the educators and toddler group's subtle changing moments, derived from mutual dialogue generated among participants and researchers. Our ontological approach of sharing one video clip, and using a screenshot technique to support analysis and synthesis, mimicked the educator's relational pedagogy.

The process of video clip interpretation through interactive discussion began as dialogue commentary, 'a technique used for showing many views that can sometimes highlight the often invisible cultural influences present' (Ridgway, Quinones, & Li, 2015, p. 181). However, we extended the dialogue commentary into mutual dialogue, merging this into the visual metanarrative methodology. The affordances for cultural-historical researchers to see different perspectives revealed specialised pedagogy embedded in toddlers' learning and development, not formerly conceptualised in the field. This makes a small, contemporary contribution to visual qualitative methodology for researching toddlers' education. Furthermore, the visual metanarrative methodology brings relational pedagogy to life by accounting for different perspectives. We extend our research beyond dialogue commentary to a meta level in search of the wholistic perspectives required for transforming video clip activity into affective scientific exploration. As a result, we offer a new, holistic, visual metanarrative methodology to reveal different dialogical and subjective processing of relational pedagogy.

11   Affordances Limitations

We used one video clip of a project participant educator from one centre. The simple moments captured in a video clip become a story of the researchers' shared relational pedagogy of cultural interpretation and reinterpretation. Visual metanarrative methodology affords researchers multiple perspectives and insights into processes of relational pedagogy.

12   Summary Statements

- The visual metanarrative methodology provides wholistic perspectives, bringing to life the dialogical processing of relational pedagogy.
- Mutual dialogue is a powerful tool in our research, placing researchers and participants as active subjects in creating valuable wholeness expression.
- Researchers' dialogue commentary and mutual dialogue provide an opportunity for open-minded collaborative experimentation.
- Different dynamic perspectives (and synthesis) offer a powerful framework for illustrating the ways in which to create metanarratives among researchers and participants, and they generalise a wholeness approach to relational pedagogy.

Acknowledgements

The researchers received a small grant from the Faculty of Education, Monash University, Australia. The university also provided the resources that enabled this study to be undertaken, including allowance for field research assistance from Cynthia Lopez Valenzuela. Furthermore, full ethics approval was granted by the Ethics Committee (CF14/2789 2014001523), Department of Education, and Training (Project ID: 2014_002500). The authors thank the participating educators and children from the three LDC centres, as well as the centre directors and curriculum leader, and appreciate the team work in mutual dialogue.

References

Bruner, J. (1991). The narrative construction of reality. *Critical Inquiry, 18*(1), 1–21.

Dahlberg, G., & Moss, P. (2005). *Ethics and politics in early childhood education*. Routledge Taylor & Francis Group.

Dawn, M. (2016). *Visual, narrative and creative research methods: Application, reflection and ethics*. Routledge.

Edwards, A., Fleer, A., & Bøttcher, L. (2019). Cultural-historical approaches to studying learning and development: Societal, institutional and personal perspectives. In A. Edwards, M. Fleer, & L. Bøttcher (Eds.), *Cultural-historical approaches to studying learning and development, perspectives in cultural-historical research* (pp. 1–20). Springer.

El'konin, D. B., & Vygotsky, L. S. (2001). Symbolic mediation and joint action. *Journal of Russian and East European Psychology, 39*(4), 9–19. http://dx.doi.org/10.2753/RPO1061-040539049

Fleer, M., & Ridgway, A. (Eds.). (2014). *Visual methodologies and digital tools for researching with young children: Transforming visuality*. Springer.

Gonzalez Rey, F. (2016). Advancing the topics of social reality, culture, and subjectivity from a cultural-historical standpoint: Moments, paths, and contradictions. *Journal of Theoretical and Philosophical Psychology, 3*, 175–189.

Gonzalez Rey, F. (2017). Advances in subjectivity from a cultural-historical perspective: Unfoldings and consequences for cultural studies today. In M. Fleer, F. Gonzalez Rey, & N. Veresov (Eds.), *Perezhivanie, emotions and subjectivity: Advancing Vygotsky's legacy* (pp. 173–194). Springer.

Gonzalez Rey, F., & Martinez, A. M. (2017). Epsitemological and methodological issues related to the new challenges of a cultural-historical-based psychology. In M. Fleer, F. Gonzalez Rey, & N. Veresov (Eds.), *Perezhivanie, emotions and subjectivity: Advancing Vygotsky's legacy* (pp. 195–216). Springer.

Hakkarainen, P., & Bredikyte, M. (2014). Understanding narrative as a key aspect of play. In L. Brooker, M. Blaise, & S. Edwards (Eds.), *Play and learning in early childhood* (pp. 240–251). Sage.

Hakkarainen, P., Bredikyte, M., Jakkula, K., & Munter, H., (2013). Adult play guidance and children's play development in a narrative play-world. *European Early Childhood Education Research Journal, 21*(2), 213–225.

Hedegaard, M. (2008). Developing a dialectic approach to researching children's development. In M. Hedegaard & M. Fleer (Eds.), *Studying children: A cultura-historical approach* (pp. 30–45). Open University Press.

Li, L. (2014). A visual dialectical methodology: Using a cultural-historical analysis to unearth the family strategies in children's bilingual heritage language development. In M. Fleer & A. Ridgway (Eds.), *Visual methodologies and digital tools for researching with young children: Transforming visuality* (pp. 35–53). Springer.

Pink, S. (2001). *Doing visual ethnography, images, media and representation in research.* Sage.

Quinones, G. (2016). 'Visual Vivencias' to understand subjectivity and affective connection in young children. *Video Journal of Education and Pedagogy, 1*(3), 1–14. doi:10.1186/s40990-016-0004-1

Quinones, G., Li, L., & Ridgway, A. (2018). Collaborative forum: An affective space for infant-toddler educators' collective reflections. *Australasian Journal of Early Childhood, 43*(2), 25–33.

Rainio, A. P., & Hilppö, J. (2017). The dialectics of agency in educational ethnography. *Ethnography and Education, 12*(1), 78–94.

Ridgway, A., Li, L., & Quinones, G. (2016). Visual narrative methodology in educational research with babies: Triadic play in babies' room. *Video Journal of Education and Pedagogy, 1*(1), 1–18. doi:10.1186/s40990-016-0005-0

Ridgway, A., Quinones, G., & Li, L. (2015). *Early childhood pedagogical play. a cultural-historical interpretation using visual methodology.* Singapore.

Rinaldi, C. (2006). *In dialogue with Reggio Emilia listening, researching and learning.* Routledge and Taylor & Francis Group.

Vygotsky, L. S. (1987). *The collected works of LS Vygotsky: Problems of general psychology thinking and speech* (Vol. 1). Plenum Press.

CHAPTER 12

Bringing Immersive Embodied Visual Methodology to Bear on Play Pedagogies for ECE Teachers

Rene Novak

1 Introduction

Immersive videos taken with a 360-degree 3D camera represent the environment from all viewing points and provide a depth of view. Combined with environmental audio, the virtual representation of the captured event provides the viewer with an immersive experience. These affordances invite new possibilities for empirical research in education that extend the analytical capabilities of the traditional video, including the application of alternative research methods. The methodology that I introduce in this chapter is firmly rooted in the phenomenological research paradigm and includes philosophical contemplation on learning from the visual experience through embodiment theory. The theory of embodiment (Fischer & Coello, 2016; Internet Encyclopedia of Philosophy, 2017; Kiefer & Trumpp, 2012; Varela et al., 1991), when grounded in the phenomenological methodological paradigm, can lead to important insights into cognitive processes that occur while learning is taking place in an immersive experience. By introducing this methodology to the field of visual pedagogies, immersive pedagogy examines the emergence of changes in human cognition as a result of the human mind being exposed to multi-sensory stimuli that are created by VR technology in order to generate new learning.

I propose that this new method is especially useful when studying ambiguous phenomena, such as play; creativity; and cultural, esoteric and spiritualistic practices, where a sense of presence is necessary to learn about a particular phenomenon. Given its ambiguous nature, play is often framed in ways that defy its basic nature (Lewis, 2017); it is thus often misrepresented and misunderstood. Such framing makes play susceptible to malicious manipulation, and it results in an alarming decrease in time and space for free play at home, in the community, in early childhood centres, in schools and in the curricula (Whitebread & O'Sullivan, 2012). To address this issue, some academics stress the need for subjecting play to more philosophical interrogations and phenomenological research (Lewis, 2017; Sutton-Smith, 1997; Whitebread & O'Sullivan, 2012).

The immersive visual methodology described in this chapter signifies a return to learning from experience. It is widely purported that learning is best attained through real-life experiences (Garrett, 1997; Hildebrand, 2016; Jarmon et al., 2009; Nebel et al., 2016), as they allow for the development of individual internal subjective knowledge that consequently alters cognition and enables personal growth (Bell, 2016; DeYoung et al., 2014; Peters, 2010; Weitz, 1956). Dewey (1986), Dale (1970) and Bruner (1966) agree that for learning to be at its most successful, the senses must be strongly involved, and emotions must be invoked. Engaging with multiple senses allows for an embodied experience, and learning through experiences involving senses uninventively causes changes in human conceptions, knowledge, views and attitudes of the world. This process is specifically investigated via embodied phenomenology theory and virtual reality (VR).

2   Embodied Phenomenology and Seeing through VR

Visual representations, such as photographs, sketches and videos, created by the researcher or the participants can become of key importance in embodied phenomenological research (O'Toole & Beckett, 2010). This tradition proposes that the world is always already there, preconstructed for the subject to reflect upon (Merleau-Ponty & Landes, 2012). This is equally true for the virtual world represented in immersive videos as a representation of the real world.

3   What Is Embodied Phenomenology?

Phenomenology was named by Edmund Husserl (Merleau-Ponty & Landes, 2012) and then further contemplated on by various other philosophers such as Heidegger, Gadamer, Satre, Kierkegaard, Hegel, Marx, Nietzsche and Merleau-Ponty (Petty et al., 2012). As often occurs in academia, some of the key concepts of the theory differ, considering theorists' divergent interpretations and views. For instance, while Heidegger and Husserl's phenomenology was sharply disconnected with the sciences, the thinking of Merleau-Ponty and Landes (2012), Dupuis and Wilson (2010) and Varela et al. (1991) engaged phenomenology with disciplines such as cognitive psychology, neuroscience and technological sciences of artificial intelligence. As a result of the favouritism towards these interlinked sciences, phenomenology assumes the embodiment theory, which is a key concept applied to this research methodology and is described next.

The phenomenology of embodiment methodology has been most thoroughly discussed by Edmund Husserl (Internet Encyclopedia of Philosophy, 2017) and later by Merleau-Ponty (Merleau-Ponty & Landes, 2012). In Husserl's phenomenology of embodiment, the body is the centre of experience, where both its movement abilities and its distinguished sensations are of key importance in the way individuals encounter phenomena or other embodied entities in a common, coherent and ever-explorable world (Internet Encyclopedia of Philosophy, 2017). Husserl focused on the importance of experiences forming knowledge production rather than merely viewing it as a form of practical action, as experiences have the ability to re-conceptualise perceptions in any world and may now include the virtual one.

Merleau-Ponty argued, through his work, that a mutual illumination should be applied among a phenomenology of direct, lived experience; psychology; and neuroscience Again – these two sentences need to be re-worked please – for laypeople and clarity On the one hand, the way in which senses biologically perceive experiences is of fundamental importance for this methodology; on the other hand, technology – another branch of science – is beckoned to research phenomena, and cognitive sciences are additionally being employed to understand changes in the cognition of individuals. This view is further supported by Merleau-Ponty's recognition that the dynamics between phenomenology and the science of experience cannot be sufficiently determined without examining the embodiment of knowledge, cognition and experience (Merleau-Ponty & Landes, 2012; Varela et al., 1991).

4 Immersive Visuality as Embodied Phenomenology

A phenomenon that is elusive in its nature in the real world can become uncovered in the metaphysical laboratory of the virtual world. It has the potential to do so through VR technology, which enables experiences to be revisited in four dimensions, with time becoming a manipulative quantity whereupon the user can revisit the same experience multiple times. Therefore, a much deeper 'trawling through' of these experiences as a phenomenological endeavour is more possible than ever before (O'Toole & Beckett, 2010, p. 61). As such, a direct description of the experience as being experienced, without a need to satisfy scientific considerations, can be endorsed in line with this methodological tradition (Merleau-Ponty & Landes, 2012).

Immersive video is a form of VR where the world is viewed as digital and fully virtual – opposite to 'reality'. Everything in between is categorised as 'mixed reality', where elements of the physical and digital are intertwined. Mixed reality can be broken down into two categories:

i.   Augmented reality, which constitutes the physical environment overlaid with a digital layer and an augmented virtuality that is mostly digital with elements from the world.

ii.   Immersive videos seek to represent the real environment in the virtual one, and are hence categorised as a form of VR, being an entirely digital representation of reality represented via a 360-degree 3D camera – the camera used for this research was the VUZE.

Once an immersive video has been created, a researcher is able to represent real-life experiences in the virtual environment. These representations can be 'played back' to viewers through VR headset devices, providing the same immersive experience to multiple individuals and, if needed, on numerous occasions (Kavanagh et al., 2016).

Once an immersive video has been created, a researcher is able to represent real-life experiences in the virtual environment. These representations can be 'played back' to viewers through VR headset devices, providing the same immersive experience to multiple individuals and, if needed, on numerous occasions (Kavanagh et al., 2016).

This development marks a new subdivision of visual methodology, with the defining element of the new tradition evolving beyond mere visual modality into an immersive experience involving a number of different senses and modalities. Through this, I was able to facilitate teachers' pedagogical reflections that were mediated through a representation of 'reality', where early childhood teachers were able to experience a representation of children involved with play at an ECE centre that was recorded in real life. Given the evolution from the visual tradition towards an immersive one, the new branch may be addressed as 'immersive methodology', while the teaching and learning that will result from this pedagogical engagement can be referred to as 'immersive pedagogy'.

5   Understanding Phenomena through Immersive Video: An
         Analytical Framework

To understand the immersive experience as pedagogy through the route of embodied phenomenology, a series of concepts can be utilised to determine how a person engages with a phenomenon from its conception until its end. Eight consecutive stages of engagement are proposed as a source of analytic alignment: ignorance, perception, feeling, craving, grasping, becoming, birth and death.

5.1   Habit/Attitude (Ignorance) Stage

This stage is set before the experience commences for the individual, and it is defined by confusion, mistaken views and emotions that derive from ignorance regarding the phenomenon (Dewey, 1986).

5.2   Contact with the Senses (Perception and Motor Response) Stage

This takes place when the experience starts and is being perceived through the senses of the body. As the sensorial and motor systems are intertwined, motor responses (movement) might be observed during the experience (Fischer & Coello, 2016).

5.3   Feeling (Affection) Stage

This stage is twofold, as it encompasses bodily feelings created through the senses and emotions developed from the contact. What this means in terms of this research is that the stronger the effect of the experienced representation of play on the teacher's feelings, the higher the possibility for changes in attitudes towards play – these should be points for discussion at the interviews.

5.4   Interest (Craving) Stage

Marked by a feeling of imbalance in the person, this stage arises when a conflict exists between current attitudes that do not match with what is being perceived through the experience. For people to change their attitudes, they must follow that craving towards preestablishing balance, which is dependent on their open-mindedness and inquisitiveness.

5.5   Grasping (Reflection)

Here, Dewey (1986) stresses the struggle within the human mind – between what our past self knows and the new knowledge that challenges our past self. Hence, this is where the process of reflection enables the change in conceptions of the mind.

5.6   Formation of New Attitudes (Becoming and Transcendence)

Grasping automatically pulls the individual into becoming (Dewey, 1986) – formatting a new situation in the future, and new attitudes, tendencies and beliefs are being formed because of the new experience.

5.7   New Mode of Being (Birth)

This is the point where comprehensions sets in and new truths about play reveal themselves to the teacher (Merleau-Ponty & Landes, 2012). Even though the experience is about to end, its aftermath has only begun, as this one change will affect a raft of other beliefs and attitudes, and questions should be asked regarding what changes to their practice these new realisations about the phenomenon are going to bring.

5.8   *Conclusion of Experience (Death)*

The experience concludes, and its end is a prelude to the beginning of a new one, for even the same experience will not be perceived in the exact same way. This finding suggests that engagement with the same immersive video on different occasions might bring forth different, or further, understandings about the phenomenon in question.

These eight orienting ways of understanding (conceptually processing) engagement with immersive visualities, underpinned by embodied phenomenology as a methodological orientation, are summarised in Figure 12.1. While play was the phenomenon in question for the present study, it might be replaced by any other phenomenon in this approach, as summarised in the conceptual framework presented in Figure 12.1.

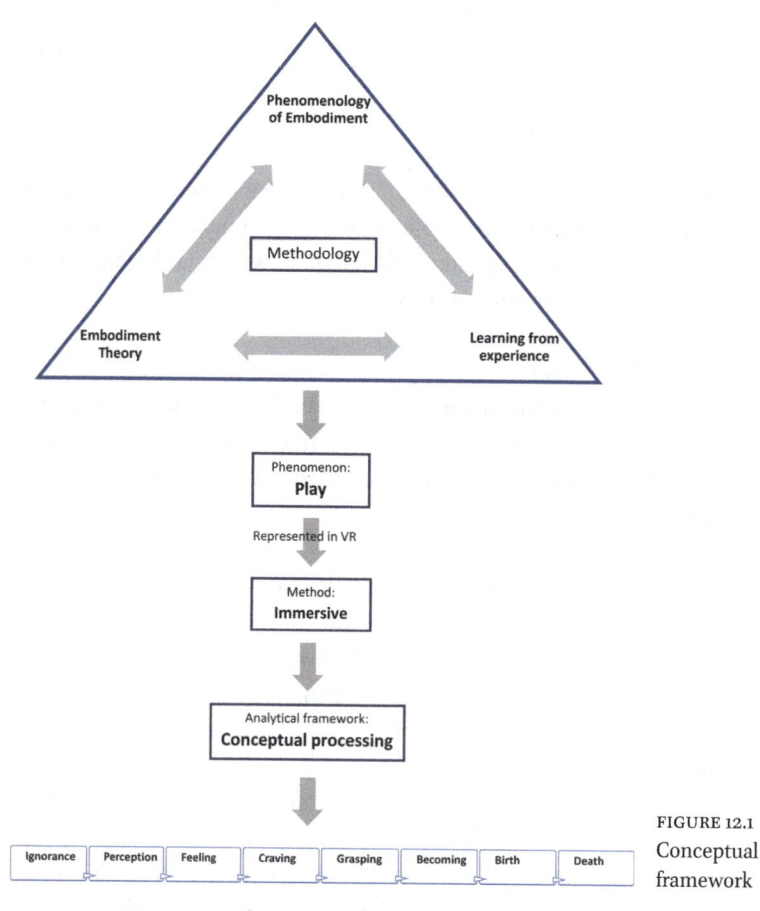

FIGURE 12.1
Conceptual
framework

6 An Application of this Methodological and Conceptual Framework in Understanding Pedagogies for Play

The research that prompted the development of this methodology arose from an inquiry into ECE teachers' understandings of play. Play is deemed to be an ambiguous concept that can best be learned about by experiencing it first-hand (Holst, 2017). Therefore, it can be challenging for adults to see – let alone interpret its significance in real-life – considering ethical constraints and the ability to access play at a certain time and space. Yet teachers are, on a daily basis, expected to make judgements based on their understandings of play and its relevance to children's learning. It was hypothesised that play experiences, represented in the form of immersive videos, might offer new insights for teachers accordingly. The study was conducted at an ECE centre in a room catering for 3- to 5-year-old children. Four teachers took part in the study.

7 Immersive Methods in ECE

An immersive video, portraying children at play at an early-years centre, was played through a VR device to trained teachers in order to establish whether their engagement with it would result in new and/or alternative insights into play.

FIGURE 12.2   Immersive video of children at play (still from video)

Probing interviews were conducted with participating teachers and video-recorded before and after the virtual experience to determine their initial attitudes towards the phenomenon in question and changes in their attitudes after the viewing. Participants were also video recorded whilst using the device to account for any embodied emotional responses that may have manifested during the experience, as well as to determine what they were looking at.

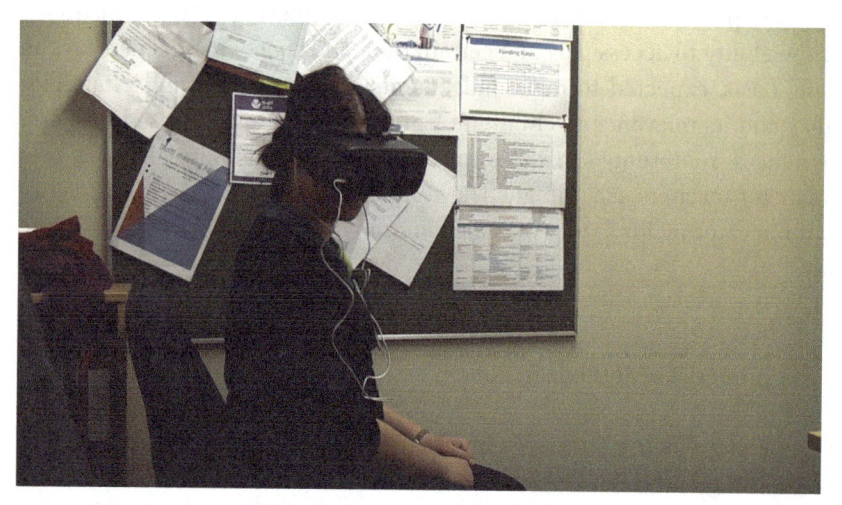

FIGURE 12.3   Teacher viewing the immersive video using the Samsung Galaxy VR device

Observations in this study were informal, as the researcher was non-participatory, and the camera –a traditional digital video camera on a stand – was the instrument recording their responses. Each observation was accompanied by individual interviews with teachers before and after the viewing of the immersive video to obtain in-depth information about their experiences with the video and corresponding views of individuals regarding how their conceptions of the phenomenon in question have changed (if at all). These interviews were conducted before and after the viewing. This method could be described as probing, which has been applied by White (2016), using a polyphonic approach to video record interviews with teachers concerning their pedagogy. Probing also enabled the participants to offer further contextual information about what they experienced in VR, thus contributing to a deeper understanding of the experience. Re-probing generates new cognitive conceptions, in the form of changed or new attitudes, that develop based on the visual surplus and the probing of the researcher, where participants are exploring past experiences from an alternative viewing angle, supported by visual representations and probing questions. Reflecting on perceived phenomena in this way is also a key component of phenomenological research. Hence, the teachers were given a few hours between the engagement with the immersive video and the second interview. Also accordingly, the interview was semi-structured, wherein some open-ended reflective questions were posed (with some opportunities for deviation). The interviews were video recorded, coded and associated with the described analytical framework, which explained the effect of VR technology on reconceptualising cognition about the target phenomenon. Interview data was then directly linked to the reconceptualised changes in cognition or perceptions (as an effect of 'viewing' – or rather experiencing – an evolved form of visual or video tradition).

Typical procedures for this tool include playing episodes of video or audio. However, in the case of this study, a pre-recorded representation of an experience was created for the VR environment in the hopes of propelling viewers' individual recollections of their conception of play beyond their current attitudes, beliefs and understandings. The challenge with interviews after watching videos is usually in distinguishing between participants' recall of and reflection on the viewed event (Cherrington & Loveridge, 2014). However, by applying probing to this study, with the aim of finding the margin between the two in order to illustrate the change in conception, this challenge paradoxically proved to be an advantage.

The interview and observation videos with recorded participants were analysed using the analytical framework above. Coding tags based on these concepts were introduced into an analytic software application (a program called V-note that had previously been tested and utilised by White in her 2020 research on play, where she examined the potential of VR to grant ECE teachers increased insights into play, among other things). The tags served as a coding reference for a number of different aspects of play, observed emotional responses and the affordances and limitations of the VR technology, and they explained the phenomenon in the form of the effects of the technology on the user. Movements of the head and body, vocalisations and facial expressions were also tagged, as were frequencies concerning how long teachers were facing the same direction (watching the same experience). The following screenshot from V-note highlights this analytic process:

A full presentation of the findings is beyond the scope of this chapter.[1] However, for the purposes of illuminating the model that has been presented, the way engaged with play through immersive video is explained.

FIGURE 12.4
V-note analysis excerpt

8   ECE Teachers' Immersive Experiences of Play

The engagement of teachers with the immersive video in this study demonstrated that the method was successful in bringing forth alternative insights about play. Information about certain defining aspects of play needed to be sought from teachers describing their views before and after the viewing of the immersive video about free play; these aspects include the teacher's role in play, space and time to play, play in the curriculum and stakeholders affecting play. For the purpose of this chapter, one example is interpreted using the suggested analytical framework. The most significant change occurred in the teachers' understanding about their role in play, and this factor is hence the focus of the below analysis.

8.1   *Habit/Attitude (Ignorance) Stage*

This stage described the initial views, habits and attitudes of teachers regarding the teacher's role in play before they had any contact with the immersive video. In the first interview, teachers explained that their role in regard to play is to provide opportunities for children to engage in play and for group interactions; to facilitate learning; to encourage; to be a role model and to support children verbally and by making the environment, equipment and resources available to them. Furthermore, they stated that teachers' focus should be on helping the children to become socially competent, confident in who they are and adept at developing relationships and to develop basic literacy and life skills, which are going to be absorbed through play.

During initial interviews (before the viewing), the teachers were mostly focused on the external factors affecting play, such as the environment (28.03% of the time); the formal curriculum (18.47% of the time); and other stakeholders, such as parents, managers and policymakers (27.43% of the time), as indicated in Table 12.1.

8.2   *Contact with the Senses (Perception and Motor Response) Stage*

While teachers were viewing the immersive videos, their movements were recorded. These observed reactions can signify the intensity of play being experienced through their senses. Teachers were quite active throughout the engagement with the immersive video, physically responding to the video in some way for at least 63.67% of the monitored time, with at least one teacher moving his or her head. A teacher was moving on his or her own for 28.11% of the observation, while two teachers moved at once for 19.71%, three at once for 11.33% and all four for 4.52% of the observation. Movement of the body,

TABLE 12.1   Quantitative results for interviews held before and after the viewing of VR content (displaying percentages of instances and total talking time of the video corresponding to the individual play category labels)

Label name	Instances (%)		Total time (%)	
	Before VR	After VR	Before VR	After VR
Free play	17.14	20	13.31	18.73
Teachers role in play	17.14	38.33	12.77	35.80
Space and time to play	26.19	21.67	28.03	21.16
Play in the curriculum	19.05	10.83	18.47	9.31
Stakeholders affecting play	20.48	9.17	27.43	15.00
Sum	100	100	100	100

excluding the head, was lower at 46.12%, with one teacher moving on his or her own for 29.44% of the observation, two together for 12.92%, three for 3.35% and all four for 0.41% of the observation. These results are important, as these physical responses affirm that contact with the senses has been established and that the physiological feelings are present, thus confirming 'perception' and 'feelings' as another two stages of the conceptual processing.

8.3   Feeling (Affection) Stage

Physical feelings were explained above. In the interviews, after the teachers interacted with the immersive videos, they talked about the emotional feelings that were present during the viewing. For example, many teachers expressed emotions they felt towards the children incepting urges to interact with them. Heim (1993) stresses that such feelings perceived through immersive videos can abruptly awaken the inner self, with the combination of physiological and affective feelings transforming the core being of an individual.

8.4   Interest (Craving) Stage

As noted this stage is marked with a feeling of imbalance in the person; this stage arises when conflict exists between current attitudes that do not match with what is being perceived through the experience. In this example, a teacher expressed the imbalance the experience caused for her regarding play, as soon as she took the headset off, saying, 'I do not know what to make of this now', referring to teachers asking too many questions and feeling that these disturbed the natural progression of play. According to Dewey (1986), this imbalance results in the experience becoming a moving force that, through a newly developed curiosity and interest, brings forth a desire to restore balance in the mind by bringing meaning to the experience.

8.5 Grasping (Reflection)

At this stage, grasping occurs through reflection, where several teachers stated that being immersed in the environment and not being able to actively engage with the children forced them to stand back and observe, which created a place for reflection for them. This can be seen as strong evidence that the virtual space can be, as Heim (1993) suggested, a space for reflection that enables seeing alternatives, rather than redundancy (ignorance).

8.6 Formation of New Attitudes (Becoming and Transcendence)

The teachers' engagement with play through this immersive process led to significant shifts concerning their ability to characterise play and their role accordingly. As noted, during initial interviews, teachers were mostly focused on the external factors affecting play, for example the environment (28.03% of the time); the curriculum (18.47% of the time); and other stakeholders, such as parents, managers and policymakers (27.43% of the time), as indicated in Table 12.1. However, by the second interview, teachers' responses shifted from an emphasis on external factors towards the teacher's role in play. Similar shifts were found in discussions concerning the role of the teacher in play. These increased from 17.14 to 38.33%, and the time they were seen to be talking about it increased from 12.77 to 35.8%.

8.7 New Mode of Being (Birth)

Teachers noted that the immersive videos made them reconsider certain aspects of play and that they were now thinking differently about play in some way. On occasion, what they were *thinking* prior to their immersive engagement was not what they were *seeing* in the immersive experience. Hence, this affirms the value the experience had for the ECE teachers, as it can only be judged by the impact it has on a person (Dewey, 1986). Dewey (1986) sees this concept as growing physically, intellectually and morally, where a new situation arises that forms a new mode of being for the teacher. Some of the new attitudes that emerged or were strongly reinforced as a result of engaging with the immersive videos for the ECE teachers included allowing the children more space, not taking over their play, joining in with the children in their play, adults asking too many questions and play looking different when adults are not there. It is worth noting that these realisations have been categorised by play theory (Education Central, 2015; Holst, 2017; Sutton-Smith, 1997;

Whitebread & O'Sullivan, 2012) as fundamental characteristics of play, which teachers were able to see and explain by viewing the virtual representations of play. Furthermore, it should also be noted that a number of teachers have gained the same or similar insights into play from the immersive video.

8.8   *Conclusion of Experience (Death)*

A teacher suggested that engaging with the same immersive video on different occasions might bring forth different, or further, understandings about play, and she thought that using this method at a staff meeting would be useful. Therefore, even though the experience itself concluded, for the teachers it provoked an openness to possibilities for further experiences that would have otherwise not been considered.

9   Affordances and Limitations

As this study has highlighted, examining pedagogical insights through immersive representations of first-hand experiences in the virtual world can be achieved through the use of filmed immersive videos. Users of the technology can indulge in specific and targeted experiences in a controlled environment, which provides researchers with a high level of control over the content and the progression of the experience. This fact accounts for a number of affordances and potentialities in various fields of research, particularly in social sciences.

Immersive videos can facilitate virtual excursions to places that would otherwise be inaccessible because of physical (e.g., visiting the inside of a human body), financial (e.g., arranging a trip to Antarctica for a large group of people), biological (e.g., a paraplegic might not be able to walk through a forest) or psychological constraints (e.g., a person with a phobia of heights might not be able to climb a mountain) (Häfner et al., 2014; Sobota et al., 2016). The technology also enables people to literally 'walk in someone else's shoes' by experiencing the world through another person's eyes via an out-of-body immersive experience, which can have significant implications for people understanding one another across race, ethnicity, profession, sexual orientation and culture (Bailenson, 2018).

However, understanding and researching complex and elusive phenomena such as play and creativity, as well as cultural, esoteric and spiritual experiences, offer additional challenges – especially if these have been mediated through second-hand mediums, such as text or other people's explanations. Nevertheless, when such phenomena are being experienced in an embodied way, alternative connections, understandings and ways of 'seeing' are established (Garrett, 1997; Heim, 1993). Such experiences can be simulated and mediated cross-modally and in multi-sensory ways by using immersive videos. Furthermore, these recorded experiences can be revisited multiple times and by several people, capacitating several research applications and creating novel opportunities in education for reflection on practice.

While experiences are simulated in VR, it is important to note that these are representations of experiences (Coyne, 1994; Heidegger, 1996) and not experiences themselves. It is thus not yet clear whether phenomena from the real world can be transposed into the real world accurately enough for them to retain their defining features, nor whether the technology is advanced enough to provide the level of immersion required for an unadulterated embodied cognition. The fact that some of the participants in the study felt slight nausea tends to signal that the body noticed a misalignment between the external and internal senses (sensory conflict), causing what has become known as VR sickness. It has been established that by improving immersion, the sickness caused by VR diminishes or disappears (Suarez, 2018). It should also be noted that the device used in the study (Samsung Gear VR) was not a high-end device; however, it was the best mobile option available at the time. High-end devices such as the Oculus Rift and HTC Vive need a highly capable computer attached to them with a number of sensors, which make its transportation and set-up more difficult, and they are also much more expensive (especially if we factor in the need for a powerful computer).

10 The 'How to' Section with Links to Relevant Software, Where Appropriate, and Examples from Research

Immersive videos are generated with the help of an omnidirectional camera that is able to capture all viewing angles (360 degree) and supports a stereoscopic (3D) perception of depth. The user of a VR head-mounted device can view immersive videos repeatedly through an immersive virtual experience of the digitised environment. Audio is usually conveyed to the user through stereo headphones that create a 3D audial environment that, along with the visual experience, provides a cross-modal and multi-sensory experience that considerably increases immersion. A number of haptic suits are in development that will provide further modalities to the immersive experience. The Tesla suit, for example, adds the modality of touch through haptic feedback and warmth or cold through its climate control system (Teslasuit Inc., 2018). Some technological advancements are also beginning to involve the senses of smell, taste and motion to further advance digitally induced immersion (Naimark, 2018).

The 360-degree 3D camera used in this research was the VUZE camera, which has eight cameras that together generate a stereoscopic 360-degree video that can be viewed in all directions and that has a separate video stream for each eye, enabling depth of perception (3D). The camera performed well for its price; however, the researcher would have still appreciated a higher resolution. Whilst the camera creates a 4K resolution video when it is stretched across the 360-degree view, the picture quality does not feel particularly sharp and hence detracts from the sense of immersion to a degree. Furthermore, the camera comes with dedicated software to download and process the video, and while the application is user friendly, a moderate video editing proficiency is still required to use some of the more advanced features to correct and enhance the video.

A suitable video playing application is required to play an immersive video, and depending on what device is being used, the availability and the brand of such software will vary. For the study in question, as previously mentioned, a Samsung Gear VR was used. It utilises a Samsung phone's screen and processing power as it fits into the device, and ear phones attach to the phone to take care of the audio. The video playback application used was 'Samsung VR', previously known as 'Samsung Milk VR'. As the researcher, I would now recommend using the HTC Vive Pro (as the currently best performing VR device on the consumer market) that provides for a higher level of immersion with a better screen, higher refresh rate, faster responses, better tracking and higher level of comfort. The device is linked in with the Steam VR and VivePort, both of which have an array of applications available to handle 360-degree video viewing.

For coding videos in this research, the V-note application was used. V-note is a collaborative video analysing software that enables multiple videos to be played while simultaneously coding and transcribing. It is an application packed with features that enables collaboration across distances with a fast and well-supported learning curve for researchers.

11   Ethical Considerations

Virtual reality technology as a new approach to research brings with it several as-yet-unexplored advantages and unknown risks. Therefore, careful considerations must be made to anticipate any unforeseen circumstances that may arise. For example, as immersive videos record in all directions, a passer-by who has not given consent might appear in the video, and there is no way to focus the view of the camera in only one direction. The researcher would need to carefully examine the videos taken in all directions for potential un-consenting people appearing or unwanted situations that may breach previously negotiated ethical conditions.

On the other hand, VR technology offers affordances that will simplify ethical approval in other circumstances. For example, an assurance of personal anonymity can be asserted if a subject appears in the VR space as an avatar, thus diminishing ethical risks when working with virtual children that may replace real children. However, such technologies have yet to find their fullest expression in ECE research.

12   Future Possibilities

Early childhood teaching practice is permeated with ambiguity (Sutton-Smith, 1997), and children's play is only one example. As this methodology has proven to be effective in enabling teachers to develop alternative insights into the true nature of an educational phenomenon such as play, it could be applied in investigating a much wider range of educational phenomena in ECE, such as culture, creativity, imagination and various other aspects of the ECE curriculum. Furthermore, the technology that was applied in this research can be seen as outdated today, as much better devices have since been developed. These advancements would make the experience more immersive and consequently strengthen all the stages of conceptual processing. Immersive videos themselves have recently evolved into interactive immersive videos, where ECE teachers could now be presented with choices in their experience that would allow them to branch off into a number of different immersive videos. This capability offers an exciting extension to the application of the immersive video in research, and it creates a need to further develop this methodology for alternative uses in ECE, in other sectors of education and more widely in other disciplines.

13   Summary Statements

- Immersive videos are a form of VR that signifies a move in research methodology from visual methodologies towards immersive ones.
- Immersive videos have the capability to simulate a real-life educational experience in a virtual representation.
- The importance of learning by experiencing the world through the body and with the mind is explained by the embodiment theory, which can be used to explain immersion in VR.

– Learning through cross-modal and multisensory experiences in VR enables shifts in conceptions and insights concerning phenomena.
– Various software applications and devices are required. Moderate ICT knowledge is thus needed to operate this methodology, and the technology itself can be costly.
– A number of ethical affordances and risks can arise with the use of VR technology for research.

Note

1   Interested readers may like to read my PhD thesis – due for submission in August 2020 to University of Waikato, NZ.

References

Bailenson, J. (2018). *Experience on demand: What virtual reality is, how it works, and what it can do* (1st ed.). W. W. Norton & Company, Inc.

Bell, D. R. (2016). Learning, play, and creativity: Asobi, Suzuki Harunobu, and the creative practice. *The Journal of Aesthetic Education, 50*(4), 86–113.

Bruner, J. S. (1966). *Toward a theory of instruction.* Belknap Press of Harvard University Press.

Cherrington, S., & Loveridge, J. (2014). Using video to promote early childhood teachers' thinking and reflection. *Teaching and Teacher Education, 41*, 42–51. https://doi.org/10.1016/j.tate.2014.03.004

Coyne, R. (1994). Heidegger and virtual reality: The implications of heidegger's thinking for computer representations. *Leonardo, 27*(1), 65. https://doi.org/10.2307/1575952

Dale, E. (1970). A truncated section of the cone of experience. *Theory into Practice, 9*(2), 96–100.

Dewey, J. (1986). Experience and education. *The Educational Forum, 50*(3), 241–252. https://doi.org/10.1080/00131728609335764

DeYoung, C. G., Quilty, L. C., Peterson, J. B., & Gray, J. R. (2014). Openness to experience, intellect, and cognitive ability. *Journal of Personality Assessment, 96*(1), 46–52. https://doi.org/10.1080/00223891.2013.806327

Education Central. (2015). Play-based learning: Producing critical, creative and innovative thinkers. Retrieved from https://educationcentral.co.nz/play-based-learning-producing-critical-creative-and-innovative-thinkers-2/

Fischer, M. H., & Coello, Y. (Eds.). (2016). *Foundations of embodied cognition. Volume 2: Conceptual and interactive embodiment.* Routledge, Taylor & Francis Group. https://www.routledge.com/Conceptual-and-Interactive-Embodiment-Foundations-of-Embodied-Cognition/Fischer-Coello/p/book/9781138805835

Garrett, L. (1997). Dewey, Dale, and Bruner: Educational philosophy, experiential learning, and library school cataloging instruction. *Journal of Education for Library and Information Science, 38*(2), 129. https://doi.org/10.2307/40324216

Häfner, P., Häfner, V., & Ovtcharova, J. (2014). Experiencing physical and technical phenomena in schools using virtual reality driving simulator. In P. Zaphiris & A. Ioannou (Eds.), *Learning and collaboration technologies. Technology-rich environments for learning and collaboration* (LNCS, Vol. 8524, pp. 50–61). Springer International Publishing. https://doi.org/10.1007/978-3-319-07485-6_6

Heidegger, M. (1996). *The question concerning technology and other essays* (W. Lovitt, Trans.). Harper and Row.

Heim, M. (1993). *The metaphysics of virtual reality*. Oxford University Press.

Hildebrand, D. L. (2016). The paramount importance of experience and situations in Dewey's democracy and education. *Educational Theory, 66*(1–2), 73–88.

Holst, J. (2017). The dynamics of play – Back to the basics of playing. *International Journal of Play, 6*(1), 85–95. https://doi.org/10.1080/21594937.2017.1288383

Internet Encyclopedia of Philosophy. (2017). *Husserl, Edmund: Phenomenology of embodiment*. Retrieved from http://www.iep.utm.edu/husspemb/

Jarmon, L., Traphagan, T., Mayrath, M., & Trivedi, A. (2009). Virtual world teaching, experiential learning, and assessment: An interdisciplinary communication course in second life. *Computers & Education, 53*(1), 169–182. https://doi.org/10.1016/j.compedu.2009.01.010

Kavanagh, S., Luxton-Reilly, A., Wüensche, B., & Plimmer, B. (2016). Creating 360° educational video: A case study. In *Proceedings of the 28th Australian Conference on Computer-Human Interaction* (pp. 34–39). ACM. https://doi.org/10.1145/3010915.3011001

Kiefer, M., & Trumpp, N. M. (2012). Embodiment theory and education: The foundations of cognition in perception and action. *Trends in Neuroscience and Education, 1*(1), 15–20. https://doi.org/10.1016/j.tine.2012.07.002

Lewis, P. J. (2017). The erosion of play. *International Journal of Play, 6*(1), 10–23. https://doi.org/10.1080/21594937.2017.1288391

Merleau-Ponty, M., & Landes, D. A. (2012). *Phenomenology of perception*. Routledge.

Naimark, M. (2018, February 16). VR/AR fundamentals – 3. Other senses (Touch, Smell, Taste, Mind). *Medium*. Retrieved from https://medium.com/@michaelnaimark/vr-ar-fundamentals-3-other-senses-haptic-smell-taste-mind-e6d101d752da

Nebel, S., Schneider, S., & Rey, G. D. (2016). Mining learning and crafting scientific experiments: A literature review on the use of minecraft in education and research. *Journal of Educational Technology & Society, 19*(2), 355–366.

O'Toole, J., & Beckett, D. (2010). *Educational research: Creative thinking & doing*. Oxford University Press.

Peters, M. A. (2010). Creativity, openness, and the global knowledge economy: The advent of user-generated cultures. *Economics, Management and Financial Markets, 5*(3), 15.

Petty, N. J., Thomson, O. P., & Stew, G. (2012). Ready for a paradigm shift? Part 2: Introducing qualitative research methodologies and methods. *Manual Therapy, 17*(5), 378–384. https://doi.org/10.1016/j.math.2012.03.004

Sobota, B., Korecko, S., Pastornicky, P., & Jacho, L. (2016). Virtual-reality technologies in the process of handicapped school children education. In *Proceedings 2016 International Conference on Emerging ELearning Technologies and Applications (ICETA)*, (pp. 321–326). https://doi.org/10.1109/ICETA.2016.7802077

Suarez, A. (2018, February 28). How and why our experiments with virtual reality motion made us ill. *VentureBeat.* Retrieved from https://venturebeat.com/2018/02/27/how-and-why-our-experiments-with-virtual-reality-motion-made-us-ill/

Sutton-Smith, B. (1997). *The ambiguity of play.* Harvard University Press.

Teslasuit Inc. (2018). *Teslasuit – Full body haptic suit.* Retrieved from https://teslasuit.io/

Varela, F. J., Thompson, E., & Rosch, E. (1991). *The embodied mind: Cognitive science and human experience.* MIT Press.

Weitz, M. (1956). The role of theory in aesthetics. *The Journal of Aesthetics and Art Criticism, 15*(1), 27–35.

White, E. J. (2020). Visual surplus of seeing play in ECE: Beyond the ontologic trap? *Beijing International Journal of Education, 3*(1).

Whitebread, D., & O'Sullivan, L. (2012). Preschool children's social pretend play: Supporting the development of metacommunication, metacognition and self-regulation. *International Journal of Play, 1*(2), 197–213. https://doi.org/10.1080/21594937.2012.693384

Index